DANGEROUS DELUSIONS

America on the Brink

DANGEROUS DELUSIONS

America on the Brink

*A Critical Solution to America's Political
and Economic Dilemma*

Michael F. Spath

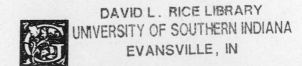

Glenbridge Publishing Ltd.

Library of Congress Catalog Card Number: LC 94-75992

International Standard Book Number: 0-944435-26-2

Printed in the U.S.A.

Contents

Introduction

The United States is on a collision course with reality. The outward appearance of a functioning democracy—campaigns waged, elections held, and legislation passed—obscures the structural flaws that have rendered America's political system incapable of solving the intractable problems that threaten the nation's future. The danger signs are evident—high levels of crime and poverty, anemic job creation, huge budget and trade deficits, and a burgeoning national debt. Solutions to these and other problems exist, but difficult decisions are required, and America's government has lost the ability to make them.

In the absence of war or economic depression, democracies are slow to adjust to changing realities. The reason for this lethargic response is that change requires consensus, and building a consensus is a typically laborious task. Unfortunately, America's warped system of campaign finance has given special interests primacy over the general interest, and, as a result, consensus building has become an almost impossible task. Confronting difficult issues and political gridlock, elected officials respond not with needed reforms, but with the empty rhetoric and false choices that are used to polarize debate and win elections.

The depth of America's political dilemma is best fathomed in a historical context, for it is the unique evolution of the nation's political economy that has created many of the obstacles to reform. Since its birth as a nation, America has had three distinct eras of political economy. The first era began with independence, when America's leaders—distrustful of a strong, centralized government—adopted the Articles of Confederation, which provided for a loose association of sovereign states. But this structure of government was too weak to function effectively and lasted just seven years. In its place, the founding fathers crafted the Constitution, which provided for a strong foundation of limited government and proved to be a perfect match for the nation's agrarian economy, where government interference was unneeded and unwanted.

The second era of American political economy, marked by a limited structure of government playing a limited role, lasted for a century and a half. As the nation spread out across the continent, the economy thrived. But when the industrial revolution began transforming the nation's economy late in the nineteenth century, the unseemly side of unregulated capitalism was exposed. For decades, the federal government failed to respond. It was not until early in the twentieth century that legislation was passed to protect the rights of workers and break up monopolistic trusts. This growing government activism, however, was interrupted by World War I, and after the war conservative politicians moved the federal government back to the economic sidelines.

America's third era of political economy began when the Great Depression made painfully clear that a larger economic role for government was needed. Franklin Roosevelt's New Deal included federal deposit insurance, social security and a broad series of public works projects. But while stopping the downward slide, the New Deal did not restore the health of America's economy. That task was accomplished by massive military spending during World War II. After the war, a baby boom, a growing consumer market, and little foreign competition combined to spark two decades of unprecedented economic growth and prosperity. The transition from limited to expanded government, a transition born of necessity, appeared to have been accomplished successfully.

But the unique postwar circumstances could not last. Foreign competitors, in both Europe and Japan, slowly emerged from the devastation of the war just as business and political leaders in the United States began taking economic prosperity for granted. In the mid-1960s, President Lyndon Johnson ended two decades of postwar fiscal conservatism by launching a series of new federal programs to assist the poor, the sick, and the elderly. His goals were worthy, but the means he chose—massive federal spending programs—were suspect. For once the doors of the federal treasury were opened, interest groups converged on the nation's capital as never before, each wanting its share of federal largesse.

During the seventies, two oil-shock recessions rocked the nation's economy. For the first time since World War II, America's elected leaders had tough economic decisions to make. But they were not up to the task. Special interest groups held too much political power, and elected officials had few incentives to make the decisions required. Equally important, the public no longer trusted the government to make the right decisions. This lack of trust was well-earned. After America's success during World War II and more than two decades of postwar prosperity, the public had strong faith in government's ability to get things done. But after Vietnam, Watergate, and countless other examples of government arrogance and incompetence, public trust in government had evaporated.

A lack of trust should have been a strong argument for political reform, but both major political parties were too entangled with the status quo. Instead, the lack of trust in government translated into strong support for the simple idea that less government was better. The idea of less government—meaning less taxes and less regulation—was popular at the polls, but during the 1980s it also led directly to massive budget deficits, a Savings and Loan crisis, and the pursuit of myopic economic and trade policies.

Today, the belief that America's government is hopelessly dysfunctional continues to provide broad political support for laissez faire and free trade, because both doctrines maintain that government should not have a role—and if government does not interfere, then it can't make things worse. The United States, however, is in the midst of a global economic competition with Japan and Germany, and in a competition where successful businesses must have ready access to skilled workers, financial capital, and efficient infrastructure, government policies play a crucial role. To simply say that government's role should be as limited as possible is no longer a tenable policy, but an abdication of responsibility.

The combination of political flaws and a lack of public trust can have severe consequences for the nation. For example, in early 1994 the nation's economy is finally emerging from three and a half years of economic recession and stagnation. What kept the economy in the doldrums so long? Consumers, worried about job security, cut back on consumption, and businesses, worried about economic conditions, kept investment low. An increase in government spending to create jobs could have stimulated the economy, but with a four trillion dollar national debt and valid public concerns about wasteful government spending, this option was unavailable. As a result, the economy was left to respond slowly to lower interest rates, and the federal government found itself in the absurd position of spending tens of billions of dollars on unemployment benefits, but no additional money to create jobs.

While it is widely recognized that political problems exist, little is being done to fix them. The main participants in American government, from the White House and federal agencies to Congress and the lobbying firms, focus their energy on daily events. The nation's news media, which must meet a weekly, daily, or even hourly reporting schedule, have a similarly short frame of reference. The need for political reform is clear to those who operate within the current system, but the incentives for reform are few and the obstacles formidable. As a result, the participants work to make incremental changes to the status quo, changes insufficient to veer America off the dangerous path it now treads.

From 1947 to 1981, the national debt grew faster than the economy in only eight fiscal years. But since fiscal year 1982, the national debt has grown faster than the economy every single year—by an annual average of 6.6%. At its current rate of growth, the national debt, which now exceeds 4.3 trillion dollars, will exceed seven trillion dollars by the year 2000. Early in the twenty-first century, as interest costs accumulate and demographic forces overwhelm the social security and health care systems, America may face the worst financial crisis in the nation's history.

The United States faces a simple, yet enormously important, choice. It can fix things now, or it can fix them later. Waiting for disaster to strike is a poor substitute for preventive action, but, absent a severe crisis, America's government is structurally incapable of responding. It is the aim of this book to make clear the flaws of America's political system, explain why the system lacks the ability of self-reform, and argue that only the concerted action of individuals, informed of both the causes and the cure, can solve our national dilemma.

The book is divided into five parts. Part I examines the flaws in America's democratic system, how they encourage disastrous policies, and how, if not fixed, they will eventually bankrupt the nation. Part II looks at the evolution of America's political and economic problems, focusing primarily on the last sixty years—America's third era of political economy. Part III details the nation's economic myopia. Part IV contains a series of proposed policy changes designed to help solve America's major economic and social ills. The political practicality of these proposals, indeed of any truly fundamental change, is dependent upon structural political reforms, which are discussed in Part V.

The reader should note that the book is not written from a particular ideological viewpoint. The author's approach is to analyze the nation's political and economic problems and offer potential solutions, some that could be labelled "liberal" and others "conservative." Solving the problems is of far greater importance than the label attached. Another point that the reader should keep in mind is that the book focuses on *long-term* economic and political problems. The economic recovery that began in March 1991 is gaining momentum in 1994 and should continue for at least the next few years. Strong economic growth in the short term will reduce public concerns about the nation's economic and fiscal problems and provide politicians with sufficient reason not to make needed reforms. While temporarily obscuring America's long-term structural problems, cyclical economic growth will not solve them.

It is both convenient and comforting to assume that, because America's political economy has worked well in the past, it can work well again in the future. But to believe that America's intractable problems are simply the result of incorrect policy decisions that the current political structure has the ability to remedy, is the most dangerous of delusions. For America's political system has developed serious flaws and the nation's future depends upon our ability to fix them. What follows is my attempt to analyze the historical causes of America's dilemma, make clear the consequences of the nation's current course, present an alternative path, and argue vigorously for a change in direction.

Part I

System Failure

Chapter 1

Democracy in Disrepair

In 1990, a year when millions of Eastern Europeans voted in free elections for the first time, two-thirds of voting-age Americans failed to cast a ballot—a disturbing sign that while democracy was on the rise throughout the world, it was deteriorating in the United States. Indeed, voter apathy is frequently cited as a major cause of America's political shortcomings. Those who do so, however, confuse cause and effect. Deep structural flaws have developed in America's democratic system, creating a perverse set of incentives that give special interests primacy over the general interest, discourage elected officials from making difficult decisions, and dramatically limit voter choice. The end result is a political system that no longer works and an electorate that no longer participates. No issue is more important to America's future success than the nation's ability to repair its malfunctioning democracy.

Demographic Change

The structural flaws that afflict America's political system have emerged slowly with the passage of time, avoiding both detection and remedy. The underlying cause has simply been demographic change. When the Declaration of Independence was signed, the thirteen colonies had roughly three million inhabitants; in 1993, over 250 million people live in the United States. An eightyfold increase in population severely tested the political system's ability to adjust. It is a test the system has failed.

In a representative democracy, population growth necessitates periodic adjustments to both the size and composition of elected legislatures. At the Constitutional Convention of 1787, the issue of representation sparked a heated debate. Delegates from the more populous states wanted seats in the federal legislature apportioned on a per capita basis, while delegates from the less populous states sought apportionment on a per state basis. A compromise between these two opposing views apportioned the Senate by state and the House of Representatives by population. While each state was given two senators, the number of representatives in the House posed more of a problem. Delegates to the Convention wanted states to have sufficient representation, but they also tried to avoid having too many representatives—a problem that plagued state legislatures at the time. As James Madison pointed out in *The Federalist Papers*, there were two sides to the coin:

> It must be confessed, that in this, as in most other cases, there is a mean, on both sides of which inconveniences will be found to lie. By enlarging too much the number of electors, you render the representative too little acquainted with all their local circumstances and lesser interests; as by reducing it too much, you render him unduly attached to these, and too little fit to comprehend and pursue great and national objects.[1]

The delegates agreed that there should be no more than one representative for every 40,000 people. But on the last day of the Convention, George Washington rose to address the issue. The delegates were all somewhat surprised, for although Washington was the president of the Convention, and everyone knew he would be the nation's first president, he rarely spoke during the proceedings. Washington asked that the ratio of representation be lowered to one representative for every 30,000 people so that the number of representatives could be increased. He explained: "I think this of so much consequence that it would give me much satisfaction to see it adopted."[2] And so it was.

The final wording of the Constitution is quite explicit: "the number of representatives shall not exceed one for every thirty thousand." A ceiling was set on the number of representatives, but not a floor. The founding fathers had implicitly assumed that a floor was not needed because the legislature would always want as many representatives as possible. Over the past two hundred years, however, this assumption has proven erroneous.

When the first Congress met in New York in 1789, there were sixty-five members of the House of Representatives. A census was taken in 1790 and the number of representatives was increased to 106. Over time, as America's population increased in size, so did the membership in the House, as shown in Table 1. From 1790 through 1840, when Congress changed the size of the House to reflect the new census information, emphasis was placed on determining the optimum size of the average Congressional district. Beginning in 1850, Congress altered its approach and began to target the total number of representatives. After Arizona and New Mexico became states in 1912, the size of the House was fixed at 435. In 1959, the number of representatives was increased to 437 after the admission of two new states, Alaska and Hawaii. In 1963, Congress lowered the number back to 435, the level that exists today.

There is nothing magical about the number 435. It just happened to be the number of representatives in the House when a majority of members decided that the House was of sufficient size. The founding fathers decided that the average Congressional district should consist of roughly 30,000 people, yet their failure to set a floor on the number of representatives left the size of future

Table 1
DEMOGRAPHIC REPRESENTATION OF THE UNITED STATES CONGRESS

Census Year	U.S. Population	House Members	Ratio	Senate Members	Ratio
1790	3,929,214	106	37,068	26	151,124
1800	5,308,483	142	37,384	32	165,890
1810	7,239,881	186	38,924	34	212,938
1820	9,638,453	213	45,251	46	209,532
1830	12,866,020	242	53,165	48	268,042
1840	17,069,453	232	73,575	52	328,259
1850	23,191,876	237	97,856	62	374,063
1860	31,443,321	243	129,396	66	476,414
1870	39,818,449	293	135,899	74	538,087
1880	50,155,783	332	151,072	76	659,945
1890	62,947,714	357	176,324	88	715,315
1900	75,994,575	391	194,360	90	844,384
1910	91,972,266	435	211,430	92	999,699
1920	105,710,620	435	243,013	96	1,101,152
1930	122,775,046	435	282,241	96	1,278,907
1940	131,669,275	435	302,688	96	1,371,555
1950	151,325,798	435	347,875	96	1,576,310
1960	179,323,175	437	410,351	100	1,793,232
1970	203,302,031	435	467,361	100	2,033,020
1980	226,545,805	435	520,795	100	2,265,458
1990	248,709,873	435	571,747	100	2,487,099

Note: House membership reflects Congressional apportionment for the census year indicated. Ratio numbers refer to the average number of individuals each House and Senate member represents.

Sources: U.S. Bureau of the Census, *Statistical Abstract of the United States: 1993* and Congressional Quarterly, *Guide to U.S. Elections*.

districts dependent upon population growth and the judgment of
future members of Congress. As a result, by 1990, the size of the
average Congressional district had exploded to 571,747 people.
Madison had warned that having too few representatives would
cause them to be "too little acquainted with all their local circumstances and lesser interests." However, the principal problem today
is not representatives who are little acquainted with local interests,
but the perverse incentives to which elected representatives must
respond.

Campaign Costs

The dramatic increase in the size of Congressional constituencies has had a profound impact on the nation's political system.
Voter-representative interaction has fallen dramatically, and, as a
result, individuals wishing to be politically involved must interact
more with special interest groups than with their own representative. At the same time, candidates can no longer meet most voters
in person and must therefore rely upon mass media advertising to
run a successful campaign. As a result, the costs of campaigns have
skyrocketed. *It is the high cost of campaigns and the increased
importance of campaign contributions that have fundamentally
transformed American democracy.*

Money and politics are not strangers. There is a profusion of
cases in American history of elected officials using public office
for personal gain. But the role of money in campaigns has
changed. In the past, a large campaign war chest was not a prereq-
uisite for running a campaign for national office. Today, the democratic ideal that any citizen can run for federal office has been
eclipsed by the hard reality that running a viable campaign requires
huge financial resources, and a successful candidate must either be
wealthy or an effective fund-raiser. In 1992, House candidates
spent an average of $389,588 on their campaigns, while Senate
candidates spent an average of $2,969,372.[3] Even after adjusting

for inflation, the cost of both House and Senate campaigns has more than doubled over the past two decades.

To raise such sizable sums, today's candidates must spend an inordinate amount of time fund-raising. The primary sources of campaign funds are the political action committees (PACs) established by corporations, labor unions, and various interest groups. Interested more in issues than in candidates or political parties, most PACs target their donations to legislators with choice committee assignments. As a result, the vast majority of PAC donations go to incumbents, not challengers. The incumbent bias of PACs is shown in Table 2, while the incumbents' overall spending advantage is shown in Table 3.

While Table 2 and Table 3 show the large and growing financial advantage enjoyed by incumbents, the picture is incomplete. For lost amid the averages are numerous races where the incumbent had an overwhelming financial advantage. Indeed, if we define a financially competitive Congressional race as one in

Table 2
AVERAGE PAC DONATIONS TO INCUMBENTS
AND CHALLENGERS ($)

	House			Senate		
	Incumbents	Challengers	Ratio	Incumbents	Challengers	Ratio
1984	142,385	31,152	4.6	625,253	210,474	3.0
1986	167,556	27,139	6.2	898,781	382,467	2.4
1988	201,360	27,519	7.3	1,225,922	288,042	4.3
1990	217,564	20,842	10.4	1,025,046	299,193	3.4
1992	261,976	27,621	9.5	1,366,423	235,982	5.8

Note: General election fund-raising by major-party candidates only. The ratio number reflects PAC donations given to incumbents for each dollar given to challengers.

Source: Compiled from studies by the *Common Cause Campaign Finance Monitoring Project*.

Table 3
AVERAGE SPENDING BY INCUMBENTS
AND CHALLENGERS ($)

	House			Senate		
---	Incumbents	Challengers	Ratio	Incumbents	Challengers	Ratio
1984	258,738	121,137	2.1	2,394,571	1,074,444	2.2
1986	309,982	118,519	2.6	3,281,015	1,767,772	1.9
1988	347,684	111,226	3.1	4,002,916	1,783,368	2.2
1990	363,986	105,373	3.5	4,037,872	1,687,871	2.4
1992	582,330	154,607	3.8	4,177,459	1,753,398	2.4

Note: General election fund-raising by major-party candidates only. The ratio number reflects dollars spent by incumbents for each dollar spent by challengers.

Source: Compiled from studies by the *Common Cause Campaign Finance Monitoring Project.*

---

which the challenger spends at least half of what the incumbent spends, then from 1984 to 1990 only 14% of House races and 34% of Senate races were financially competitive. An even more disturbing statistic, however, is that during those same four elections, 18.5% of House incumbents *faced no major-party opposition.*[†] Voters in those districts were not even given a choice of who would represent them in Congress.

Democracy cannot exist without choice. Races with only one candidate running are not the hallmark of a democracy, but of dictatorial regimes.

[†] In Louisiana all primary candidates run on the same ballot; if one candidate receives a majority of the vote, then that candidate wins. If no candidate wins a majority of the vote, then the two top vote recipients are placed on the general election ballot. As a result of this law, Louisiana has a high number of unopposed candidates in the general election. Not counting Louisiana's races, the percentage of unopposed House incumbents from 1984-1990 falls to 17.4%

Elections: The Linchpin of Democracy

The 1992 elections were heralded as a time for political change. With the economy stuck in neutral and the government mired in gridlock, a visibly enraged electorate would finally send a clear message that they wanted action, not excuses. Results of the 1992 Congressional elections seemed to reflect this sentiment. Indeed, 110 new members won seats in the House—the largest freshman class in over forty years. Even the number of House incumbents facing no major-party opposition dropped dramatically—to 7.7%.[†]

Beneath these encouraging signs, however, was evidence that the system's resistance to change remained intact. The high turnover rate in Congress was primarily the result of redistricting and retirement, not challenger electoral success. Reflecting the

---

[†] Excluding Louisiana, the percentage of House incumbents running unopposed was 6.5%.

1990 census, reapportionment redistributed nineteen seats in the
House (thirteen states lost seats; eight states gained seats). Redistricting dramatically altered the geographic shape of many Congressional districts, and, as a result, many incumbents chose
retirement over a tough race in unfamiliar territory. Two other
events—the House bank scandal and the imminent expiration of a
law allowing the legal conversion of unused campaign funds to
personal use—also increased the number of retirees. In total, sixty-
seven House members did not seek re-election in 1992.† Of the
368 House incumbents who sought re-election, 325 or 88.3% were
successful. While it was the first time since 1974 that House
incumbents had failed to attain at least a 90% reelection rate, it was
hardly a harbinger of significant change.

   If voters truly wanted change in 1992, why did they return
incumbents to Congress in typically large numbers? Campaign
finance plays a critical role in keeping competition light, but
another important reason exists. Opinion polls consistently show
that, while voters don't like Congress as a whole, they generally
like *their* representative in Congress. This ambivalent attitude
toward Congress results from the perception that while it is *their*
representative who brings federal money and pork barrel projects
to the district, it is the *entire* Congress that can't balance a budget
or reform the health care system. At election time, however, when
individual voters act in their own interest (voting to re-elect their
representative or senator) the collective result is undesirable (having the same Congress as before). This electoral dichotomy com-
bines with the current campaign finance system to make the United
States Congress a bastion of incumbency, as seen in Table 4.

   The dichotomy between individual actions and collective
results cuts both ways. In the current system, a member of

---

† Of this number, 52 retired, 13 sought other political office, and 2 died in office.
Statistics from *Congressional Quarterly Almanac 1992*, Volume XLVIII,
p. 20-A.

Table 4
CONGRESSIONAL INCUMBENTS'
REELECTION SUCCESS

| | House | | | Senate | | |
	Running	Reelected	Percent	Running	Reelected	Percent
1980	398	361	90.7%	29	16	55.2%
1982	393	354	90.1%	30	28	93.3%
1984	412	393	95.4%	29	26	89.7%
1986	394	385	97.7%	28	21	75.0%
1988	409	402	98.3%	27	23	85.2%
1990	407	391	96.1%	32	31	96.9%
1992	368	325	88.3%	28	23	82.1%

Source: U.S. Bureau of the Census, *Statistical Abstract of the United States: 1993.*

Congress can turn one term in office into a long and successful political career by following a few simple steps: respond effectively to constituents and campaign contributors, aggressively raise campaign funds, and avoid taking unpopular actions. But while these steps make sense for an individual, when every member follows the same set of rules, America ends up with a Congress that likes to spend money, cut taxes, run large deficits, and avoid difficult decisions.

Historically, members of Congress had to balance the interests of voters in their home state or district with the interests of the nation as a whole. Even under the best circumstances, it was a difficult balancing act. During the postwar era, a third set of interests—those of campaign contributors—has emerged and taken a prominent role. Members of Congress are left in the difficult position of attempting to balance three, usually conflicting, sets of interests. Over the last few decades, this balancing act has been a losing proposition—the short-term interests of campaign donors and voting constituencies are being met, but the long-term interests of the entire nation are being ignored. The clearest indication that America's political system is structurally flawed is that when all of the participants—voters, campaign contributors, and politicians— act in their own best interest, then elected officials have strong incentives *not* to make the difficult decisions required to solve the nation's long-term problems.

Fund-Raising

The role of money in politics is not a Democratic or a Republican problem, but a structural problem. And it is a structural problem that is not limited to the legislative branch of the federal government. Presidential candidates are equally dependent upon campaign contributions, particularly during the primary season. In 1992, six major Democratic candidates competed for their party's nomination, but a lack of financing quickly drove three candidates from the race. Former Massachusetts Senator Paul Tsongas won the New Hampshire primary on February 18, but he did not have the financial resources to campaign adequately in the twenty-four states that held primaries and caucuses in the succeeding three weeks. After losing primaries in Illinois and Michigan on March 17, Tsongas withdrew from the race. While former California Governor Jerry Brown, armed with a toll-free number and a multitude of small donations, continued to wage his guerrilla campaign until the end, Arkansas Governor Bill Clinton effectively had the Democratic nomination sewn up when Tsongas left the race. But what about voters in the twenty-two states that held primaries and caucuses after March 17? Democratic voters in those states, which contain more than fifty-one percent of the nation's population, were given a choice between their party's nominee and a protest vote. Throughout the primary season, Republican voters were given a similarly limited choice.

The hard reality is that America's exclusionary presidential primary system places overwhelming emphasis on fund-raising and gives a majority of voters little or no choice in selecting their party's nominee. Federal law prohibits presidential campaign donations in excess of $1,000; yet a gaping loophole allows unlimited funds, referred to as "soft money" donations, to be passed through state political parties. Presidential candidates of both parties rely heavily on "soft money" donors during the primary season's rapid winnowing out process. For example, in 1988 candidate George Bush built a huge campaign war chest by recruiting 249 individuals to join his "Team 100." Membership in this exclusive club had but one requirement—donating $100,000 to Bush's campaign.

What do financial backers of presidential campaigns receive for their generosity? Publicly, politicians will acknowledge only one benefit—access. And at George Bush's President's Dinner, held on April 28, 1992, access was readily available. After having paid $1,500 a plate, attendees were given a "menu" of contribution choices. For a $15,000 contribution, a donor could "purchase" a table of ten and would receive two tickets to a private reception hosted at the White House by President and Mrs. Bush or two tickets to a reception hosted by the President's Cabinet. In addition, a table buyer would receive two tickets to a luncheon at the Vice President's residence hosted by Vice President and Mrs. Quayle and two tickets to a breakfast hosted by Senator Bob Dole (R-KS) and Congressman Bob Michel (R-IL). The tablebuyer also had the option to request a member of the House of Representatives to complete the table of ten. For those in a really generous mood, $92,000 or more bought a photo opportunity with President Bush. The dinner was quite successful, raising a record nine million dollars.[4]

Access, however, is not the only benefit contributors receive. In return for their donations, contributors receive favorable regulatory rulings, generous tax breaks, and well-padded pork barrel projects. A more prevalent, and more insidious, benefit is the ability of campaign contributors to water down or block legislation contrary to their interests. The proliferation of this "veto" power is a major cause of America's political paralysis.

A Monetary Democracy

The growing importance of campaign fund-raising has transformed America's electoral system in fundamental ways. First, for many potential candidates, the high cost of elections has become an insurmountable hurdle. They simply cannot raise the money required for a viable campaign. As a result, fewer candidates run, and elections are less competitive. Second, an elected official must constantly spend time raising funds for his next election. This takes time and effort away from dealing with the nation's problems. Third, and most important, candidates are not oblivious to where the money is coming from. Their views on issues are influenced by campaign contributors, for few candidates will risk alienating potential financial supporters.

A fundamental transformation has occurred in the American political system. The campaign dollar has displaced the individual vote as the primary source of political power. In effect, America's representative democracy has evolved into a monetary democracy where money, not votes, is of primary importance.

The rise of America's monetary democracy has had a profound impact on voters. As the influence of campaign contributors increased, the competitiveness of elections fell. Voters were given fewer choices, and, as a result, voter alienation increased and voter participation fell, as shown in Table 5.

In 1992, for only the second time since 1960, voter participation in a presidential election increased. The five percent increase was the largest increase in forty years. It would be comforting to think that this increase reflects a new spirit of political activism on the part of the American people and the start of a trend toward higher voter participation. It would be more accurate, however, to

Table 5
VOTER PARTICIPATION (PERCENTAGE OF VOTING-AGE POPULATION)

Midterm Elections		Presidential Elections	
1962	45.4%	1964	61.9%
1966	45.4%	1968	60.9%
1970	43.5%	1972	55.2%
1974	35.9%	1976	53.5%
1978	34.9%	1980	52.6%
1982	38.0%	1984	53.1%
1986	33.4%	1988	50.1%
1990	33.1%	1992	55.2%

Source: U.S. Bureau of the Census, *Statistical Abstract of the United States: 1993.*

attribute most of this rise to the independent presidential candidacy of Ross Perot. If Ross Perot did not re-enter the race, then how many of the 19,741,048 people who voted for him would have cast a vote for president? It is an unanswerable question, but if half of them had stayed home, then the voter participation rate in 1992 would have been as low as it was in 1988.

Periodically held free elections are the cornerstone of democracy, yet elections require real choices. American democracy is failing in this fundamental respect. Reforming the current system will not be easy, for no matter how distorted the system has become, it works for those who benefit from it. Candidates seek out campaign contributors as a needed source of funds, while contributors actively seek to influence the political agenda. While privately condemning the current system, neither elected officials nor campaign contributors have incentives to change it. *Elected officials can rationalize the current system because they were able to get elected under it, and contributors can rationalize the current system because of the access and government benefits they readily receive.*

America's democratic system is two hundred years old and has weathered much, but the insidious disease that now afflicts it threatens the nation's future as never before. The gradual transformation from a representative democracy to a monetary democracy has taken political power away from the people and placed it in the hands of campaign contributors. As a result, narrow interest groups are able to exert a political influence much greater than their numbers would warrant. While interest groups are an integral part of any democracy, a political system dominated by interest groups quickly loses the ability to act in the national interest. Unfortunately, the United States has developed this dangerous political flaw. And, as we shall see in the next chapter, such a flaw encourages disastrous and costly government policies.

Chapter 2

Government Guaranteed:
The Savings and Loan Debacle

The disturbing implications of having a monetary, rather than representative, democracy were made clear during the Savings and Loan (S&L) crisis. How a historically conservative, government-regulated industry was so quickly and dramatically transformed into a taxpayer sinkhole provides a vivid illustration of America gone astray. With the American public facing a $100 billion bailout bill, millions of Americans asked: "what the hell happened?" Having ignored the S&L industry's growing problems for most of the decade, the nation's news media belatedly bombarded the public with stories of high-rolling Savings and Loan executives using the taxpayers' money to support outrageously lavish lifestyles. Although successful at generating public outrage, these news stories generally ignored the real cause of the crisis—disastrous government policies. Congress and the Reagan administration bear ultimate responsibility for the Savings and Loan debacle, for if they had looked after the general interest instead of the special interests, the crisis need not have occurred.

17

The Federal Government's Role

The federal government's role in the Savings and Loan industry began in the wake of the Great Depression—a depression whose length and severity was greatly increased by massive banking failures. As banking reform was debated in Congress, deposit insurance emerged as a pivotal issue. During the first three decades of the twentieth century, many states had instituted deposit insurance funds to increase public confidence and mitigate the impact of banking failures. But all of the state-sponsored funds eventually ran dry during economic downturns. In the wake of the Great Depression, progressive politicians wanted any banking reform bill to include federal protection for small depositors, but the large Eastern banks were against the proposal because they did not want to subsidize the losses of other banks. President Franklin D. Roosevelt was also against federal deposit insurance because he felt it would encourage risky lending practices. But after thousands of bank failures across the country, public opinion was overwhelmingly in favor of deposit insurance, and Roosevelt relented.

The Glass-Steagall Act, passed on June 12, 1933, created the Federal Deposit Insurance Corporation to insure deposits at the nation's banks. A year later, the Federal Savings and Loan Insurance Corporation (FSLIC) was created to insure deposits at Savings and Loan associations. The 1934 Act also restricted Savings and Loans to mortgage lending and placed strict restrictions on interest rates. As a result, the S&L industry became a government-regulated, government-protected industry. Years later, after deposit insurance had proven to be instrumental in restoring financial stability, President Roosevelt, the master politician, proclaimed that his administration's strong support for the measure had been justified.

Over the next four decades America's thrift industry changed little.[†] Government regulation provided the industry with a steady,

---

[†] The term *thrift* is a common name for either a mutual savings bank or a savings and loan association.

if unspectacular, flow of profits. The industry was characterized by the "3-6-3 rule"—pay depositors 3%, lend money at 6%, and be on the golf course by 3 p.m. Running an S&L in this comfortable environment required little skill. But while providing for easy profits, government regulation was shielding institutions from the interest rate risks they undertook every day. Savings deposits typically have short maturities, anywhere from a daily savings account to a certificate of deposit (CD) maturing in a few years. In contrast, mortgage loans typically have thirty-year maturities. The maturity mismatch between deposits and mortgages carried tremendous interest rate risk. For example, if interest rates paid on deposits rose above the interest rates earned on home mortgages, then the steady flow of S&L profits would quickly turn into a stream of losses. But there was no need to be concerned about such risks, because government regulation determined the level of interest rates. So, Savings and Loan executives continued to work on their golf game, oblivious to the changes taking place in the world around them.

A Liquidity Crisis

During the seventies, government regulation of the S&L industry began to unravel. The catalyst for change was not conscious deregulation, but inflation. Lyndon Johnson's fiscal mismanagement of the Vietnam War and the nation's foreign oil dependency unleashed market forces that altered the nation's financial structure. As inflation rose, keeping money in a savings account paying five percent interest began to look less attractive. When inflation was higher than five percent, there was a strong economic incentive *not* to put money in a savings account. With inflation eroding the attractiveness of government-regulated investment vehicles, individuals looked elsewhere for higher returns to protect their savings.

The vehicle of choice was the money market mutual fund (MMMF). First appearing in 1972, the funds purchased treasury securities and large bank deposits and then sold shares to the public. Investors were able to get a much higher return than was available in passbook savings accounts. An early drawback, a rule that required investors to lock up their money for eight years, was removed by the government in June 1978. As a result, money flooded out of passbook savings accounts and into MMMFs. Table 6 shows the magnitude of this shift. As many people withdrew their deposits, Savings and Loans faced a liquidity crisis. Inflation had fundamentally transformed America's financial markets, leaving thrifts unable to compete effectively for the nation's savings.

Deregulation and Its Consequences

Congress responded to this dilemma by passing the Depository Institutions Deregulation and Monetary Control Act of 1980, which, among other things, deregulated the interest rates that thrifts could pay to depositors. The 1980 Act also increased deposit insurance from $40,000 to $100,000 per account, creating a new market for brokered deposits. Large retail brokerage firms, such as Merrill Lynch and Prudential Bache, pooled the deposits of small investors into groups of $100,000 each and then placed the deposits with the federally insured institution offering the highest interest rate. At the time, regulations limited brokered deposits to

Table 6
INFLATION'S IMPACT ON SAVINGS ACCOUNTS

| | Average Balances ($ Billions) | |
	MMMF Accounts	Savings Accounts
1978	9.5	481.8
1980	76.8	400.1
1982	236.3	356.7

Source: *Economic Report of the President, 1991.*

five percent of an institution's total deposits. In addition to actively competing for deposits, thrifts had also been given greater flexibility in making mortgage loans. In December 1979, the Federal Home Loan Bank (FHLB), the Savings and Loan regulator, adopted a rule allowing thrifts to make adjustable rate mortgages.

By removing the interest rate restrictions on both assets (mortgage loans) and liabilities (savings deposits), the federal government had completed the *interest rate* deregulation of the Savings and Loan industry. Although interest rate deregulation solved the liquidity crisis, it exposed the nation's Savings and Loans to a more fundamental problem—interest rate risk. The interest rates needed to attract new deposits were significantly higher than the interest rates thrifts were receiving on the mortgages they held. By 1982, the steady stream of profits had been replaced by a torrent of losses. If the entire S&L industry had been forced to adjust their assets and liabilities to market prices at this time, the industry would have had to face facts—it was bankrupt. But bankruptcy was not an immediate problem, because most institutions still reported positive net worth and, more importantly, they were not required to mark their portfolios to market (i.e. change the value of their assets to reflect current market interest rates). Nevertheless, substantial losses were quickly eroding the net worth of the nation's Savings and Loans.

Having deregulated both deposit rates and mortgage rates, Congress had two choices to deal with the S&L industry's deteriorating net worth. The first choice was to sit tight and do nothing. Under most normal circumstances, Congress is quite adept at this tactic. And, in this case, there were strong arguments for doing nothing. The S&L industry's losses in 1980 and 1981 were caused solely by high interest rates, which, in turn, were a result of the Federal Reserve Bank's fight against inflation. When inflation began to abate, the Fed would lower interest rates, and thrifts would start to make money again. The downside of waiting was that more thrifts would fail, and the industry would be forced to

consolidate. The second choice for Congress was to find other revenue sources for thrifts to offset the losses that remained on their
balance sheets. The idea was to keep as many institutions as possible afloat until more normal interest rate conditions returned. Having been regulated for forty years, the S&L industry had a strong
lobbying presence in Washington. With so many member institutions in trouble, the U.S. League of Savings Institutions, the industry's lobbying group, turned up the pressure for Congress to act.
Unfortunately for the American people, both the administration
and Congress responded to the heavy lobbying of the Savings and
Loan industry.

Government Incompetence

In another manifestation of the Reagan administration's policy
of deregulation, the Federal Home Loan Bank Board (FHLBB)
decided to eliminate the five percent limit on brokered deposits in
1982. The policy was to let market forces determine where money
was invested and what interest rates will be. However, brokered
deposits were still regulated because they were insured by the government. In effect, the Reagan administration only partially deregulated the industry and, by doing so, created a potentially explosive
situation. A thrift institution, with a couple of telephones and a sign
in the window which said "FSLIC-insured," could raise hundreds
of millions of dollars by simply offering the highest interest rates.
Problems did not occur immediately because Savings and Loans
were still restricted to the historically safe arena of mortgage lending. Unfortunately, Congress was about to change that forever.

In 1982, Congress passed the Garn-St Germain Depository
Institutions Decontrol Act. It was a historic piece of legislation. In
the crowded field of financial mismanagement, it had no equal in
the nation's history. Having decided that the thrift industry should
be allowed to grow out of its problems, Congress removed the
investment restraint on Savings and Loans. S&Ls were no longer

restricted to just mortgage lending; they could now invest in commercial real estate, shopping malls, raw land, and—what was to become the media favorite—"junk" bonds.

This new lax regulatory environment highlighted an additional problem, the dual charter system. Savings and Loan institutions could be chartered at either the state or federal level. While being regulated by state regulators and operating under state law, state-chartered institutions could still qualify for federal deposit insurance. Unfortunately, some states, most notably California and Texas, adopted even less restrictive rules regarding S&L investments. With the limit removed from brokered deposits, the new investment freedom was a prescription for financial disaster. Like many government actions during the 1980s, the Garn-St Germain Act was a conscious suspension of reality.

The United States has the most efficient financial markets in the world. While constantly searching for new investment opportunities, investors assess both the potential risk and the potential return of any investment. During the eighties, the government acted as if there were no relationship between risk and return. Congress decided to take a near-bankrupt industry, whose executives had operated in a totally regulated environment for decades, and give it almost limitless access to funds and few restrictions on investments. To raise money, thrifts had to offer high interest rates; to generate profits, thrifts had to invest in projects with higher potential return. But with the higher potential return came higher risks.

Federal deposit insurance is a two-sided issue. Protection of individual savings accounts from loss is essential to public confidence in the nation's financial system. However, this protection is not free. The federal government and, ultimately, the American taxpayer are financially responsible to make up for any losses not covered by the insurance funds. Congress and the Reagan administration had the responsibility to make sure that federally insured deposits were invested soundly. In 1982, the federal government abdicated this responsibility. Deregulation of the industry caused federally insured deposits at S&Ls to jump from $560.5 billion in 1982 to $932.6 billion in 1987.[1] Most of this five–year increase of $372.1 billion was invested in unsound ventures or lost due to fraud and insider abuse.

The government's unbroken streak of incompetence was not yet complete. Federal thrift regulators were concerned about industry accounting practices. Under generally accepted accounting principles (GAAP), the thrift industry was generating huge losses. Corrective action was needed, so the administration decided to change the rules. To replace GAAP, the regulators created regulatory accounting principles (RAP), which essentially provided thrifts with a government-approved way of deferring losses into the future. With new investment powers and new accounting rules, it would have been appropriate to increase the number of thrift regulators and to increase their funding. However, the Reagan administration, again preaching the benefits of deregulation, actually *cut* funding and *reduced* the number of regulators.

In a few short years, the federal government had transformed the nation's S&L industry. Thrifts could now raise hundreds of millions of dollars simply by taking in brokered deposits. They could then turn around and invest the money in just about any type of real estate or financial security, no matter how risky the investment. It was a no-lose situation. If the investments worked out, the thrift owner made a fortune. If the investments did not work out and the thrift went out of business, the government would take over the institution and absorb the losses. By recklessly deregulating the S&L industry, the United States government offered, at taxpayer expense, a no-risk business opportunity. It was an opportunity that attracted a new breed of thrift "entrepreneur."[2]

Congress and the Thrift Industry

Admitting that a problem exists, especially one caused by past mistakes, has never been easy for a government. The Savings and

Ronald Reagan's "Free" Market Approach

Loan crisis was no exception. Edwin Gray, appointed chairman of the Federal Home Loan Bank Board in 1983, started warning Congress of growing problems in 1984. He introduced new rules to curb the explosive growth of brokered deposits, but the rules were rejected. He asked for more money to increase the number of regulators, but he was ignored. The political forces that had set in motion the poorly conceived deregulation of the industry were too well entrenched.

The thrift lobby had powerful allies in Washington, such as House Banking Committee Chairman Fernand St Germain (D-RI) and Majority Leader Jim Wright (D-TX). In March 1986, FHLBB Chairman Gray asked Congress for the authority to borrow $15 billion to recapitalize the FSLIC fund so that some of the most insolvent thrifts could be closed. At the behest of the S&L lobby, Wright and St Germain blocked the legislation. Why? The plan called for raising $15 billion through higher fees on healthy thrifts. Industry officials privately told Gray that they wanted to wait, so that the situation would deteriorate and a taxpayer bailout would be required.[3] The legislation started to move only after a flurry of news reports documented the close ties between Congress and the thrift industry. The legislation was finally passed by Congress on August 4, 1987, and signed by President Reagan a week later. The bailout legislation was a year late and provided only $10.8 billion in additional borrowing authority. The government response was totally inadequate. The thrift industry insurance fund was bankrupt, and the federal government did not want to acknowledge the problem. As each day passed the problem simply grew worse.

On June 30, 1987, Edwin Gray's term as chairman of the FHLBB ended. In choosing a replacement, the federal government had one priority—it wanted someone who could keep a lid on the true size of the Savings and Loan crisis until after the 1988 elections. The administration found its man in Melvin Daniel (Danny) Wall. Wall was the senior staff member of the Senate Banking Committee, and he had played an active role in drafting the disastrous Garn-St Germain Act. It was somehow only fitting that an individual who shared responsibility for the legislative blunder that had caused the S&L crisis would now oversee the industry's final demise.

Although the magnitude of the Savings and Loan crisis was apparent to all in 1988, neither political party wanted it to become a major campaign issue. The reason was simple: both parties were to blame for the debacle. A comprehensive bailout plan was quietly drafted during 1988, but it would not emerge publicly until after the election. As point man for this conspiracy of silence, Danny Wall did a wonderful job. As late as June 1988, when private economists were estimating a cost to taxpayers between fifty and one hundred billion dollars, Wall stated that "I have no reason to change my position that we can manage the problem with the resources that we have. We have made very conservative calculations."[4] Truth and credibility are the sacrificial lambs of presidential campaigns. Since it was ignoring the problem, the government certainly was not going to appropriate money to solve it. Wall then was given the responsibility to clean up a problem whose true magnitude could not be revealed and do so without spending any money. In response to this dilemma, Wall unveiled the Southwest Plan in March 1988.

The Southwest Plan

The Southwest Plan was just another sorry chapter in the Savings and Loan tragedy. It made no attempt to fix the problems that had caused the disaster: brokered deposits, few investment restrictions, and lack of supervision. Instead, it focused on combining the sickest thrifts and selling them to outside investors. Again, government regulators ignored economic reality. The only way an outside investor would want to invest in a bankrupt S&L was if the opportunity provided high returns with relatively little or no risk. To attract investors, therefore, the government had to make the investments more attractive. Since the FHLBB had little money available to help make the sick thrifts more attractive, the regulators offered tax breaks. A number of deals were completed during 1988, but the real free-for-all occurred at the end of the year. During the last five days of the year, lawyers at the FHLBB worked around-the-clock, making deals in order to take advantage of tax breaks that were to expire at year's end. In that short period of time, the government completed fourteen transactions selling thirty-four institutions with a total of almost $62 billion in assets. To help expedite the deals, the regulators not only gave out tax breaks, but committed to spending $13.8 billion over ten years to protect the new owners from losses. These new investors brought high-paid corporate lawyers to the table to negotiate with underpaid and understaffed government lawyers.[5] The government and, by default, the American taxpayers got taken to the cleaners again.

After the elections, the government finally passed a Savings and Loan bailout bill. On August 9, 1989, George Bush signed the Financial Institutions Reform, Recovery and Enforcement Act, which established the Resolution Trust Corporation (RTC) to sell off failed thrift institutions and called for spending $166 billion over ten years and a total of $300 billion ($225 billion from tax-payers) over thirty years. During the next few years, even these projections seemed too optimistic. After having spent $32 billion on the crisis in fiscal years 1988 and 1989, the federal government spent an additional $124 billion in fiscal years 1990 and 1991. By late 1991, with commercial real estate prices still in a tailspin, cost projections for the S&L crisis routinely topped $300 billion. By 1992, the RTC needed additional money to close down more ailing thrifts. But with an election coming up, no new money was allocated.

At this point, the tab for America's Savings and Loan debacle actually began to shrink. Falling interest rates provided a double benefit—they reduced the cost of thrift deposits while providing a floor for real estate prices. By 1993, the RTC was selling off sub-stantially more assets than they were taking over from failed thrifts. Indeed, after having spent $159 billion from fiscal years 1988-1992, the federal government received $28 billion in asset sales during fiscal year 1993. The federal government currently projects another $30 billion in asset sales over the next four years, which would put the total cost of the S&L crisis at roughly $100 billion in current dollars ($106 billion in 1990 dollars).[6] While lower interest rates have slashed its cost, the Savings and Loan crisis is still the most expensive financial disaster in the nation's history. And it need not have happened.

America's Monetary Democracy in Action

The federal government bears ultimate responsibility for the S&L crisis. The mistakes made by the Congress and the Reagan administration were on a scale never before seen in the annals of American finance. It could have been a case of simple incompe-tence, but it was not. The Savings and Loan crisis was a direct result of America's monetary democracy. Both the S&L lobby and individual campaign contributors lobbied hard to have the thrift industry deregulated. After deregulation occurred, a corrupt flow of money developed—federally insured deposits were used to encourage politicians not to reform a system that was generating billions of dollars of losses that American taxpayers ultimately had to make good.

How the purchase of political influence caused the S&L crisis can best be shown by looking at the examples of Congressmen Fernand St Germain and Jim Wright. Both men had no qualms about using their public positions for personal financial gain. As a member of the House Banking Committee, St Germain developed a mutually beneficial relationship with both real estate developers and the S&L lobby. For example, in 1971 St Germain invested $3,000 for a 15% share in a partnership established by Roland Ferland, a real estate developer in Rhode Island. In 1980, St Germain sold 13% of the partnership for $184,799, an average annual return of over 60%. In another transaction, St Germain purchased a string of pancake restaurants for $1.3 million, all of it borrowed money. He sold one of the restaurants in 1984 for a profit of $315,995.[7]

St Germain reciprocated. Utilizing the House Banking Committee's oversight responsibility over the Department of Housing and Urban Development, St Germain funnelled numerous federally subsidized housing projects to Ferland. When he became chairman of the House Banking Committee, St Germain kept the favors flowing. When the 1980 interest rate deregulation was passed by both houses of Congress, a joint committee had to iron out the differences in the two bills. The Senate proposed increasing the limit on deposit insurance from $40,000 to $50,000, while the House bill had not proposed an increase. At the behest of industry lobbyists, St Germain pushed the limit up to $100,000, setting the stage for the subsequent explosion of the brokered deposit market.[8]

After the 1986 elections, the House ethics committee looked into allegations that St Germain had broken House rules and cheated on his taxes. The ethics committee, officially called the

Committee on Standards of Official Conduct, is made up of twelve members, six from each party. In theory, the committee is supposed to enforce the House's ethical standards. In practice, the committee falls far short. Typically, the committee fails to enforce many rules, and accused members usually receive only a "slap on the wrist." The committee did not question St Germain's income tax avoidance or even ask for his tax returns. Nor did they question anyone under oath. When the committee was done, it cited St Germain for understating his assets and for taking too many free rides on corporate jets, but recommended no punishment. St Germain responded to the report by saying it had "confirmed what my constituents, my friends, and I have known all along—that I adhere to the highest standards of conduct in both public office and private business affairs."[9] The ethics committee failed to punish St Germain because the sweetheart deals from which he profited were common among House members.

When Savings and Loans were given broad investment freedoms in 1982, real estate developers around the country bought these institutions to finance their development projects. The sharp rise in oil prices in 1979 and 1980 had sparked a Texas real estate boom, and the 1982 Garn-St Germain Act added fuel to the fire. A few years later, as oil prices were dropping, new real estate projects were still being started. In 1986, however, oil prices plummeted, and, at the same time, the bottom fell out of the Texas real estate market. Hundreds of savings institutions, whose portfolios contained heavy exposure to commercial real estate projects in Texas, became hopelessly insolvent. Their only hope for survival was to delay actions by federal regulators until oil prices went back up and the real estate market rebounded. And the best way to delay the regulators was to have politicians on your side. The price was high, but thanks to the legislative blunders of the early 1980s, thrift owners had easy access to brokered deposits and, as a result, became huge campaign contributors to the Democratic Congressional Campaign Committee (DCCC) and to Jim Wright.

The list of Wright's largest financial supporters reads like a "who's who" of notorious Texas thrift owners: Ed McBirney, owner of Sunbelt Savings, who used federally insured deposits to throw lavish parties and finance gambling trips to Las Vegas; Don Dixon, owner of Vernon Savings and Loan, who kept the yacht *High Spirits* on the Potomac River to throw parties for Washington politicians; and Wright's largest contributor, Thomas Gaubert, owner of Independent American Savings and Loan, who actually served as the finance chairman of the DCCC during 1985 and 1986.[10] Jim Wright knew them all and was more than happy to intervene with regulators on their behalf, even though their high-rolling lifestyles were financed at taxpayer expense. Belatedly, the government closed down Sunbelt Savings in 1986, while both Vernon and Independent American were seized in 1987. The total cost to taxpayers for these three institutions easily exceeded $3 billion.

In 1988, Wright became the target of an investigation by the House ethics committee. At issue were Wright's actions on the part of Texas thrift owners and the marketing of his book, *Reflections of a Public Man*. This book was sold in bulk to lobbying groups and political supporters. Indeed, more books were sold than were actually printed. Wright earned $55,000 from the book. Although it found no violations of House ethics laws, the ethics committee, reeling from public criticism of its handling of the St Germain case, hired lawyer Richard Phelan to conduct an independent investigation. Phelan, who had a different view of Congressional horse trading, filed a secret report that accused Wright of 117 violations of House rules. The committee ignored many of the violations concerning intervention with federal regulators, but it could not ignore Wright's lucrative financial deals with Texas real estate developer George Mallick and the book deal. On April 17, 1989, the committee released a 279-page report alleging sixty-nine violations of House rules.[11] Under a hailstorm of public criticism, Wright resigned as Speaker on May 31, and left the House for good at the end of June.

In one way, the cases of Fernand St Germain and Jim Wright were typical of the cases reviewed by the ethics committee: members using political power for personal financial gain. However, Congress failed to focus on a more significant problem: the use of political influence in return for campaign contributions. Both St Germain and Wright played significant roles in the S&L crisis. Their actions were in response to campaign contributors, not constituents. Congress avoided this issue in both cases because, in some way, shape, or form, the vast majority of members was guilty of the same thing. *It was an institutional, not an individual, problem.*

It is the nature of America's monetary democracy that strong incentives exist to ignore the conflicts inherent in the system. Members of Congress constantly provide constituent service, while at the same time, they seek campaign contributions. Deciding whether certain actions of constituent service are appropriate or not is an area of ethics that Congress has handled in typical government fashion—it has ignored the existence of the problem.

The Keating Five

St Germain's personal finance troubles finally cost him an election in 1988. As a result, the chairmanship of the House Banking Committee went to Henry Gonzalez (D-NM) who had few financial ties to the thrift industry. Soon after the passage of the Bush bailout bill, Gonzalez held public hearings on the failure of Lincoln Savings and Loan, based in Arizona. The hearings unearthed a broad array of questionable financial and political actions by the management of Lincoln Savings. On October 13, 1989, Common Cause, a citizens' lobbying group, asked the Senate ethics committee and the Justice Department to examine whether five senators—Alan Cranston (D-CA), Dennis DeConcini (D-AZ), John Glenn (D-OH), John McCain (R-AZ), and Donald Riegle (D-MI)—violated ethics rules when they intervened with thrift regulators on behalf of a campaign contributor, Charles Keating, owner of Lincoln Savings. The preliminary investigation began on December 22, and the five senators became known as the Keating Five.

It was not the first time that Keating had problems with federal regulators. In 1979, the Securities and Exchange Commission (SEC) charged Keating with violations of securities laws. The SEC filing claimed that, over a five-year period, Carl H. Linder, president of American Financial Corporation, and Keating, a vice president, had provided officers and directors with fourteen million dollars in uncollateralized personal loans. Without admitting guilt, both Linder and Keating signed consent orders stating that they would not violate securities laws in the future.[12] Keating's insider dealings at American Financial Corporation were nothing compared to what he would do a decade later. The "anything goes" environment of the S&L industry during the eighties was particularly attractive to those individuals who knew how to use corporate funds creatively for personal gain. And Keating knew how to do that.

Having purchased Lincoln Savings and Loan in 1984 for $51 million, Keating placed numerous family members on the payroll and paid them excessively. During the five-year period in which he ran Lincoln, Keating paid himself and family members $41.5 million in salary, bonuses, and perks. But the thrift was, under normal accounting rules, actually losing hundreds of millions of dollars. When Keating purchased Lincoln, it had roughly $2.2 billion in assets. Three years later, the company had grown to $4.2 billion in assets. The vast majority of this growth was due to investment in hotels, commercial real estate, and speculative securities. When the real estate market in Arizona began to collapse, Keating sought to raise new capital for American Continental, the holding company of Lincoln Savings, by selling $230 million in high yield or "junk" bonds. These bonds were not sold to sophisticated institutional investors, but to individuals whose certificates of deposit were maturing. A total of 23,000 Lincoln customers, many of them retirees, purchased these risky securities.[13] Most of these people were falsely led to believe that their investments were government guaranteed. When Lincoln was seized by thrift regulators in April 1989, these bond holders lost all of their investment and, in some cases, their life savings.

What sets the case of Charles Keating apart is not the securities fraud committed against retirees; it is not the rampant insider dealing that took place; and it is not that the bailout cost taxpayers more than $2 billion, the costliest failure to date. What truly sets the case apart is the amount of political influence Keating was able to purchase with his campaign contributions. Keating and his associates, using federally insured deposits, gave the five senators $334,850 in direct campaign contributions and an additional $1,135,000 was given to groups established by the senators to promote voter registration in their states.[14] Did Keating expect to receive special treatment for his generous financial support? When asked a similar question by reporters at a news conference in April 1989, his response was unambiguous: "I want to say in the most forceful way I can; I certainly hope so."

Keating did receive preferential treatment. In early 1987, regulators from the San Francisco office of the Federal Home Loan Bank petitioned the FHLBB to have Lincoln Savings shut down. Keating's response was to call in his political chips. At his behest, Senators Cranston, DeConcini, Glenn, and McCain met with Chairman Gray on April 2, 1987, to discuss Lincoln Savings. The senators wanted to know why the regulators were giving Lincoln Savings such rough treatment. Gray suggested that they talk directly with the San Francisco regulators. On April 9, the four senators, now joined by Senator Riegle, met with the regulators from the San Francisco office responsible for oversight of Lincoln Savings. They pressed the regulators to find out what the problem was with Lincoln. The regulators responded that Lincoln was operating in an unsound manner and that a criminal referral to the Justice Department had been made.[15] At that point, Senators Glenn,

McCain, and Riegle all broke off relations with Charles Keating. Senators Cranston and DeConcini, however, continued to work on Keating's behalf.[16]

Keating's political muscle was still sufficient to go shopping for more lenient regulatory treatment. On July 1, 1987, Danny Wall had replaced Ed Gray as head of the FHLBB and Keating petitioned Wall to have the San Francisco regulators removed from oversight responsibility over Lincoln. In May 1988, Wall allowed the petition to go through, insisting at the time that he was not giving Keating or Lincoln Savings any special treatment. The responsibility for examining Lincoln's financial position was taken from the San Francisco office and transferred to the Washington office. Keating's political influence had emerged victorious, but the political winds in Washington were slowly shifting. As the true magnitude of the Savings and Loan crisis publicly emerged early in 1989, regulators and politicians could no longer afford to be seen as too lenient toward freewheeling thrifts. On April 14, 1989, the government finally shut down Lincoln Savings and Loan. Keating's campaign contributions had bought him a two-year delay in closing his institution. During that time, losses at the thrift continued to soar and more than $230 million of worthless junk bonds were sold to unsuspecting investors.

The Senate ethics committee opened public hearings on the Keating Five on November 15, 1990. The primary issue facing the ethics committee was: where is the line between constituent service and undue political influence? The committee decided that the line existed far from where the Keating Five had stepped. The committee found that Senators Glenn and McCain had exercised poor judgment and that Riegle had exercised poor judgment and had acted in a manner that gave the appearance of impropriety. Deconcini's aggressive conduct was deemed inappropriate. After making these declarations public, the committee recommended no further action against any of the four senators. In Cranston's case, the committee found that the senator had acted in an impermissible pattern and that further action by the entire Senate was warranted. More than eight months after issuing the preliminary report, the committee voted to rebuke Cranston for his actions. A rebuke is a public form of Congressional wrist slapping. In effect, the six senators on the ethics committee were unwilling to hold any of their colleagues truly accountable for operating in a system that caused tremendous conflicts of interest.

The Savings and Loan crisis exemplifies the most fatal flaw of America's monetary democracy—the structural inability of the federal government to place the long-term public interest ahead of short-term special interests. As we have seen in this chapter, the short-term impact of this political flaw is high cost and disastrous policies. The long-term implications, however, are much worse, for in the 1980s the federal government adopted fiscal policies which, if left unaltered, will essentially bankrupt the United States within the next twenty years. To this important issue, we now turn.

Chapter 3

The Fiscal Abyss

When President Ronald Reagan took the oath of office in January 1981, the national debt was approximately $925 billion. At the end of fiscal year 1992, the national debt was $4 trillion.[1] Twelve years of Reagan, Bush, and a spendthrift Congress more than quadrupled the national debt. The bitter irony is that Reagan ran his 1980 campaign on a promise to balance the federal budget by 1984. Once elected, Reagan found it easy to follow through on some campaign promises—such as increasing defense spending and cutting taxes—but difficult to make the unpopular decisions required to reduce the deficit. Reagan's failure to keep his deficit promise carried no political penalty—indeed, he won a landslide reelection victory in 1984. The stark reality is that in America's monetary democracy, the *political* incentives required for deficit reduction simply do not exist. A continuation of current fiscal policies, however, is unacceptable, for the long-term result will be financial disaster.

The Debt and the Deficit

Just how bad are America's fiscal problems? Before answering that question, it is important, with numbers like billions and trillions, to review some basic terminology. Many people, including members of Congress, frequently confuse the words *budget deficit* and *national debt*. The budget deficit, or budget surplus as last seen in 1969, is the difference between government receipts and government expenditures during a fiscal year. Fiscal years begin on October 1 and end on September 30.[†] To pay for a budget deficit, the United States Treasury sells bonds, commonly called treasury securities. The national debt is the total of outstanding treasury securities and debt issues of other government agencies. On September 30, 1993, the *reported* budget deficit for the 1993 fiscal year was $255 billion, while the outstanding national debt stood at $4.35 trillion. I use the word "reported" in front of budget deficit because, as we shall see later, the government's penchant for accounting gimmicks understates the true size of the deficit.

There is a common misconception that government borrowing, for any purpose, is inherently bad. History, however, teaches otherwise. In the depth of the Great Depression, with businesses unwilling to invest and consumers unable to spend, only deficit-financed government spending could get the economy going again. During World War II, heavy federal borrowing was crucial to America's military success and helped the economy boom as never before. On the other hand, government borrowing can also be used as a politically painless and fiscally irresponsible substitute for higher taxes. No, government borrowing is inherently neither good nor bad. What matters is how much money is being borrowed and what it is used for.

The size of a debt is best measured relative to income. For example, a $3,000 debt is small for an individual making $200,000 a year, but rather large for an individual making $15,000 a year. A

[†] Before 1976, fiscal years were July 1 through June 30.

debt's purpose can typically be categorized as either investment or consumption. For example, an individual who borrows money to attend college is investing in her future, while an individual who borrows money for a vacation is living for today. Likewise, a company that borrows money for expansion creates jobs and raises future profits, while a company that borrows money to pay out dividends is simply increasing the current income of shareholders.

How Bad are America's Fiscal Problems?

The two borrowing tests, size and purpose, can assist us in examining the magnitude of America's fiscal problems. Let's begin with size. Chart 1 shows America's fiscal year budget deficits from 1940 to 1993. The *nominal* budget deficits of the Reagan-Bush years are higher than any in American history, but this measure ignores both inflation and the growth in the economy. Chart 2 shows the same budget deficits as a percentage of gross domestic product (GDP).[†] Under this measure, America's largest budget deficits were during World War II. While much smaller than the deficits of the war years, the Reagan-Bush deficits are still the highest in fifty years.

Measuring deficits compared to GDP, however, provides only a snapshot of a particular fiscal year. The total outstanding national debt provides us with a cumulative measure. Chart 3 shows that the national debt has grown at an accelerated pace since 1975. But again, the outstanding debt should be compared to gross domestic product, as shown in Chart 4. The national debt as a percentage of GDP peaked at a high of 127.6% at the end of FY 1946. Between

---

[†] Gross Domestic Product (GDP) includes all the goods in services produced in the United States by individuals, corporations, and government. The measure includes both American and foreign-owned domestic production. In contrast, Gross National Product (GNP) includes the goods and services produced by America's government, corporations and citizens, whether based in the United States or overseas. The federal government used GNP as its main economic measure until 1992, when it switched to GDP.

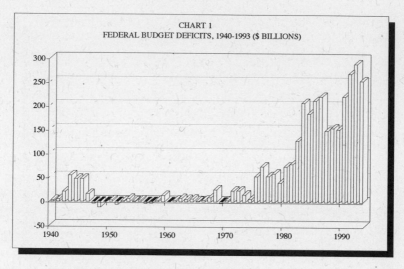

CHART 1
FEDERAL BUDGET DEFICITS, 1940-1993 ($ BILLIONS)

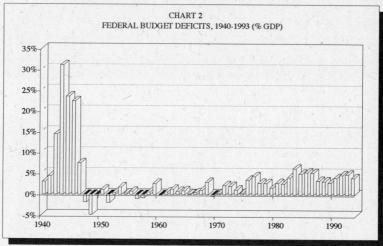

CHART 2
FEDERAL BUDGET DEFICITS, 1940-1993 (% GDP)

1946 and 1981, while the debt was rising from $271 billion to $994 billion, it was falling as percentage of GDP—to a low of 33.5%. During this thirty-five year period, the economy grew much faster than the national debt. But in 1981, the trend was reversed. By 1993, the national debt as a percentage of GDP had increased to 69%, returning the ratio to a level last seen in 1955. *The*

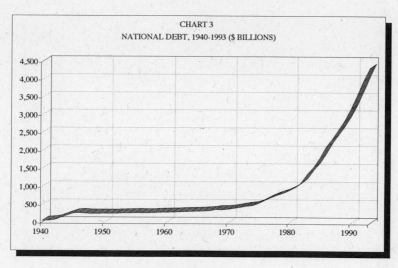

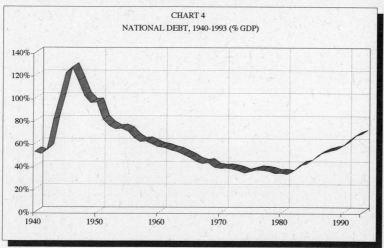

Reagan-Bush fiscal policies reversed twenty-six years of relative debt reduction.

A final measure of national indebtedness is required to provide an accurate picture of America's fiscal condition. When the government borrowed heavily to finance World War II, it sold government bonds at very low interest rates—averaging around 2%.

Today, the government must borrow at much higher rates. As a result, interest payments on the debt have increased as a percentage of GDP, as shown in Chart 5. From the immediate postwar peak of 2.2% in 1946, interest payments on the debt rose to a record 5% of GDP in 1991, before falling to 4.6% in 1993 as interest rates fell dramatically. Critics of this measure will point out that of the $292.5 billion in interest paid in FY 1993, $93.7 billion was paid to other government accounts. Unfortunately, even if we look at just the $198.8 billion in net interest paid to the public, this amount is still 3.2% of GDP.[2] *Under this measure, America's debt load in the early 1990s is higher than at any time in the nation's history.*

Having examined the issue of size, we now turn the second issue: what are these deficits being used for? Federal spending can be divided into two different categories—current spending and capital spending. Or in other words, consumption and investment. The major categories for federal investment expenditures are: physical capital, research and development (R&D), and education and training. Table 7 shows a breakdown of federal spending for fiscal year 1993.

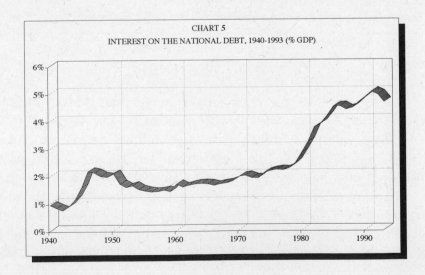

CHART 5
INTEREST ON THE NATIONAL DEBT, 1940-1993 (% GDP)

Table 7
FEDERAL SPENDING CATEGORIES - FY 1993

	Spending ($ Billions)	Percent of Total
Social Security	304.6	21.6%
National Defense	291.1	20.7%
Income Security	207.3	14.7%
Medicare and Medicaid	206.4	14.7%
Net Interest on the National Debt	198.8	14.1%
Other Consumption	80.0	5.7%
Total Federal Consumption	*1,288.1*	*91.5%*
Physical Capital	50.2	
Research and Development	28.0	
Education and Training	41.9	
Total Nondefense Investment	*120.1*	*8.5%*
Total Spending	*1,408.2*	*100.0%*
Total Receipts	*1,153.5*	*81.9%*
Budget Surplus (Deficit)	*-254.7*	*18.1%*

Note: Numbers may not add up due to rounding.

Source: *Budget of the United States Government, FY 1995, Historical Tables.*

During FY 1993, the federal government spent $116.5 billion of the defense budget on capital investment and R&D. While increasing America's ability to project military power, defense-related investment has little impact on the nation's future productivity and has therefore been included with government consumption expenditures. Total nondefense investment expenditures during FY 1993 were $120.1 billion, or 8.5% of total federal spending. The Reagan-Bush tilt away from public investment was substantial. During the 1970s, federal nondefense investment expenditures were 12.7% of total federal spending; during the 1980s, they fell to 8.6%.[3]

Deficit-financed government spending can play an important role in pulling the economy out of recession or in improving future productivity by increasing public investment. Government borrowing, however, can also be used to finance a higher standard of living today at the expense of a lower standard of living tomorrow. The two tests—size and purpose—help determine whether deficits are being used wisely or not. The fiscal policies of the Reagan-Bush era failed both tests. The federal government borrowed record sums of money not to increase investment, but to increase consumption spending and cut taxes. America is only now starting to confront the long-term implications of this irresponsible fiscal policy.

The Budget Process

There is no law that requires a balanced federal budget. Since the nation's birth, the understanding has been implicit: it is unfair and irresponsible for one generation to pass its bills on to future generations. During America's first century and a half of limited government, balancing the budget was relatively easy; except during times of war or economic recession, the federal government typically ran either a small deficit or a small surplus. It was not until the late seventies, when expansive government collided with economic stagnation, that large peacetime budget deficits became a problem.

The OPEC oil price hikes in 1973 sent inflation soaring and the American economy into a deep recession. The recession's budgetary impact was huge—reducing tax revenues while driving up the cost of unemployment insurance. In addition, most government entitlement programs had recently been indexed to the consumer price index. In 1974, the index rose 11%, sending the cost of these programs soaring. In fiscal year 1974, the federal government ran a $6.1 billion federal deficit. A year later, the deficit was $53.2 billion.

Economic stagnation and high inflation did not account for all of the problem, however. In 1974, in response to the Watergate scandal, an activist Congress sought to curb the powers of the presidency. On July 12, 1974, less than a month before he resigned, President Richard Nixon signed the Congressional Budget and Impoundment Control Act of 1974. The law prohibited the president from impounding funds without the approval of Congress. Impounding funds was Nixon's way of not spending money authorized by Congress. But the law went far beyond this one issue. It established a Congressional Budget Office and budget committees in both the House and the Senate. It gave Congress a much more active role in the budget-making process and provided a framework for its new role. The new budget structure gave little focus to budget deficits, however, because at the time deficits were still relatively small.

In general terms, the budget process was supposed to work like this: The president would submit a budget to Congress in January or February for the new fiscal year, which started on October 1. Congress would use the president's budget as a starting point, making numerous changes to reflect its own priorities. Congress would then work to pass a series of spending resolutions which, in total, would compose the new budget. While the 1974 law provided for a budget framework, it created an environment almost guaranteed to create larger deficits. Each Congressional committee decided upon spending levels primarily by looking at three things: the amount spent the previous year, the level of inflation in the past year, and any new spending programs that had been proposed. Noticeably absent from this list was any reference to how much money was available to spend, which was a rather important issue. The budget process actually started by determining how much to spend. Any shortfalls in tax revenue were then to be met through borrowing.

Now imagine if you crafted a family budget in the same fashion. First, you would decide what you wanted to buy: maybe a new car, a new house, a trip to Australia, and a few nice presents for your relatives. After adding up all the things you might possibly want to spend money on, you look at your family's income and find, much to your surprise, that you can't pay for all of these things with this year's salary. What would you do? Cut out a few of the items that you wanted to spend money on, right? Not if you work in Congress you don't. Instead, you simply borrow money to make up the difference. As an individual, you typically would not budget your money this way unless you had a strong desire to spend some time in personal bankruptcy court a few years down the road. This, however, is the way that Congress creates a budget for the nation. Before the Reagan-Bush years, economic stagnation and a flawed Congressional budget process opened the doors for large budget deficits.

Government Attempts at Deficit Reduction

In 1982 and 1983, when Reagan's early budget deficits were significantly higher than projected, there was no large public outcry. Mired in a painful recession, the American people were much more concerned with the state of the economy. Once the economy began to grow again, however, Congress reluctantly turned its attention to the issue of deficit reduction. Congress's early attempts at deficit reduction reflected the institution's desire to find a responsibility-free method of deficit reduction. In 1985, Congress passed the Balanced Budget and Emergency Deficit Control Act, better known as Gramm-Rudman-Hollings, which established deficit targets that had to be met or the president was required to impose across-the-board budget cuts. Congress thought it had solved the deficit problem, but when the deficit targets were not met, Congress avoided across-the-board spending cuts by passing the Balanced Budget and Emergency Deficit Control Reaffirmation Act of 1987, which simply revised the targets upwards.

Both the original and revised Gramm-Rudman-Hollings (GRH) targets projected steady decreases in future budget deficits, as shown in Chart 6. However, the budget deficits in fiscal years 1987, 1988, and 1989 all hovered around $150 billion, showing little tendency to decline. In FY 1990, higher government spending combined with the recession to increase the deficit to $220 billion. In FY 1991, the budget deficit hit $268 billion and rose again in FY 1992 to $290 billion. It took Congress a while to figure out that simply setting a deficit target provided no assurance that the target would be met.

The Gramm-Rudman-Hollings charade came to an abrupt end in 1990. On January 29 of that year, President Bush presented to Congress his budget for FY 1991, which would begin on October 1. The budget estimated a FY 1991 deficit of $64.7 billion, right in line with the Gramm-Rudman-Hollings target of $64 billion. On March 5, the Congressional Budget Office (CBO) released its own

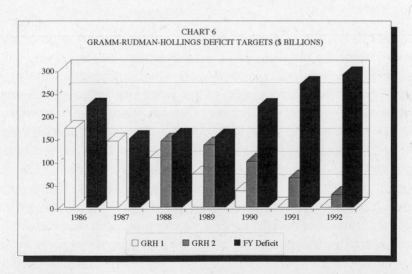

CHART 6
GRAMM-RUDMAN-HOLLINGS DEFICIT TARGETS ($ BILLIONS)

Note: Fiscal year deficit numbers include the costs of the Savings and Loan bailout (FY 1988, $10 billion; FY 1989, $22 billion; FY 1990, $58 billion; FY 1991, $66 billion; FY 1992, $3 billion), which were exempted by law from the Gramm-Rudman-Hollings calculations.

analysis of the Bush budget. The CBO estimated a FY 1991 deficit
of $131 billion. Meanwhile, the economy continued to slow down.
With each passing month, the deficit for the current year, FY 1990,
exceeded the projections of the administration. It was becoming
clear to the Bush administration that its economic projections were
too optimistic. As they planned for FY 1991, the administration
realized that the Gramm-Rudman-Hollings target would never be
met. Concerned about rising deficits in an election year, President
Bush met with Congressional leaders on May 6. They agreed to
discuss a bipartisan budget compromise, and negotiations began
nine days later.

The budget negotiations stalled on the issue of raising taxes.
During the 1988 election campaign, Bush got tremendous political
mileage out of his slogan "read my lips, no new taxes." Under-
standably, Congressional Democrats were not willing to take sole
responsibility for any tax increases. Bush had to decide between
getting a budget agreement and keeping his campaign pledge. On
June 26, he broke his pledge. Three weeks later the Office of
Management and Budget (OMB) updated its estimate of the FY
1991 budget deficit. The OMB now projected a deficit of $168.8
billion (not including expenditures on the Savings and Loan crisis).
On September 30, President Bush and Congressional leaders
announced a budget deal that would reduce the deficit by $40 bil-
lion in FY 1991 and by $500 billion over five years. After four
months of negotiations a deal had been reached, or so it seemed.
On the same day as the agreement was struck, Congress passed a
stopgap spending bill, which kept the government open until October 5, so that there was sufficient time to debate the agreement. On
October 2, President Bush gave a nationally televised address calling on the American people to support the budget agreement.[4]

For nine years Presidents Reagan and Bush had made little
effort to reduce the nation's huge structural budget deficits. They
told the American people that economic growth would slowly
reduce deficits to a manageable level. Painless deficit reduction

was quite easy for politicians to say, and it was appealing for voters to hear. Unfortunately, it never happened. Instead, both the government and the American public grew addicted to the fiscal drug of budget deficits. The government enjoyed spending money it didn't have, while the public grew accustomed to receiving more government services than it actually paid for. During the eight Reagan budgets and the first Bush budget (fiscal years 1982-1990), total federal spending was $8.8 trillion, while receipts were $7.2 trillion, leaving nine years of budget deficits which totalled $1.6 trillion. During this nine-year period, the American taxpayer paid only eighty-one cents for every dollar of federal spending.

In 1988, Bush realized that the American people were unwilling to make up that nineteen-cent gap by paying more in taxes. His campaign pledge of "read my lips, no new taxes" was a direct recognition of this. Yet here he was, a mere twenty-one months into his administration, speaking on national television to ask the public to support a budget package that not only broke his main campaign promise, but also sought to reverse nine years of massive deficit spending. During the speech, he made a few worthwhile points:

> When you get a bill, that bill must be paid. And when you write a check, you're supposed to have money in the bank. But if you don't obey these simple rules with common sense, there's a price to pay. But for too long, the nation's business in Washington has been conducted as if these basic rules did not apply.

Bush's words were quite prescient. A year after the speech was given, the public learned that House members had bounced more than 8,000 checks in a single year at a private bank for House members only. If this was not bad enough, it was also revealed that current and past members had more than $200,000 in outstanding bills at Congressional restaurants. Members of Congress seemed to be living in their own little world where the "basic rules did not apply."

Bush's sudden appeal to the American people for sacrifice was met with a simple answer—No! Bush had not made the case for sacrifice, and it would take more than one national address to overturn the nine-year addiction to deficit spending. Newspapers ran stories about how much more people would have to pay in new taxes and where their services would be cut. And for what? To reduce the deficit? The same deficit that the Reagan and Bush administrations had so purposefully ignored? Calls to Congress came in heavily against the budget deal. Special interest groups turned up the heat. With elections only one month away, Congress wilted.

The bipartisan budget agreement, supported by the President and the Congressional leadership, was rejected by the House on October 5. On the same day, Congress approved another stopgap measure to keep the government running until October 12. The next day, Bush vetoed the measure, and the House failed to override the veto. The government closed down for the weekend. On October 8, the House passed a bill that set general spending levels for the various committees and included a stopgap measure. Bush signed the measure and the government reopened. But details still needed to be worked out. Over the next three weeks, specific issues were hammered out among the various factions. It was during this period of time that President Bush flip-flopped on a number of tax and spending issues. It was a disturbing sight, for the government seemed rudderless. Bush's approval rating plummeted. It took until October 27, a mere two weeks before the elections, until a budget for FY 1991 was finally passed. On November 5, thirty-five days after the new fiscal year had already begun, Bush signed the Budget Enforcement Act (BEA) of 1990.

The BEA changed the deficit reduction focus from setting deficit targets to slowing the growth in federal discretionary spending. The belief was that if spending growth slowed, then economic growth would slowly reduce the size of the deficit. This new approach had two significant problems. First, it set caps only on discretionary spending, which accounted for just 40% of the FY 1991 budget, while making no effort to rein in mandatory spending, which accounted for the other 60% (and was rising rapidly). Second, the recession that began in July 1990 continued to send the budget deficit higher. If the economy is not growing and tax revenues are not increasing, then slowing the growth of discretionary spending will not reduce America's budget deficits.

Federal Spending Patterns

In the mid-seventies, when expansive government collided with economic stagnation, fiscal responsibility disappeared. Facing difficult decisions, government officials simply substituted borrowing for taxes. Table 8 shows that, while federal spending has been rising steadily as a percentage of gross domestic product, federal tax receipts have barely increased since the 1960s. Reversing these fiscal trends will be extremely difficult, for America's monetary democracy provides few incentives for elected officials to make the difficult decisions required.

Table 8
FEDERAL BUDGET TRENDS
(PERCENTAGE OF GDP)

	Federal Receipts	Federal Spending	Budget Deficit
1950s	17.7%	18.1%	0.5%
1960s	18.4%	19.2%	0.8%
1970s	18.5%	20.7%	2.3%
1980s	18.9%	23.0%	4.1%
1990-93	18.5%	22.9%	4.4%

Note: Numbers may not add up due to rounding.

Source: Calculated from statistics in *Economic Report of the President, 1994*.

And while current budget trends are bad, a closer look at how the federal government spends the taxpayers' money reveals other dangers. Table 9 provides a historical breakdown of federal spending. Since the fifties, federal spending on social security, net interest on the debt, health care programs (medicare and medicaid), and federal employee retirement has grown rapidly. In contrast, defense spending as a percentage of GDP has been shrinking since the fifties, with the exception of a slight blip upward in the eighties. All other federal spending rose from the fifties through the seventies, before beginning to fall in the eighties. Table 9 illustrates a vitally important point. *If the United States is to get its fiscal house in order, then it must reduce the growth in spending on social security, net interest on the debt, health care programs, and federal employee retirement.*

Table 9
HISTORICAL BREAKDOWN OF FEDERAL SPENDING (PERCENTAGE OF GDP)

	1950s	1960s	1970s	1980s	1990-93
Social Security	1.2%	2.7%	4.1%	4.7%	4.7%
Net Interest	1.3%	1.3%	1.6%	3.0%	3.3%
Medicare and Medicaid	—	0.3%	1.3%	2.2%	2.9%
Federal Employee Retirement	0.2%	0.4%	0.8%	1.0%	1.0%
Subtotal	*2.7%*	*4.7%*	*7.8%*	*10.8%*	*12.0%*
Defense	10.8%	8.9%	5.7%	6.0%	5.0%
All Other Spending	4.6%	5.6%	7.3%	6.1%	6.0%
Total	*18.1%*	*19.2%*	*20.7%*	*23.0%*	*22.9%*

Note: Federal employee retirement includes federal employee disability. Numbers may not add up due to rounding.

Source: Calculated from statistics in *Budget of the United States Government, FY 1995, Historical Tables.*

The federal government, however, has little direct control over net interest costs on the national debt. These costs are determined by the interest rates the United States Treasury sells its securities to the public. In the previous chapter, we saw how the dramatic drop in interest rates from 1991-1993 had a large beneficial impact on the cost of the Savings and Loan crisis. This interest rate drop also caused net interest on the federal debt to fall slightly from FY 1992 to FY 1993—the first such drop in more than thirty years.† The danger, of course, is that a future rise in interest rates will cause net interest on the debt to increase substantially.

Short-term variations in interest rates aside, the basic facts of budget math are straightforward—if the federal government continues to run large budget deficits over the long term, then net interest costs on the debt will continue their upward climb. To reverse this dangerous trend, the federal government must therefore focus on reducing the growth of spending on social security, health care, and federal employee retirement. But in all three of these areas, federal expenditures are dependent not only upon government policy, but on the number of Americans reaching retirement age. And America's current demographic trends have ominous implications for the nation's future.

America's Demographic Dilemma

Between the years 1994 and 2010, the number of Americans age sixty-five or over will increase from thirty-three million to thirty-eight million, but as a percentage of the total population, this group will actually decrease from 12.6% to 12.2%. In the year 2010, however, the baby boom generation—the large group of

---

† It is important to note that while lower interest rates have many positive impacts—such as lower net interest costs on the federal debt and greater activity in the crucial housing sector—these benefits are not costless. Individuals receive less interest on their savings, and for those on fixed incomes this impact can be substantial.

Americans born between 1945 and 1960—will begin to retire. Between 2010 and 2030, the number of Americans age sixty-five or over will jump from thirty-eight million to sixty-six million, or 17.1% of the entire population.[5] As a result, federal expenditures for social security, health care, and federal employee retirement will soar, pushing the American economy to the breaking point.

The aging of the baby boom generation is like a ticking demographic time bomb. And at the moment, government officials are making no efforts to insure that the bomb does not go off.

A closer look at the social security system illuminates America's demographic dilemma. In 1983, the federal government raised payroll contribution taxes to stop the social security system from going bankrupt. As a result, the social security trust funds began to run sizable operating surpluses. At the end of FY 1993, the main social security trust fund had assets of $356 billion.[6] These assets are sufficient to pay roughly sixteen months of current benefits. But while the social security trust fund has an operating surplus, it has also been undertaking huge financial liabilities for future benefits.

Three different actuarial measures provide a portrait of the social security system's financial health. The first method, called the currently accrued method, calculates the liabilities that have been accrued to date and compares them with the money currently set aside to meet those liabilities. This is the method used by private corporations. The second method, the closed system method, assumes that no new workers are added to the system in future years. The present value of all current and future benefits is compared to the present value of all current and future taxes paid into the system. The third method, the open system method, is similar to the closed system method except that it includes new participants who will enter both the work force and the social security system in the future.

How does the social security system look under these three measures? I estimate that as an open system, the most favorable measurement, the social security system has an actuarial deficiency of $1.5 trillion. Under the currently accrued method, a deficiency of $2.6 trillion, and under the closed system method, the social security system is short a whopping $7.4 trillion.[7] Under any measure, it is poignantly clear that the social security system faces a massive actuarial deficiency. The government's retirement funds for military, civil service, railroad, and post office employees all face similar, though somewhat smaller, problems. Confronted with this harsh reality, politicians point with pride to the operating "surplus" in the social security trust funds, while conveniently ignoring the system's huge long-term liabilities.

The government's failure to reserve sufficient funds to meet future liabilities is worrisome enough, but deceptive accounting practices compound the problem. It would seem logical that the difference in the outstanding national debt from one fiscal year to another would simply be the budget surplus or deficit for that fiscal year. However, this is not the case. Federal agencies and trust funds are required by law to invest their excess cash in government treasury securities. Federal debt securities issued to government agencies and trust funds, while increasing the national debt, are treated as inter-government transactions for accounting purposes and are not included in calculating the federal budget deficit. As a result, treasury securities issued to government agencies and trust funds reduce the size of *reported* budget deficits. What is the impact of this accounting practice? By double counting the "surplus" funds in its trust and retirement funds, the federal government has been able to understate the size of its budget deficits by $738 billion over the past seven fiscal years (FY 1987 to FY 1993).

Fixing these problems will be politically difficult. The beneficiaries of social security and medicare—elderly Americans—are a potent political force. Indeed, the American Association of Retired Persons (AARP) is arguably the most powerful special interest group in the country. Founded in 1958, the AARP had five million members in 1981; today, its membership exceeds thirty-four million. The benefits received by most current social security recipients are typically multiples of any contributions they actually paid into the fund. Attempts to curb costs, such as means testing to reduce benefits to wealthy retirees, are political nonstarters, for few politicians wish to raise the ire of the AARP. Presidents Reagan and Bush both frequently proclaimed "now is not the time to mess with social security," which was exactly what the AARP wanted to hear. But the political realities do not change the financial facts: although currently running an operating surplus, the social security system is dangerously underfunded.

America's short-term demographics, however, encourage the government to continue its current accounting practices. Over the next decade, operating surpluses in the social security and other trust funds will continue to grow, allowing the federal government to hide incrementally larger portions of future budget deficits. By the year 2010, a huge supply of treasury securities will have been built up in the social security trust funds. But when the social security trust funds begin to "cash in" their treasury securities, the harsh reality will set in. There is no real money in the social security trust fund, only federal IOUs. The payroll taxes paid by workers in earlier years would have already been used to pay for previous budget deficits.

When the baby boom generation begins to retire in the year 2010, two forces will combine to cause severe economic and fiscal stress on the United States. To pay off the treasury securities held in the social security trust fund, the government will have to borrow more money from the public (i.e. run larger budget deficits), pushing up interest rates and inflation. In addition, as the number of retirees increases dramatically, the costs of social security and medicare will soar. Contentious disputes will erupt between the generations over benefits and responsibilities. The end result will be a dramatic rise in tax rates, a sharp curtailment in benefits, or, most likely, a combination of both. Elected officials will be in the unenviable position of choosing between frequent recessions and high inflation. America's demographic time bomb will have exploded and the nation will have fallen into the fiscal abyss.

Gauging America's Fiscal Health

The simplest gauge of America's fiscal course is to compare the growth of the nation's economy with the growth of the national debt. As long as the economy grows faster than the national debt, then budget deficits should not be a significant problem. But if the federal debt increases faster than the economy, then, at some point in the future, interest payments on the debt will begin to choke off economic growth and spark rapid inflation.

How is the United States doing by this measure? During the thirty-four year period from 1947 to 1981, the national debt grew faster than the economy in only eight fiscal years. And in five of those years the difference in growth rates was less than 1%. Since fiscal year 1982, however, the national debt has grown faster than the economy every single year, and at no time has GDP growth come within 2.5% of debt growth. Indeed, during the twelve fiscal years from 1982 to 1993, the national debt grew faster than the economy by an annual average of 6.6%.

History is replete with examples of nations that have worked hard to reach the pinnacle of economic success only to grow complacent and enter a long period of economic decline.[8] Indeed, nothing can insure a nation's demise faster than irresponsible fiscal policies. There exists no natural correction mechanism for a nation that has embarked on a downward path, for once the economic pie begins to shrink, interest groups focus more on keeping their share than on trying to make the pie bigger. Brazil provides a modern day example of this dangerous phenomenon.

A democratic nation of 160 million people, Brazil has the world's tenth largest economy, but its political system has been crippled by special interests and a massive public bureaucracy. Persistent large budget deficits and a $40 billion foreign debt have combined to hamper economic growth and produce hyperinflation (over 1,000% in 1992). Real GNP—in dollar terms—grew at an average rate of 2.1% from 1980 to 1989, but per capita GNP actually fell.[9] While the indexation of most workers' incomes to inflation has prevented major civil unrest, severe economic problems exist. Although Brazil has the highest per capita income in Latin America, its income distribution is wildly skewed—the top 20% of the population earn twenty-six times what the bottom 20% earn (in the United States the ratio is nine to one). Economic stagnation and a skewed income distribution have fueled a rapid escalation in crime and a further deterioration in the public's confidence in Brazilian democracy. The spectre of a return to military rule looms on Brazil's horizon.[10]

This is not to argue that America is in imminent danger of becoming another Brazil. But that nation's experience teaches an important lesson. Brazil's leaders did not plan to have hyperinflation, high crime rates, and sluggish economic growth. After decades of myopic fiscal and economic policies, however, the present predicament was almost inevitable, and their political system does not have the ability to make the difficult decisions required. The Brazilian lesson is that in a democracy there is no natural correction mechanism for political myopia other than public determination to no longer tolerate it. Today, America's leaders do not plan on having high inflation, high unemployment, and sluggish economic growth in the future. Yet for the last two decades the United States has pursued economic and fiscal policies that have set the nation on a clear course for eventually reaching such outcomes.

Budget Deficit in the Political Spotlight

During the 1992 presidential campaign, independent candidate Ross Perot made reducing the nation's budget deficit his primary issue. The need for greater fiscal responsibility hit a responsive chord with American voters, helping Perot garner nineteen million votes—the best showing of an independent candidate in eighty years. By successfully tapping into voter disenchantment with the political status quo, Perot proved that a large constituency for fiscal responsibility does exist in the United States.

As a result of Perot's efforts, reducing the size of the federal budget deficit has become a high priority for the Clinton administration. The administration's first budget (for FY 1994) included a deficit reduction package aimed at reducing the federal deficit by $500 billion over five years. In its second budget (for FY 1995), the administration trumpets its deficit cutting success by stating that "if the declines we project in the deficits for 1994 and 1995 take place, it will be the first time deficits have declined three years running *since Harry Truman occupied the Oval Office.*"[11]

On the surface, it seems like the Clinton administration has been able to make the difficult decisions required to restore the nation to fiscal health. The reality, however, differs from the rhetoric. The recent decline in federal budget deficits (from $290.4 billion in FY 1992 to $254.7 billion in FY 1993 to a projected $234.8 billion in FY 1994) is primarily the result of lower interest rates and an improving economy. And while it is true that the administration's efforts—the elimination of some unnecessary programs, the reduction in the growth rate of others, and the increase in tax rates on the wealthiest Americans—will reduce the size of budget deficits in future years, these actions make only a small dent in the nation's fiscal problems.

The Clinton administration currently predicts that the national debt will increase by $1.6 trillion over the next five fiscal years (1994-1998). A national debt increasing at the rate of over $300 billion a year indicates that substantial additional steps need to be taken to restore America to fiscal health. The current dangers, however, are twofold. First, after having waged a difficult budget battle and with low interest rates and an improving economy, strong incentives exist for the Clinton administration to claim victory and not seriously address the deficit issue again until after the 1996

I think we finally have this deficit thing under control.

elections. Second, and more importantly, the focus has been on short-term deficit reduction and not on the political flaws which encourage irresponsible fiscal policies. If these flaws are not fixed, then America will be unsuccessful in its attempts to reign in the powerful forces, both political and demographic, which will push budget deficits to dizzying heights during the next two decades. A closer look at government budget projections, both past and present, can be found in Appendix A.

This point bears repeating. Federal budget deficits are not inherently bad. Deficit spending for investment purposes can help create jobs, improve productivity, and increase economic growth. With good reason, however, the American people no longer trust government to act in a fiscally responsible fashion, for recent budget deficits have not been used for investment purposes, but as a politically painless substitute for taxes. Large budget deficits are not simply the result of a few poor decisions, but a manifestation of the perverse incentives of America's monetary democracy. In reversing America's dangerous fiscal trends, political reform is not simply a welcomed addition, but an absolute necessity. To see why, we now turn to the journey which America has taken—from limited government, to expansive government, to a government that no longer works.

Part II

An American Evolution

Chapter 4

The Breakdown of Laissez Faire

Beliefs long held are not easily discarded. Since the nation's birth, Americans have generally opposed government intervention in the economy. This opposition reflects not only a strong belief in the benefits of a free market system, but also a deep-seated distrust of government involvement. For over one hundred and fifty years, American government played little role in the national economy. During the twentieth century, however, the government's role has grown rapidly. In 1929, government spending at all levels— federal, state, and local—accounted for slightly less than ten percent of the nation's gross domestic product. Over the next sixty years, government spending more than tripled as a percentage of GDP. Today, while the reality of non-intervention has long since disappeared, the illusion lives on. Instead of focusing on how to make government's economic role more effective, America's political debates are still dominated by rigid ideology and empty rhetoric. A look at the evolution of America's political economy reveals why the United States has failed to adjust to the political and economic realities of the 1990s.

America's Political Economy

America's first era of political economy was conceived in rebellion. After declaring independence from Great Britain in 1776, delegates to the Continental Congress debated how to structure the new government. One group wanted a strong central government patterned after the British model, while a second group wanted strong state powers and a weak central government. It is not surprising that the prevailing sentiment, in the midst of a war with England, was with the latter. America's first constitution, the Articles of Confederation, provided for a loose association of sovereign states. On November 17, 1777, the Articles were sent to the states for ratification; support was not overwhelming. It took more than three years, until March 1781, for the Articles to be adopted. Seven months later, George Washington's troops defeated the British at Yorktown.

The conclusion of the Revolutionary War shifted the nation's attention to growing domestic problems. The central government could not pay off the war debt because it had no power to tax, and the states ignored its financial requisitions. Contentious disputes erupted between the states over trade and Western land claims. On July 8, 1786, Daniel Shays, a former Revolutionary War officer, led a revolt in Western Massachusetts to protest excessive state taxes. Although suppressed in January 1787, the revolt reinforced a growing consensus that the Articles of Confederation were not working.

A Philadelphia convention was called to propose amendments to the Articles. Scheduled to begin on May 14, 1787, the proceedings were delayed for eleven days until seven states were represented. During those eleven days the delegates from Virginia, including George Mason, Edmund Randolph, James Madison, and George Washington, met daily to develop ideas for change. Their proposals, the Virginia Resolves, called not for amendments to the Articles, but for an entirely new system of government. The consensus for dramatic change was strong, for the Virginia Resolves became the working blueprint of the convention. When completed in September 1787, the new Constitution provided for a strong central government and a separation of powers. A mechanism for amendment was also included so that future generations, benefitting from experience, could remedy its defects. On June 21, 1788, the second era of American political economy began when New Hampshire became the ninth state to ratify the Constitution.

Adam Smith and Laissez Faire

In 1776, the year America declared political independence, a Scottish philosophy professor published a book that became the foundation of modern economics. In *The Wealth of Nations,* Adam Smith described in detail a new dynamic shaping the world around him. It was the dynamic of capitalism. Smith's historic work not only set forth the basic concepts of capitalism, but also argued persuasively for a new approach to organizing a national economy.

One fundamental goal of political economy is to increase national wealth. During the seventeenth and eighteenth centuries, European nations sought to achieve this goal through the policies of mercantilism. Under this system, governments created large trading monopolies and made liberal use of regulations and duties to encourage exports and discourage imports. By maintaining a favorable balance of trade, nations increased their wealth through the accumulation of gold and silver bullion. Although an improvement over the feudal system that characterized the Middle Ages, mercantilism had serious flaws.

The Wealth of Nations was a frontal assault on the tenets of mercantilism. Smith described how government regulations and duties, while helping specific producers, often reduced the flow of trade and increased consumer costs. In addition, the emphasis on bullion accumulation was misguided because gold and silver were valuable only in exchange for other goods. Smith explained that the real source of national wealth was the annual produce of the nation's workers. He argued that the government, by focusing on managed trade and bullion accumulation, was actually impeding the increase in national wealth.

Smith's alternative to mercantilism arose from his observations of human nature: "It is not from the benevolence of the butcher, the brewer, or the baker, that we expect our dinner, but from their regard to their own interest."[1] Economic self-interest was the driving force of capitalism. From this starting point, Smith described how competition and the interaction of supply and demand determined prices, profits, and the allocation of resources. The beauty of this natural economic order was that it was self-regulating; the market acted like an "invisible hand" to guide individual economic pursuits into promoting the common good. Because the economy was self-regulating, the optimal way for government to increase national wealth was to not intervene. Smith's philosophy, known as non-interventionism or laissez faire, became the mantra of Europe's growing business class.

The writings of Adam Smith found a receptive audience in the United States. As an agrarian nation, the United States had little need for government intervention in the economy. Distrustful of authority, Americans wanted limited government powers. Therefore, from both a philosophical and practical standpoint, laissez faire capitalism was a natural choice for the young American nation. Under the Constitution, the federal government was given the power to levy excise taxes, coin money, and regulate interstate commerce. Beyond these basic functions, government involvement was unneeded and unwanted.

America's Economy Evolves

During the nineteenth century, America's economy flourished under laissez faire. Plentiful natural resources, a growing population, technological advancements, and an expanding Western frontier all contributed to strong economic growth. The rate of growth, however, was uneven. The economy would grow for a number of years, then contract, then grow again. In other words, the economy exhibited a cyclical pattern of boom and bust. Today we call this pattern the business cycle. Although never identical, business cycles often exhibit common traits. Economic growth usually stops when a period of overproduction causes a "general glut:" too many products and not enough buyers. Prices fall. Companies lay off workers. Demand drops. Savings increases. Interest rates fall. Inventories are slowly reduced. The economy hits bottom. When production has dropped enough so that it can no longer meet demand, production is increased. New workers are hired. Demand increases and the economy begins to expand.

The level of aggregate demand drives the business cycle. In an agrarian economy, aggregate demand is a function of population—a relatively stable variable. But in a manufacturing economy, aggregate demand is a function of both consumer and business spending—much more volatile variables. As the industrial revolution transformed the American economy in the late nineteenth century, Americans discovered that capitalism exacted a price for economic progress. Growth in manufacturing required ever increasing levels of economic interdependence, but that same interdependence exacerbated the highs and lows of the business cycle. Nevertheless, because economists and business leaders saw the business cycle as a natural phenomenon, the cycle's self-correcting nature simply reinforced their belief in laissez faire.

Was the American economy operating as Adam Smith had envisioned? To a great extent it was, but the passage of time slowly transformed the economic landscape. Smith lived in an agrarian society where manufactured goods were produced by thousands of small companies. If a manufacturer, seeking to promote his own self-interest, was overcharging for a particular good, then competitors would enter the market and force the price of the good down to its natural price. Competition was a vital part of Smith's "invisible hand." Smith assumed that no manufacturer would be able to dominate a particular industry unless the government granted the company a monopoly. This assumption, while true in Smith's day, was no longer valid in late nineteenth century America. As predatory companies bought out competitors and drove others out of business, small manufacturers gradually disappeared. By monopolizing a particular industry, a company could charge high prices and earn exorbitant profits. In the late nineteenth century, monopolies emerged in most major American industries.

But, as Adam Smith pointed out, political economy seeks the increase of *two* objects: national wealth *and* social welfare.[2] During America's first hundred years, laissez faire worked well. Competition acted as a restraining mechanism, keeping the pursuit of self-interest from resulting in public exploitation. But as businesses grew larger, competition began to disappear. The stark excesses of unregulated capitalism, such as horrible working conditions and an unequal distribution of wealth and income, emerged throughout the nation. Smith's natural economic order slowly gave way to a Darwinian jungle, where issues of social welfare were consistently ignored. As the nineteenth century came to a close, America's policy of laissez faire needed a drastic overhaul.

One hundred years of economic success, however, created strong support for laissez faire. The most ardent supporters, not surprisingly, were the monopolies that thrived in the unregulated environment. Using their formidable political power, big business interests were successful in hampering government efforts to intervene in the economy. Legislative attempts to improve working conditions—such as prohibiting child labor, reducing the work week, establishing a minimum wage, and allowing unions to organize—were regularly defeated. The Sherman Antitrust Act, passed on July 2, 1890, prohibited monopolies, but the Supreme Court consistently ruled in favor of big business. Nevertheless, the gradual rise of labor unions and growing public outrage over corporate greed slowly changed the political climate. President Theodore Roosevelt successfully prosecuted a number of antitrust cases, and President Woodrow Wilson passed additional legislation to curb some of the worst monopolistic abuses. But just as government efforts to curtail the excesses of laissez faire were gathering steam, events in Europe seized the nation's attention.

World War I

When the First World War began on June 28, 1914, the United States had no intention of getting involved and declared its neutrality. To Americans, the war seemed like all the other conflicts that had periodically erupted on the European continent. President Wilson won re-election in 1916 partly based on the cry of supporters that "he kept us out of war." But on February 1, 1917, the German government declared a policy of unrestricted submarine warfare against all shipping in the war zone. Wilson's hand had been forced, and on April 2, 1917, Wilson asked Congress to declare war saying, "the world must be made safe for democracy." The entrance of America into the war turned the tide against Germany and its allies. On January 8, 1918, Woodrow Wilson presented Congress with his "Fourteen Points," which provided the world with a statement of American war aims. On October 4, 1918, Germany began negotiations for an armistice based upon Wilson's pronouncements. The armistice was signed on November 11, 1918.

While the United States won the war, it did not win the peace. Wilson sought a fair and just peace, a "peace without victory."†
This idealistic theme was found throughout Wilson's "Fourteen Points," which included the phrases "open covenants of peace,

---

† This sentiment was first expressed by Wilson in a speech before the Senate on January 22, 1917 (before America entered the war), in which he stated "victory would mean peace forced upon the loser, a victor's terms imposed upon the vanquished. It would be accepted in humiliation, under duress, at an intolerable sacrifice, and would leave a sting, a resentment, a bitter memory upon which the terms of peace would not rest permanently, but only on quicksand. Only a peace between equals can last."

openly arrived at," and "a free, open-minded, and absolutely impartial adjustment of all colonial claims." Wilson's views, however, were not shared by America's allies. After the long conflict, the French and British wanted to punish their defeated foe. French leader Georges Clemenceau wanted to extract a high payment from Germany, just as Germany had done to France in 1871.[†] Lloyd George, the prime minister of the United Kingdom, called for an election shortly after the war's close, and the major campaign issue was how high the German reparation payments should be. At the peace negotiations held at Versailles in 1919, Wilson's idealism and lack of foreign diplomacy experience led to a series of grave errors. Wilson became fixated on his "fourteenth point," the establishment of a league of nations to arbitrate international disputes and eliminate the need for war. In pursuit of this goal, Wilson abandoned the core of his remaining points and acceded to the demands of Britain and France. Included in the treaty were heavy reparations to be paid by the Germans—a staggering sum of $40 billion—and other oppressive measures.

Wilson's fixation on the League of Nations blinded him to reality. In the 1918 elections, the Republicans had gained control of both houses of Congress. Nevertheless, Wilson refused to bring any senior Republican senators to Versailles—an action that only intensified the animosity between himself and Senator Henry Cabot Lodge (R-MA), chairman of the Senate Committee on Foreign Relations. During the ratification debates, the Republicans attempted to attach a number of amendments to the treaty limiting America's future international involvement. A majority of senators supported the Republican version, but Wilson encouraged Democratic senators to oppose it because he wanted the treaty passed with no reservations. Wilson hoped to use the 1920 elections as a

---

[†]Under the terms of the Treaty of Frankfurt, signed on May 10, 1871 to conclude the Franco-German War, France agreed to pay five billion francs in reparations and cede the provinces Alsace and Lorraine to Germany.

referendum on both the treaty and the League. Taking his case to the people, Wilson traveled across the country in an effort to convince the public of the League's importance. However, the trip was cut short when Wilson suffered a stroke. A few weeks later another stroke paralyzed the left side of his body. Wilson's declining health prohibited a re-election run, and, as a result, the referendum he sought was never held. America did not sign the treaty or enter the League. By failing to take on new international responsibilities, the United States lost any opportunity to remedy the deficiencies of the Versailles treaty.

At the Versailles conference, economist John Maynard Keynes was part of the British delegation. Disgusted at the resulting treaty, Keynes resigned his position in the British Treasury Department and wrote a seething book entitled *The Economic Consequences of the Peace*. Keynes argued that the reparations being required of Germany were unrealistically severe. According to Keynes, Germany's prewar economic prosperity rested on three pillars: its coal industry, its manufacturing base, and its international trade. However, the economic clauses of the treaty required Germany to surrender its merchant marine and a large portion of its annual coal output. Its international trade suffered further from restrictions imposed by other nations. Keynes argued that while reparation payments were based on German prewar economic activity, the treaty stripped Germany of its ability to return to those levels. Politics, in its infinite wisdom, had reduced economic logic to dust.

The war left America's allies with huge debts, which hung like a dark cloud over Europe's economy. The United States was owed $10 billion; the United Kingdom owed the United States $4.2 billion, but was owed $8.7 billion by its other allies; France owed $5.3 billion to the United States and the United Kingdom, but was owed $1.8 billion by its other allies.[3] Keynes proposed three reforms: a revision of the treaty, a cancellation of inter-ally debts, and a program of international loans to spur economic development. Debt cancellation would have been the single greatest form of economic aid available, but it required a great deal of foresight and generosity on the part of the United States and the United Kingdom. At a crucial point in the economic history of the world, the United States decided to let its European allies fend for themselves.

Keynes's economic analysis of the treaty proved to be prescient. Germany, its economy devastated by inflation and unemployment, soon defaulted on its reparation payments. In response, French and Belgian troops occupied the Ruhr in 1923. Twice during the 1920s, German reparation payments were revised downward, but the damage had already been done. The fragile German democracy that emerged after the war was shattered, and the seeds were sown for the emergence of the Nazis in the 1930s. The few German reparation payments made were paid for, not by its own economy, but by private foreign loans, mostly from the United States. This was just one part of a farcical flow of international credit emerging after the war. America's allies had no real chance to make payments on their debt unless they received payments from Germany. Germany borrowed money from American investors to pay reparations to the allies. The allies turned around and sent the money back to the United States. Soon, reality would call a halt to that charade.

The Roaring Twenties

During the 1920s, laissez faire capitalism was again embraced by America's government. Warren Harding was elected president in 1920 and immediately began to reduce the government's role in the economy. He appointed big business supporters to federal regulatory bodies, and his four Supreme Court nominees were all staunch advocates of limited government. After Harding's death in 1923, President Calvin Coolidge continued Harding's laissez faire approach. As long as the economy was doing well, conservative politicians did not notice that laissez

faire capitalism was not improving the social welfare of a growing number of Americans.

After the 1920–21 recession, the American economy grew
strongly. The nation's steel and auto industries, utilizing mass-
production techniques, boomed as never before. The Federal
Reserve Bank's easy money policies kept interest rates low, while
sizable increases in worker productivity kept inflation under control. The nation's strong economic growth was reflected in rising
stock prices. From 1922 to 1927, the New York Stock Market, as
measured by the Dow Jones Industrial Average (DJIA), increased
at an average annual rate of 16.5%.[4] However, trouble was brewing
just below the surface.

This period of growth, expansion, and constantly rising stock
prices created a euphoric environment, aptly named the Roaring
Twenties. A growing number of people wanted to get rich quickly,
and the stock market was the place to do it. As the stock market
kept rising, more and more people began to join the party. The
Federal Reserve Bank's easy money policies, so instrumental in
creating economic growth and prosperity, were now used to fuel
rampant speculation. In 1928, caution was thrown to the wind and
the DJIA soared 48.2%.

Wall Street capitalized on this unrestrained optimism by
providing individual investors with easy access to borrowed
money and investment trusts, which were companies established
solely to purchase stock in other companies. Investment trusts were
similar in concept to today's mutual funds, but with one crucial
difference—the use of leverage. By borrowing money, both
investors and investment trusts could obtain a higher return from
anticipated price increases. At the time, a stock purchase required
at least half of the purchase price be paid for in cash. Under ordinary circumstances, fifty percent is a fairly conservative margin
requirement, but the proliferation of investment trusts rendered this
constraint impotent. For example: an individual could borrow half
of the money needed to buy shares in an investment trust; the trust

could then borrow half of the money needed to buy shares in a second investment trust; the second trust could in turn borrow half of the money needed to purchase shares in a third investment trust. A pyramiding scheme of endless height could be created, all of it legal, and all of it generally unregulated. As long as prices kept increasing, everyone was happy. But the stage was being set for a dramatic reversal.

By 1929, the speculation had taken on a life of its own. The New York Stock Exchange was drawing money from around the world to finance the speculative frenzy. On September 3, 1929, the great bull market of the twenties reached its peak when the DJIA closed at a high of 381.17. The market drifted lower during the month of September and early October. On October 24, the market began to fall on heavy volume, and on October 29—Black Tuesday—the stock market began a free fall. The DJIA hit a low of 212.33 on that day. The market would recover over the next few days, but would begin to fall again in November, hitting a low for the year when the DJIA closed at 198.69 on November 13. In a short span of ten weeks, the DJIA had lost almost half its value. Many individuals lost everything in the wake of the crash as they discovered that leverage was a double-edged sword, magnifying both gains *and* losses.

America's economy had already stopped growing before the crash. The Federal Reserve Bank's indices for both industrial activity and factory production had peaked in June 1929.[5] By the end of the year, the economy was demonstrating all the signs of a normal recession; overproduction had increased inventories, and, in response, businesses were slowly cutting production levels. The economy needed to go through a short recession before it could begin to grow again. At the bottom of previous economic downturns two things happened. First, savings increased. Second, demand stopped falling and businesses responded by increasing production to restock inventories. In 1930, neither of these things happened.

For more than forty years the federal government had dragged its feet in dealing with the economic and social excesses of laissez faire. During the twenties, as stock market speculation reached a fever pitch, the government quietly sat on the sidelines. When the bubble burst in 1929, a shock wave was sent through America's economic system. The business cycle, brought to record highs by speculative excess, was whipped sharply in the opposite direction, and the cycle's self-correcting mechanism snapped. As a result, what began as a normal recession turned into the Great Depression.

The Great Depression

Strong economic growth during the twenties had dramatically increased the interdependence of the nation's economy. Nowhere was this more true than in the nation's banking system. Banks played a crucial role in the national economy by acting as a bridge between individual savings and business investment. In the wake of the stock market crash, this bridge collapsed. As Table 10 shows, bank failures increased dramatically.

Table 10
BANK FAILURES
DURING THE GREAT DEPRESSION

	Bank Failures	Deposits at Failed Banks ($ Millions)
1921-29 Avg.	635	181
1930	1,352	853
1931	2,294	1,690
1932	1,456	715
1933	4,004	3,599

Source: *Federal Reserve Bank Annual Report, 1937.*

In 1929, federal deposit insurance did not exist. As a result, the torrent of banking failures devastated national savings. Gross private savings fell from $15.9 billion in 1929 to a low of $400 *million* in 1932, a 97.5% decline. Personal savings collapsed from $2.6 billion in 1929 to a *negative* $1.3 billion in 1932.[6] America lost confidence in its banking system. People began taking money out of banks and hiding it in mattresses and cookie jars. Worried about the future, individuals slashed their spending. The sharp drops in savings and consumer spending created a deflationary spiral that fed on itself. Savings fell. Demand fell. Production was cut. Workers were fired. Banks closed. Demand fell again. More production cuts. More workers fired. The two natural brakes to a recession—increased savings and a stabilization of demand—were broken.

Political actions exacerbated the downward spiral. In an attempt to help domestic producers, Congress passed the Smoot-Hawley Tariff Act in June 1930, which significantly raised duties on imported products. Foreign nations retaliated with higher tariffs of their own, and the resulting trade war reduced American exports from $7.1 billion in 1929 to $2.4 billion in 1933.[7] In addition, the debt legacy of World War I came back to haunt the United States. The merry-go-round of international loans, already threatened by the crash, came to a complete halt in the wake of the new tariff. First the Germans defaulted, then America's main allies, and by 1933 only Finland was still making debt payments to the United States.

President Herbert Hoover repeatedly told the American people that the economy would correct itself. By 1932, the American people had grown tired of waiting and elected Franklin D. Roosevelt president. Roosevelt's approach was in sharp contrast to his predecessor's. Roosevelt stressed the positive, had a wide smile for the cameras, and was able to appeal to the voters as a leader who would bring them out of the depths of economic despair. He was also willing to make dramatic changes. To correct structural flaws in the economy, Roosevelt established the Federal Deposit Insurance Corporation (FDIC) to protect depositors and the Securities and Exchange Commission (SEC) to regulate the securities industry. To improve working conditions, he pushed through legislation that eliminated child labor, established a national minimum wage, and set a maximum work week. To help retirees and those in need, he sponsored the Social Security Act. And to fight widespread unemployment, he launched an unprecedented series of public spending programs to create jobs.

In fiscal year 1932, the federal government spent $4.7 billion, of which $2.7 billion was borrowed money.[8] During the presidential campaign, both President Hoover and Governor Roosevelt had, in accordance with the clearly stated positions of their respective political parties, proclaimed their firm support for a balanced federal budget. Accepted economic theory held that a balanced budget was essential to financial stability. Once elected, however, Roosevelt ran large budget deficits to finance his programs. With one quarter of the work force unemployed, Roosevelt was motivated more by politics than by economic theory. He did, however, receive enthusiastic support from one economist—John Maynard Keynes. In an open letter to Roosevelt in December 1933 Keynes stated that "as the prime mover in the first stage of the technique of recovery, I lay overwhelming emphasis on the increase of national purchasing power resulting from government expenditure which is financed by loans and is not merely a transfer through taxation, from existing incomes. Nothing else counts in comparison with this."[9]

Failure of Classical Economics

Conventional economic thought failed to explain the causes of the Great Depression. This failure can be traced to the path economic thought had taken in the one hundred and sixty years since Adam Smith wrote *The Wealth of Nations*. Smith's work was the result of more than a decade of personal observations of the economic forces transforming the world around him. When David Ricardo published *Principles of Political Economy* in 1817, however, economic thought took a decidedly theoretical turn. In order to develop his economic principles, Ricardo relied heavily upon simplifying assumptions. A core assumption was Say's law, which held that supply created its own demand and, as a result, overproduction and involuntary unemployment could not exist.[10] As Keynes noted in his 1936 book *The General Theory of Employment, Interest, and Money*, "the idea that we can safely neglect the aggregate demand function is fundamental to the Ricardian economics, which underlie what we have been taught for more than a century."[11]

The Great Depression, however, made painfully clear that involuntary unemployment could indeed exist. Laissez faire had broken down and classical economists had no explanation. But Keynes did. He argued that classical economic theory was

No, we're still confident that it will be able to fix itself.

applicable only in a special case, whose characteristics "happen not to be those of the economic society in which we actually live, with the result that its teaching is misleading and disastrous if we attempt to apply it to the facts of experience."[12] He argued that the level of employment was dependent upon the level of aggregate demand, which was the total spending of all three economic entities—individuals, businesses, and government. The economic dilemma during the Great Depression was that individuals were reducing consumption, businesses were cutting investment, and the government was not increasing spending because of concerns over the budget deficit. As a result, aggregate demand plummeted and unemployment soared.

The Great Depression made clear the fragile nature of America's interdependent economy. From their incomes, individuals typically consume a portion and save a portion. Individual consumption is therefore dependent upon wages and, subsequently, employment. An increase in employment raises aggregate wages and consumer consumption, which, in turn, causes aggregate demand to increase and allows employment to expand further. Conversely, a drop in employment reduces aggregate wages and consumption, causing a decrease in aggregate demand and, potentially, a further drop in employment.[†] This circular dependency between individual income and employment exacerbates the highs and lows of the business cycle.

Business investment has its own dependencies. In contrast to consumption, which impacts employment indirectly, a change in business investment (for example, opening a new manufacturing plant or closing an existing one) has a direct impact on the level of employment. Business leaders make investment decisions based on

---

[†] Businesses can react to small changes in aggregate demand by adjusting production schedules instead of the level of employment. Large changes in aggregate demand, however, will encourage businesses to change their employment levels.

the level of interest rates, the level of current business activity (dependent upon aggregate demand), and prospects for future business. High interest rates stifle investment, while low interest rates encourage it. Interest rates alone, however, are not enough. Interest rates were low throughout the Great Depression, but business leaders, concerned about a contracting economy, had few incentives to expand production or to hire more workers.

To Keynes, the economic dilemma was clear. As unemployment rose, consumer consumption and individual savings were both falling. Businesses could increase investment to create jobs, but with the economy contracting there existed no incentive to do so. Keynes argued that "the weakness of the inducement to invest has been at all times the key to the economic problem,"[13] and he concluded "that the duty of ordering the current volume of investment cannot safely be left in private hands."[14] Of the three economic entities—individuals, businesses, and government—only government had the ability to act in a strong countercyclical fashion and break the downward economic spiral. Classical economics failed on two counts: it waited for the system to fix itself, and it argued strongly against the one measure that could get the economy going again—deficit spending. Without increased government spending, the economy would have continued to contract until it reached some minimum subsistence level of activity.

Roosevelt's New Deal programs stopped the economic slide in 1933 and set the stage for a slow, though anemic, recovery. The civilian unemployment rate, which had risen from 3.2% in 1929 to 25.2% in 1933, slowly began to fall. Although unemployment dropped to 17% by 1936, nine million Americans were still out of work.[15] At this point, the government began to curtail spending in an attempt to reduce the budget deficit. In fiscal year 1936, the federal government spent $8.2 billion. Over the next two years, federal spending was cut to $6.8 billion, reducing the deficit from $4.3 billion to less than one hundred million.[16] Although deficit reduction was successful, the spending reductions precipitated a recession. After falling to 14.3% in 1937, the unemployment rate shot back up to 19.1% in 1938, as 2.7 million more Americans lost their jobs.[17]

The government's ill-conceived attempt at deficit reduction in 1937 and 1938 provided clear, and painful, evidence of the importance of deficit-financed government spending to increasing both aggregate demand and employment during sluggish economic times. As we shall see later in the book, it is a lesson easily forgotten with the passage of time.

World War II

In the late 1930s, the drumbeats of war were again heard on the European continent. In the early part of the decade, as most European economies were mired in a worldwide depression, the German economy began to show signs of life as the nation embarked on a huge rearmament program. Preoccupied with their own troubles, Germany's weakened neighbors ignored violations of the First World War treaties. When Adolf Hitler took control of Austria and then demanded the Sudetenland region of Czechoslovakia, British prime minister Neville Chamberlain and French premier Edouard Daladier met with Hitler and Italy's Benito Mussolini in Munich in September 1938. Chamberlain and Daladier, following the general public opinion of their nations, avoided war through the policy of appeasement, giving Hitler the Sudetenland in return for his solemn promise not to expand again. Six months later, Hitler took all of Czechoslovakia. The inevitable military clash began when Germany invaded Poland on September 1, 1939.

The United States, having fought a European war twenty years earlier, was in no hurry to fight another one. For twenty-seven months, the United States sat on the sidelines. France fell. Germany dominated Europe and attacked Russia. Japan occupied Korea and most of China's coastal areas. President Roosevelt pushed through higher levels of defense spending to prepare the nation for a war it probably could not avoid. Sooner or later, the United States would have to enter the conflict. The Japanese attack on Pearl Harbor accelerated the process and galvanized the nation. The full economic and military capabilities of the United States were tapped to win the war.

While the Great Depression showed the depths to which the American economy could sink, World War II demonstrated the economy's productive capability. Massive government military spending, financed by higher taxes and heavy borrowing, created the greatest period of economic growth in American history. Table 11 shows the economy's wartime performance. From 1940 to 1945, unemployment plummeted and real (inflation-adjusted) GDP grew by an annual average rate of 11.4% (from 1941-44, real GDP growth was 16.5%). Most economists view this type of economic performance as obtainable only under wartime conditions. However, the mechanics of a war-time economy—high levels of savings and investment, reduced levels of consumption, and

Table 11
GOVERNMENT FINANCE
AND ECONOMIC PERFORMANCE, 1940-45
($ BILLIONS)

	1940	1941	1942	1943	1944	1945
Federal Spending	9.5	13.7	35.1	78.6	91.3	92.7
Federal Receipts	6.5	8.7	14.6	24.0	43.7	45.2
Budget Surplus (Deficit)	-2.9	-4.9	-20.5	-54.6	-47.6	-47.6
Real GDP Growth (%)	7.8	18.2	20.0	19.9	8.4	-4.0
Unemployment (%)	14.6	9.9	4.7	1.9	1.2	1.9

Note: Growth and unemployment statistics are for calendar years; government figures are for fiscal years. Numbers may not add up due to rounding.

Source: *Economic Report of the President, 1994.*

increased levels of production—are applicable under other circum-stances. We shall return to this important issue in Chapters 10 and 13.

Riding the Currents of History

The sixteen-year period from 1929 to 1945 was a roller coaster ride for America's political economy. At each turn, the government struggled to keep up with the dramatic pace of change. When the speculative bubble burst in 1929, the economy spiralled down-ward. The government, recognizing neither the nature nor the severity of the problem, waited for the economy to revive itself. After four years of depression, a new administration orchestrated a more active role for government. And although the New Deal breathed life into the moribund economy, the problems of high unemployment and slow growth were not solved until the war.

America's political economy was in uncharted waters. Limited government, as established by the founding fathers, was no more. The third era of American political economy—an era when the government would play an activist economic role—had begun. But there was no blueprint, no plan. Laissez faire had been an appeal-ing government policy not only for economic and philosophical reasons, but also because it was simple. It required the government to *do nothing*. During both the Great Depression and World War II the government was forced to respond.

World War II was a defining period in American history. The nation's economic and military successes restored public confi-dence and instilled the government with tremendous confidence in its own abilities. Yet wartime conditions were unique. Creating a consensus is usually a long and drawn out process in a democracy, but after Pearl Harbor the nation's task was clear. There were no ambiguities, no gray areas.

In the postwar era, favorable economic conditions—a baby boom, a growing consumer market, no foreign competition, and a fiscally conservative government—combined to usher in more than two decades of unprecedented prosperity. The transition from limited government to expanded government, from the second to the third era of American political economy, seemed to have been accomplished successfully. But as the unique conditions of the postwar era began to disappear and the government was confronted with more complex and difficult issues, the nation's political flaws began to emerge.

Chapter 5

The Cold Winds of War

There is no greater unifying force in a democratic nation than the need to wage war against a foreign enemy. But after the Second World War, America's political leaders were—in both foreign and domestic affairs—without a compass. In foreign affairs, the cold war became America's policy guide. In domestic affairs, the government initially curtailed its economic role, limiting it to public works and defense spending. In both foreign and domestic affairs, however, initial success bred complacency. Sound policies became rigid philosophies that were soon outdated in a rapidly changing world.

Foreign Policy

At the conclusion of the Second World War, Europe lay in ruins. The economies of the individual nations were in shambles, devastated from years of war. As the world's leading power, the United States faced a familiar question —should it help out its European allies? Twenty-five years earlier the United States had left Europe to fend for itself after the war. Should it do so again?

President Franklin D. Roosevelt decided that America should not. In June 1944, the United States sponsored an economic conference in Bretton Woods, New Hampshire, to discuss international economic issues. From that conference came the blueprint for the International Monetary Fund and the World Bank. In the fall of 1944, representatives from Great Britain, the Soviet Union, China, and the United States met in Washington to discuss a new international organization to promote peace and stability in the world. Tentative proposals were made for the organization that would become the United Nations. America was on its way to playing a very active international role in the postwar era.

However, events quickly changed the nation's course. President Franklin D. Roosevelt died on April 12, 1945. While his presidential successor, Harry Truman, capably led the United States for the remainder of the war, Truman's vision of American postwar involvement was significantly more conservative than Roosevelt's. Throughout 1946, as the charters for the United Nations, the International Monetary Fund, and the World Bank were being completed, the United States demilitarized rapidly. Europe needed significant help rebuilding, yet American financial assistance was not immediately forthcoming. Strong public support for an activist international role for the United States simply did not exist.

But America's foreign policy soon took another sharp U-turn. As the iron curtain descended across the continent of Europe, the United States saw that its own interests were at stake. When Great Britain announced that it could no longer act as military protector of Turkey and Greece, the United States stepped in with a $400 million aid package. To push the legislation through a reluctant Congress, President Truman emphasized the Communist threat. The choice, Truman stated, was between freedom and repression. He made his choice perfectly clear. "I believe that it must be the policy of the United States to support free peoples who are resisting attempted subjugation by armed minorities or by outside pressures. . . . If we falter in our leadership, we may endanger the peace of the world—and we shall surely endanger the welfare of the nation."[1] The Truman Doctrine was born, and America's cold war commitments had begun.

Three months later, on June 5, 1947, Secretary of State George C. Marshall spoke at Harvard University where he outlined the problems facing Europe and promised American assistance in drafting a European economic recovery program. Between April 1948 and June 1952, the United States provided Western European nations with $11.8 billion in grants and $1.5 billion in loans.[2] The economies of Western Europe rebounded strongly, and the American economy boomed. Today, the Marshall Plan is recognized for its economic generosity and its importance in the rebirth of Western Europe.

A month after Marshall's Harvard speech, George Kennan, a leading Soviet expert at the State Department, wrote *The Sources of Soviet Conduct*, published under the pseudonym "X" in the July 1947 issue of *Foreign Affairs*. The article argued that strong financial, economic, and political support for America's allies could keep the expansionist nature of Soviet Communism in check. Containment became the centerpiece of America's cold war foreign policy.

In 1949, Mao Tse-Tung's army defeated the nationalist forces of Chiang Kai-shek and took control of mainland China. The most populated nation in the world had become Communist. In the United States, there was growing concern about a monolithic Communist power emanating from Moscow, a power seeking to control the entire world. Journalist Joseph Alsop wrote a three-part series in the *Saturday Evening Post* entitled "Why We Lost China."[3] Alsop believed that the Communists had won because the United States had failed to back adequately Chiang Kai-shek's regime. Alsop inferred that the State Department failed to support Chiang Kai-shek's regime, not because the regime was corrupt or inept—it was both—but because the State Department was sympathetic to the Communists. He did not view the Communist victory as the resolution of an internal Chinese dispute, but as a failure of

American resolve against the growing forces of communism. He was not alone in this view. The Communist victory in China had a profound impact on the role the cold war would play in American politics. The Republicans, losers of the past five presidential elections, found anti-communism to be a domestic issue that could be exploited for partisan political reasons. Over the next four decades, America's foreign and domestic policies were to be dominated by the politics of the cold war.

On January 7, 1950, Republican Senator Joseph McCarthy had dinner with three friends and asked for their help. He needed to find a good campaign issue to get the voters' attention. The ideas flowed freely. How about the St. Lawrence Seaway? No, too boring. How about a national pension plan? No, too idealistic. After the dinner, the issue arose—how about communism? McCarthy had found his issue.[4] Two days later, McCarthy gave a speech in Wheeling, West Virginia, where he declared that he had a list of State Department officials who were members of the Communist party. The McCarthy era had begun. He had no evidence of his charges, but that did not stop him from launching a series of personal attacks on a wide range of American citizens and government officials. His attacks ruined the reputations and lives of many Americans, but his most devastating legacy was the hardening of anti-Communist sentiment in American foreign policy. No politician wanted to be viewed as "soft on communism."

The Korean War

On June 25, 1950, North Korean troops crossed the 38th parallel and invaded South Korea. Superior in manpower, training, and equipment to their South Korean neighbors, the North Korean forces had good reason to believe that the United States would not intervene. A year earlier, in keeping with United Nations' resolutions, the United States had withdrawn the last of its occupation forces and had left behind just 500 military advisors.[5] More importantly, on January 12, 1950, Secretary of State Dean Acheson gave a speech in which he excluded South Korea from America's "defensive perimeter."[6] But in response to the North Korean invasion, President Harry Truman appealed to the United Nations, and a U.N. force, consisting mostly of Americans, was quickly sent to help the beleaguered South Koreans.

In the first six months of the war the United Nations forces, led by General Douglas MacArthur, stopped the North Korean advance in the South and pushed the Communists back over the 38th parallel. By late fall, MacArthur had pushed the North Koreans almost off the peninsula, and his troops were approaching the Yalu River, which divided North Korea from China. The Chinese threatened more than once that they would intervene, but these warnings were dismissed as bluffs. MacArthur told Truman that there was little chance the Chinese would enter the war, and he predicted that American troops would be home by Christmas.

On November 25, however, three hundred thousand Chinese troops attacked. MacArthur's troops were caught off guard. Overextended, they were forced to retreat. As a result of Chinese intervention, the war raged on for another two and a half years. Of the 54,246 Americans who died in Korea, 44,000 died after the Chinese entered the war.[7] When the truce ending the war was signed on July 27, 1953, the line dividing North and South Korea was essentially the same as it was before the war started.

The Korean War ended in a stalemate, but it provided a number of important lessons for the United States. First, if the United States had an appropriate foreign policy prior to the start of the conflict, the North Koreans would probably not have invaded. The North Koreans had assumed that the United States would not intervene militarily if they attacked South Korea. If the United States felt the defense of South Korea was important enough to risk American lives, then it should have let its potential adversaries know from the start. There was no risk in eliminating ambiguity. Forty years later, Saddam Hussein invaded Kuwait because he had no reason to believe the United States would intervene. Foreign policy ambiguity again cost American lives.

Second, America's military commanders should never under-estimate the strength of the enemy. America's success in World War II and early success in the Korean War bred military arrogance —it was assumed that the Chinese would not dare to challenge the Americans. MacArthur's complete disregard for Chinese warnings about their intervention led to a significant military defeat, which lengthened the war by two and a half years. In the aftermath of the war, however, America's military leaders blamed the stalemate, not on MacArthur's miscalculations, but on Truman's failure to wage full-scale war with China.[8]

A third lesson from Korea was that the cold war had changed the nature of military conflict. During the two world wars, America went on a domestic "war footing," and waged total war with all the nation's resources. The only other type of military engagement with which America's twentieth century leaders were familiar was small armed interventions that were typically over in a matter of days or weeks. The cold war and the risk of a nuclear conflict cre-ated a third category—a regional war that required a large commit-ment of men and resources, but would be waged on a limited scale. This new type of conflict was the most dangerous of all, for it required explicit goals, a firm understanding of the enemy and its goals, and a plan for winning. Failure to understand all of these issues could lead to a costly military stalemate, a characteristic of the last two years of the Korean War.

In World War I, the United States fought for nineteen months and was victorious; in World War II, the nation fought for forty-four months and defeated the enemy in Africa, Europe, and the Pacific; in the Korean War, the nation fought for thirty-seven months, and the war ended where it started. Stalemate was a shock to a nation accustomed to victory, especially after the successes of the first six months. Americans were not in a hurry to get involved in another such conflict. As he took office in 1953, President

Dwight Eisenhower realized that the nation was weary of war, and he worked diligently to keep America out of future conflicts. The next administration, however, sought to broaden America's international role.

In his 1961 inaugural address, President John Kennedy declared "let every nation know, whether it wishes us well or ill, that we shall pay any price, bear any burden, meet any hardship, support any friend, oppose any foe, to assure the survival and the success of liberty." This promise of support was soon tested. On April 17, 1961—a mere ninety days into office—Kennedy approved an invasion of Cuba by American-backed Cuban exiles. The Kennedy administration believed that once the 1,500 exiles landed, a popular revolt would break out and Cuban dictator Fidel Castro would be deposed. It was a calculation based more on wishful thinking than on fact. American intelligence failed in other ways. The landing site, a beach located next to a large swamp, was poorly suited for an invasion. Success depended upon complete surprise. However, Castro found out about the invasion in advance and easily turned back the invaders. In the aftermath of the Bay of Pigs debacle, the Kennedy administration felt it needed an opportunity to show its resolve against the forces of communism. As Kennedy remarked to James Reston of *The New York Times*, "now we have a problem in making our power credible, and Vietnam is the place."[9]

Vietnam

The Vietnam era stands as a dark chapter in American history. For nine years, America fought a war in order to stop the spread of communism. In pursuit of this goal, America's leaders ignored the lessons of history, backed a series of corrupt regimes, fought a war without a plan to win, and consistently lied to the American public. Step by step, America sank deeper into a quagmire of its own making. Blind adherence to the anti-Communist line cost the lives of more than 57,000 Americans and divided the country. No single event in American history demonstrates the dangers of delusion more than the Vietnam War.

The history of Vietnam provided fair warning about the dangers of armed intervention. Vietnam was a French colony from the late 1800s until falling under Japanese control in 1940. A year later, Ho Chi Minh started an active resistance movement—the Vietminh—to fight for Vietnamese independence. At the end of World War II, France wanted to reclaim its former colony and the United States assented.[†] Lacking other options, Ho Chi Minh reached an agreement with the French on March 6, 1946. Under the terms of the accord, France would recognize Vietnam as a free state within the French Union. In return, Ho Chi Minh would allow the presence of French troops in Vietnam for five years. But the agreement was never formally signed. After a number of skirmishes and attempts at negotiation, war broke out on December 19, 1946.

America's support of the French effort shifted with the winds of the cold war. Initially, the United States provided only small amounts of military aid to the French. Substantial support was not forthcoming because American policymakers did not want to become closely associated with French colonialism. However, the Communist victory in China prompted a policy change. American policymakers now viewed the French war in Indochina, not as a

---

[†] On August 14, 1945, Ho Chi Minh sent a message to President Truman, asking him to make Vietnam an American protectorate "on the same status as the Philippines for an undetermined period" before granting Vietnam full independence. Two weeks later, on September 2, 1945, Ho Chi Minh declared the Independence of the Democratic Republic of Vietnam before 500,000 people in Ba Dinh Square in Hanoi. He began with the familiar words "all men are created equal." Over the next eighteen months, he sent eleven telegrams and letters of appeal to Truman and Truman's secretary of state, James Byrnes. There was no response. See Neil Sheehan, *A Bright Shining Lie* (New York: Vintage Books, 1988), pp. 147-149.

colonial war of independence, but as another example of expanding communism that had to be stopped. Aid to the French was increased dramatically, and by the end of the war the United States was paying most of France's military costs.

The war did not go well for the French. The Vietminh were elusive and unconventional. They avoided confrontation and focused on slowly wearing down the desire of the French to fight. It was an effective strategy. The French advantage in weapons was neutralized by geography. In early 1954, the French established a base on the plain at Dienbienphu in order to launch attacks against the Vietminh. But it was the Vietminh who did the attacking. The French had walked into a trap. For three months, the Vietminh had prepared. Not only did the Vietminh outnumber the French five to one, but they had dragged artillery pieces through the jungle to the mountains surrounding the base where they blasted the French and hindered resupply by air. The battle raged for almost two months, but the outcome had been decided before the battle began. The French had made the same mistake that the United States had made in Korea—they underestimated their adversary. After nine years, France had suffered more than 90,000 casualties and lost the war.[†]

The Geneva Conference of 1954 ended the French Indochina War. The accord called for a cease-fire, a division of the country along the seventeenth parallel, and elections to be held in two years to reunify the country. The French forces would leave the North, and the Vietminh would leave the South. The Eisenhower administration reluctantly agreed to the Geneva accords, but Ngo Dinh Diem, Prime Minister of the newly created South Vietnam, had no intention of complying. Any free election would have meant a

---

[†] This total reflects losses of all troops under French command, including French, Vietnamese, Algerian, Moroccan, Senegalese, German, Cambodian, and Laotian troops. Losses of French nationals totalled roughly 20,000. See Paul Marie La Gorce, *The French Army* (New York: George Braziller, Inc., 1963), pp. 376-377.

clear victory for the Vietminh. The United States, again following a strict anti-Communist policy, backed Diem in his refusal to hold free elections.

The Diem regime had no political legitimacy. Those in power had assisted the colonial French. They tolerated no political opposition, and the few elections that were eventually held were staged for propaganda purposes. Corruption was rampant, and political intrigue was a national pastime. The few soldiers who showed real skill were often placed in obscure assignments, for they were a potential threat to lead a coup. The United States overlooked these danger signs in the name of containing communism. Anti-communism had become a dark prism through which the light of reality became heavily distorted.

In 1957, the remaining Vietminh troops in the South organized and started an assassination campaign against South Vietnamese officials. In 1959, North Vietnam began infiltrating troops into the South, and the level of guerrilla activity slowly increased. In response, the United States sent additional military aid to the Saigon government. During 1962, Kennedy increased the number of American military advisors from 700 to 12,000.[10] Although officially restricted from engaging in combat, the Americans were very active in offensive operations and what they saw was not reassuring. Though well equipped by the Americans, the Army of the Republic of Vietnam (ARVN) fought poorly, refused to fight at night, and spent most of its time in the field avoiding direct contact with the Vietminh, who were now called Vietcong—short for Vietnamese Communists—for propaganda purposes. The new name was a creation of the United States Information Service.[11]

At the battle of Ap Bac on January 2, 1963, all the incompetence of the ARVN was exposed. The South Vietnamese troops failed to commit troops to battle, delayed engaging the enemy, and fought atrociously. They had the opportunity to surround and completely destroy three Vietcong companies, but, fearing a bloody confrontation, they provided the Vietcong with an easy escape path. Although the battle was well covered by the American press corps, General Paul Harkins, America's top advisor, refused to see the battle as a disaster. In fact, he claimed the battle was a victory because the target had been secured. In a war of attrition however, the goal was to kill as many of the enemy as possible so they would quit fighting. Harkins had claimed success for capturing a hamlet that the Vietcong had abandoned. Unfortunately, Harkins viewed his role as reporting "successes" back to Washington, whether or not the reports were an accurate portrayal of reality. Harkins's lack of candor marked the beginning of a press controversy that raged for the next decade in Vietnam. Journalists in the field reported the incompetence of the ARVN and the political problems of the Saigon government, while the military provided glowing reports of its successes and wondered aloud why some members of the press were so sympathetic to the Communists.

A war of independence was being fought in Vietnam. The United States, blinded by its anti-Communist fixation, was backing the wrong side. The Vietminh had been fighting for independence since 1941, first against the Japanese, then against the French, and now against the American-supported Saigon regime. *The world had changed dramatically, but the United States had not changed with it.*

As early as 1950, George Kennan, the author of the containment policy, had grown increasingly concerned with the militarization of American foreign policy and the simplistic approach of viewing communism as a single unified force. He wrote a memo to his boss, Secretary of State Dean Acheson, in which he warned that the French would lose in Vietnam and that the United States should decrease its involvement. Kennan issued this warning because he realized that the forces of nationalism were far stronger than the forces of communism or anti-communism.[12] Kennan was able to look beyond the rhetoric of the cold war and see the French Indochina War for what it was—a war of independence against a colonial power. The issue of communism was secondary. By the early 1960s, the Chinese-Soviet split was becoming apparent to the whole world, and the time had come to challenge the old theories of monolithic communism upon which America's foreign policy was based. The Kennedy administration was just beginning to wake up to this reality.

In November 1961, Averell Harriman was named Assistant Secretary of State for Far Eastern Affairs. In his new position, Harriman found an Asian desk decimated by the McCarthy era. As he told friends, "it's a disaster area filled with human wreckage."[13] Harriman slowly improved the quality of State Department reporting from Vietnam. In the past, the State Department had simply confirmed the sugar-coated success stories written by the military. Now it began to give a more accurate portrayal of reality in South Vietnam.

A growing number of officials in the Kennedy administration began raising questions about America's involvement in Vietnam, resulting in a large split in the Kennedy administration, a split that mirrored the dichotomy in reporting. The Pentagon and the Joint Chiefs of Staff wanted to commit American combat troops to achieve a military solution. The State Department, with the exception of Secretary of State Dean Rusk, backed military disengagement, believing the corruption of the Saigon regime made any military efforts pointless. A telling example of these opposing views: in early September 1963, Kennedy sent General Victor Krulak and Joseph Mendenhall, a State Department official, on one of the government's many fact-finding missions to Vietnam. On his return, Krulak gave a glowing report of the military successes in the field. However, Mendenhall reported that the Diem regime had little popular support, corruption was rampant, and the government was on the verge of collapse. Kennedy's response was to ask "You two did visit the same country, didn't you?"[14]

By the fall of 1963, the Kennedy administration had lost patience with the corrupt and ineffective government of Ngo Dinh Diem. When Henry Cabot Lodge became American Ambassador to

South Vietnam on August 22, he let it be known that the United States had grown tired of Diem and would have no objection to a change in leadership. On November 1, 1963, the Diem regime was overthrown and replaced by a group of generals. The United States had foolishly hoped a change at the top would improve stability and eliminate many of the political problems facing South Vietnam. However, corruption and incompetence were ubiquitous. The fall of Diem was followed by a succession of leaders equally incompetent, underscoring the fragility of a nation created around the negotiating table at Geneva. The administration was slowly turning to a reduction of American involvement when President Kennedy was assassinated on November 22, 1963.

Kennedy's successor, Lyndon Johnson, had not been kept informed of the ongoing debate over America's Vietnam policy. While he had inherited an administration split over Vietnam, Johnson's personal view was strongly anti-Communist. He didn't want to be the American president who lost Southeast Asia to the Communists. To form a consensus among his advisors, Johnson simply began transferring officials who supported disengagement. Henry Cabot Lodge resigned as Ambassador to Vietnam in order to seek the Republican presidential nomination, and Johnson replaced him with General Maxwell Taylor, an advocate of the use of military force.

Johnson avoided major decisions about Vietnam during his first year as president; he was facing an election in 1964 and did not want Vietnam to be a major issue. Nevertheless, he did obtain Congressional authority for military action. On August 7, 1964, Congress passed the Gulf of Tonkin Resolution, which gave Johnson broad powers to commit American forces in Vietnam. The resolution was passed in response to two attacks by North Vietnamese patrol boats on an American destroyer. Later investigations revealed that the North Vietnamese were acting in response to a South Vietnamese raid, and that the second patrol boat attack did not actually occur. Like so many events during the Vietnam era, there was a large gulf between perception and reality.

The stage was set. Johnson had his Congressional resolution and, by switching personnel, he had achieved a consensus of his advisors. Ultimately, America would make a stand against Communist expansion in Vietnam. That the French had fought for nine years before withdrawing in defeat was ignored. The nature of the enemy, the history of prior conflict, and the corruption and ineptitude of the Saigon regime were all secondary issues. The facts, at this point, were irrelevant. The Johnson administration was viewing the world as it wanted to see it, not as it actually was. It was myopia on a monumental scale.

Johnson did not wage war in the traditional manner. Against the advice of many of his advisors, he did not call up the reserves because he did not want to heighten public awareness. In 1965, the American escalation began with Operation Rolling Thunder, which called for bombing runs on North Vietnam. The purpose of the bombing was to convince Ho Chi Minh that the United States was serious and that North Vietnam had better stop its operations in the South. The idea was essentially flawed—the bombing focused on industrial targets because it was assumed that the Hanoi regime wouldn't want to lose its industrial base. However, North Vietnam was still an agrarian nation, and most of its military supplies were coming from China and the Soviet Union. As a result, the bombing of North Vietnamese factories had little impact. After fighting the Japanese for four years, the French for nine years, and waging an active guerrilla war for five years, the Vietminh were not about to stop trying to unify Vietnam because the United States was dropping bombs.

Once started, the military escalation took on a life of its own. The presence of American bombers in South Vietnam necessitated the presence of American Marines to protect the bombers. Once attacked, the Marines were given the opportunity to strike back. General William Westmoreland, the American commander, utilized a strategy of "search and destroy" missions. The United States had become involved in a war of attrition with the Vietcong. It was the type of war the Vietcong wanted to fight. In 1946, Ho Chi Minh had warned the French: "you can kill ten of my men for every one I kill of yours. But even at those odds, you will lose and I will win."[15] America's war plan was to wear the other side down, but the Vietnamese had already demonstrated a tremendous ability to withstand hardship and death. The belief that America had a greater tolerance for such a war was sheer folly.

The American public clearly had little tolerance for the war. During past wars, Americans could follow the progress of the war on maps printed in their local newspapers. The battle lines were clearly marked, and everyone knew the ultimate objectives. In Vietnam, the measure of success was not in changing lines along a front, but in the body count. While the American military was willing to swap American lives for those of Vietcong guerrillas, a growing number of Americans were not. Public support for the war relied heavily upon the continuous flow of positive reports coming from the military. But during the Vietnam War, for the first time in history, Americans were able to watch war film footage on television. What the people saw in their own living rooms often contradicted the military's assessments of the war. As a result, the Johnson administration began to suffer from a growing credibility gap.

On January 31, 1968, the Vietcong attacked major cities and military installations throughout the South, including the capital city of Saigon. Launched during Tet, the Vietnamese New Year, the attacks caught the American military by surprise. In the days following the attacks, Johnson launched a major public relations campaign claiming a great victory for the American and South Vietnamese forces. He had finally gone too far. The Tet offensive exposed the hollowness of the military's claims of success. Although the Vietcong suffered heavy losses, the Tet offensive ended up being the turning point of the war because it brought reality into the American policy discussion and eroded public support for both Johnson and the war.

The war in Vietnam was the main issue in the 1968 presidential campaign. After Johnson almost lost the New Hampshire primary to Senator Eugene McCarthy, Robert Kennedy entered the race. With his support waning, Johnson announced he would not seek re-election. A heated race for the Democratic nomination ensued. After winning the California primary, however, Kennedy was assassinated. Ultimately, Vice President Hubert Humphrey became the nominee. But conflict within the Democratic party over the war and civil rights opened the door for the Republicans. In a three-way race between Humphrey, Republican Richard Nixon, and independent candidate George Wallace, Nixon won with 43.4% of the popular vote.

Nixon had no real plan for Vietnam. He knew the American public would not back further escalation, but he did not want to "lose" the war. He authorized military activities in Cambodia and Laos, which were not only unsuccessful, but further destabilized both nations. Nixon later adopted a program of "Vietnamization," which aimed to turn the task of fighting over to the South Vietnamese. He also began secret negotiations with the North Vietnamese to bring an end to the war. An armistice was finally signed, but not until January 27, 1973, four years after Nixon had taken office. In total, the American War in Vietnam lasted nine years and cost the lives of over 57,000 Americans, over 20,000 of whom died during the Nixon years.[16]

The Lessons of Vietnam

American success in World War II had inspired confidence, hope, and pride. The victory over aggression reinforced the ideals of freedom and democracy set forth by the founding fathers. Americans had faith in their government to do the right thing. Though each had their faults, the Truman, Eisenhower, and Kennedy administrations all worked toward keeping the public trust. While Kennedy's assassination shocked the American people, the nation still had faith in its government. The Vietnam War changed all that, for it not only tore apart the nation's social fabric, it also betrayed the American people's trust in their own government.

America's cold war mentality polarized debate and excluded honest consideration of vital issues. The driving force behind the actions of the Vietminh was not Communist expansion, but nationalism. The Vietnamese wanted to be free from foreign domination, and the Saigon regime was a remnant of French colonialism. The United States, for all its anti-Communist rhetoric, had simply replaced the colonial French. Both Western powers fought wars in Vietnam with roughly the same results—nine years of war, over 50,000 casualties, and, ultimately, defeat.

America's Vietnam experience provided important lessons. No amount of positive thinking or media manipulation can change the flow of events. If problems exist, then ignoring them or denying their existence will only court disaster in the future. Ample evidence existed that communism was not a monolithic force emanating from Moscow. But the United States government had its own simplistic world view, and contrary evidence was ignored. It took nine years and 57,000 American lives to prove that the policy of containment needed to be modified.

The Vietnam War hangs heavy over America's collective conscience. The true lessons of Vietnam are not about winning and losing, but about the differences between perception and reality. The cold war had a devastating impact on American politics. Rigid adherence to the simplistic, anti-Communist line caused a systemic failure of American government. Ideology overwhelmed rational thought. This failure was not an isolated case, for the dangers of delusion continue to haunt the United States.

Chapter 6

Postwar Pitfalls

As we have seen, America's second era of political economy came to an end during the Great Depression, when laissez faire's natural correction mechanism broke down. The government's economic role grew during both the New Deal and the Second World War. At the conclusion of the war, the government's economic role contracted as America demilitarized and politicians pursued fiscally conservative policies. Few could argue with the results—after a short postwar recession, economic growth surged. The rebuilding of Europe, an expanding consumer market, and a baby boom all created a large demand for goods. With no foreign competition, American companies met with unprecedented success. The transition from the second to third eras of American political economy seemed to have been completed successfully. But when the unique economic conditions of the postwar era began to disappear, America's ability to adjust to changing economic conditions was put to the test.

America's Postwar Economy

America's economic success during World War II owed much to the development of mass-production techniques. The idea that manufacturing efficiency could be improved by breaking down jobs into simple discrete tasks and standardizing equipment and production lines was first put forth by Fredrick Winslow Taylor in his 1911 book entitled *The Principles of Scientific Management.* Taylor's ideas soon became an integral part of American manufacturing. After the success of high-volume, standardized production during World War II, America's large corporations utilized these same techniques to meet the needs of the nation's rapidly expanding consumer market.

The economic conditions of the fifties and sixties were ideal for the United States. Preoccupied with industrial rebuilding, Japan and Western Europe not only provided little economic competition, but provided a significant market for American goods. In almost every industry, the United States produced the highest quality goods in the largest quantity. American workers, many with just a high school education, were able to find high-wage jobs in America's thriving manufacturing industries. Economic times were good.

During the Truman and Eisenhower administrations, government's role in the economy continued to be restrained. With the status quo working so well, there was little impetus for change. President Truman proposed a wide range of legislation in many areas—labor, education, civil rights, housing, and national health—but the Republicans had won control of both houses of Congress in 1946 and were in no mood to expand government's role. Even when the Democrats regained control of Congress in 1948, however, conservative Southern Democrats continued to resist more expansive government.

In 1952, Republican Dwight Eisenhower was elected president. Eisenhower was a strong proponent of fiscal conservatism, but he did expand the government's role in a few areas, notably the development of a national highway system. To make such an expenditure politically acceptable to conservatives, the program was promoted as necessary for national security. An efficient highway system would assist evacuation in case of enemy attack. From the end of World War II to the mid-sixties, the only large scale government spending efforts that passed through Congress were those believed to be vital to America's national security interests.

In his farewell address on January 17, 1961, President Eisenhower talked about the growing "military-industrial complex." While conceding the need for a permanent military establishment to fight the cold war, Eisenhower warned the American people about the huge potential for abuse. In addition, Eisenhower warned that the country "must avoid the impulse to live only for today, plundering, for our own ease and convenience, the precious resources of tomorrow." Unfortunately, both of Eisenhower's warnings went unheeded.

President Kennedy spoke eloquently of the need to expand the helping hand of government both at home and abroad. He proposed numerous government programs to increase domestic employment, and he established the Peace Corps to help overseas. But conservative members of Congress, both Democrat and Republican, blocked most of his proposed programs. It was not until after Kennedy's assassination that this resistance to expanding the role of the federal government began to erode.

Kennedy's successor, Lyndon Johnson, was a New Deal Democrat. First elected to Congress in a special election in 1937, Johnson was an ardent supporter of Franklin D. Roosevelt's policies. Like many Democrats, Johnson felt that the promise of the New Deal had not been completely realized. As president, Johnson wanted to complete the mission; as a former senate majority leader, he knew how to push legislation through Congress. He declared a war on poverty and proposed a whole series of spending programs that he named the Great Society.

At the height of America's economic power, Lyndon Johnson fundamentally altered the role of the federal government. Although patterned after the New Deal, the Great Society did not focus on creating jobs but on raising incomes. New government spending programs were created to solve the nation's social and economic ills. But by swinging open the doors of the federal treasury, Johnson ended two decades of postwar fiscal restraint. As the money started flowing, demands for more government spending increased. With a decision-making process no longer tempered by economic concerns or fiscal restraint, political expediency became the driving force of America's "interest-group liberalism." Most of the programs created during the sixties started small, but once created they developed a life of their own.

Signs of Fiscal Strain

Johnson proposed the Great Society with the best of intentions, but the same cannot be said of all his actions. While the United States was escalating the war in Vietnam in 1965 and 1966, President Johnson and Secretary of Defense Robert McNamara both purposefully underestimated the true costs of America's military involvement. McNamara assumed, against all evidence to the contrary, that it would be a short war. Johnson's rationale was that he did not want to frighten the American people about the cost of the commitment. In his 1966 State of the Union address, Johnson told the American people: "I believe that we can continue the Great Society while we fight in Vietnam."

But Johnson's economic advisors laid it on the line—the economic reality was that Johnson could not finance the war, create the Great Society, and balance the budget without a tax increase. Johnson was not swayed. He went to Capitol Hill and, showing the legislators artificially low estimates for the war, Congress decided that there was no reason to raise taxes. The charade became an annual event. As the war dragged on, Johnson began to hide the true military cost estimates not only from Congress, but from his own economic advisors.[1] The result was predictable—the budget deficit, which had been only $1.4 billion in fiscal year (FY) 1965, grew to $8.6 billion in FY 1967, and then spiked to $25.2 billion in FY 1968, the highest deficit since FY 1945.

The tragedy was that the American economy was strong enough to pay for both the Vietnam War and the Great Society, but Johnson was worried that a tax increase would undercut public support for his programs. Instead of taking his case to the American people, Johnson decided to keep the true costs secret. His actions not only led to large budget deficits, but a sharp rise in inflation. From 1960 to 1964, the consumer price index (CPI) rose at an annual rate of 1.2%. In 1967, it grew by 3.1%, and in 1969, it shot up by 5.5%—more than a fourfold increase from five years earlier. Johnson had planted the seeds for an insidious force that would ravage the American economy during the seventies and early eighties.

The Nixon Administration

Johnson's successor, Richard Nixon, failed to adequately address America's growing economic problems. As Nixon slowly reduced America's involvement in Vietnam, the nation faced the twin problems of unemployment and inflation. In response to these difficulties, Nixon announced a new economic program on August 15, 1971. The program had three stated goals: increase employment, fight inflation, and stabilize the dollar in foreign exchange markets. It was a short-term approach to economic policymaking. With elections only a year away, the emphasis, not surprisingly, was on jobs. To promote jobs, Nixon proposed an investment tax credit for business, a repeal of the seven percent excise tax on automobiles, and a reduction in personal income taxes. The centerpiece of his fight on inflation was a ninety-day wage and price freeze, which was nothing more than a temporary political gimmick to keep inflation low until after the elections. Once the controls were removed, inflation returned, for its root causes had not been addressed.

As the 1972 elections approached, the economy was growing slowly and Nixon knew his re-election would not be easy. After being Dwight Eisenhower's vice president for eight years, Nixon had lost to Kennedy in 1960 by the slimmest of margins—a mere 119 thousand votes out of a total of 68.8 million.[2] Two years later, Nixon ran in the California gubernatorial race and was again defeated. On the day after the election, he retired from politics and told reporters that "you won't have Nixon to kick around any more." The comment provided a revealing look at Nixon the candidate—in his own eyes he had not lost the races, but was the victim of hostile enemies, especially the press.

As president, Nixon's paranoia about hidden enemies led him to conduct covert investigations on individuals opposed to his war policy. As the Vietnam War wound down, these espionage teams became involved in his re-election campaign. They carried the tradition of campaign trickery to new heights—initially with great success. They harassed the campaigns of Democratic contenders to undermine their political support. An example of their handiwork was the so-called "Canuck letter," which appeared on February 24, 1972 in the *Manchester Union Leader*. The anonymous letter stated that Edmund Muskie had slurred Americans of French-Canadian origin. The next day, editor William Loeb reprinted a two month-old *Newsweek* article about Muskie's wife, claiming that she drank, smoked, and used off-color language. During a snowstorm the next morning, Muskie gave a speech in which he attacked Loeb, but, while giving an emotional defense of his wife, he appeared to cry. The "crying incident" undermined the Muskie campaign, and the potentially formidable challenger to Nixon left the race a month later.

Proving quite effective, the operations continued. Unfortunately for Nixon, his minions were caught while breaking into the

Democratic headquarters at the Watergate hotel. The resulting investigations revealed the most blatant evasion of the law by an American president in the nation's history. Nixon used every resource at his command to cover up the break-in, derail the investigation, and attack his opponents. But on August 9, 1974, after a parade of former aides was convicted on various charges and the House of Representatives voted to begin impeachment proceedings, Nixon resigned. Only a pardon by Gerald Ford kept Nixon from spending considerable time in court and possibly some time behind bars. The American people's confidence in its government, already devastated by the war in Vietnam, fell further in the wake of Watergate.

Oil Crises

October 1973 was not a banner month in American history, as other troubling events competed with Watergate for space in the nation's newspaper headlines. On October 6, Egypt and Syria attacked Israel. On October 10, Vice President Spiro Agnew resigned as part of an agreement with the Justice Department in which Agnew pleaded guilty to federal income tax evasion in order to avoid imprisonment. On October 17, Arab oil producing nations agreed to cut exports of oil by five percent, with the reduction being aimed at the United States and other nations friendly to Israel. On October 18, Saudi Arabia announced an immediate ten percent cut in oil production. On October 20, Saudi Arabia joined Libya in an oil embargo against the United States. Other Arab nations joined the embargo over the next few days.

The 1973 oil crisis compounded Johnson's inflation legacy and Nixon's failure to deal strongly with the problem. In a mere six months, the price of gasoline at the pump rose over 48%.[3] Not only were prices higher, but an inefficient oil distribution bureaucracy caused shortages in many areas. Americans suffered the double blow of having to wait in long lines to pay higher prices. The oil

embargo sent inflation dramatically higher and exposed the economic dangers of America's foreign oil dependence. The economy
fell into a deep recession, and the consumer price index increased
11% in 1974 and 9.1% in 1975.

By the presidential election year of 1976, voters were ready for
a change. Their choice was a Washington outsider, Georgia Governor Jimmy Carter. But Carter's presidency, despite his best intentions and efforts, was overwhelmed by outside events. In January
1979, the Shah of Iran fled his country, and a new provisional government took over. The immediate result of this change in government was that Iran stopped exporting oil. The second oil crisis in
six years rocked the American economy. Gasoline prices rose 44%
in nine months.[4] Inflation accelerated and economic growth slowed.

In the wake of energy price increases, Carter called for
increased energy conservation. On July 15, 1979, Carter gave a
nationally televised speech entitled "Energy and National Goals."
Carter discussed the crisis in American confidence, a crisis caused
by the tragedy of Vietnam and the economic turmoil of the 1970s.
He did not mince words. "This is not a message of happiness or
reassurance, but it is the truth and it is a warning." He observed
that "the people are looking for honest answers, not easy answers;
clear leadership, not false claims and evasiveness and politics as
usual." Carter made it clear that there would be no easy answers,
and that it was going to require time and effort to solve America's
problems. It was an unusual political speech because it was both
accurate and blunt. However, Carter made the political mistake of
pointing out large problems without offering effective solutions.
The speech came to be known as the "malaise" speech.

Iranian Hostage Crisis

Other events soon captured the nation's attention. In October
1979, the Shah of Iran was allowed into the United States to
receive medical treatment. On November 4, 1979, fifty Americans

at the United States embassy in Tehran were taken hostage by radical "students." While the admission of the Shah triggered the seizure, the underlying reason was Iranian bitterness over decades of American support for the Shah. In addition, the moderate government of Mehdi Bazargan, which had taken over in January, had collapsed. The Iranian government was now ruled by a revolutionary council whose leader, Ayatollah Khomeini, referred to the United States as the "Great Satan" and used the hostage seizure to eliminate domestic opposition and consolidate power.[5]

For six months, Carter tried unsuccessfully to find a diplomatic solution to the crisis. He then approved a hostage rescue attempt, Operation Eagle Claw. Eight helicopters flew to an isolated point in the Iranian desert to use as a staging area. During the long helicopter flight, one helicopter developed mechanical failure and another returned to base after its guidance instruments failed. Upon reaching Desert One—the first stage of the mission—a third helicopter suffered from mechanical failure. Because six helicopters were required for the mission and only five helicopters were in working order, the mission was scrubbed.

A failed mission now turned into disaster. During the withdrawal, a helicopter crashed into a transport plane, leaving eight men dead and many badly burned. In the days that followed, pictures of the burned-out aircraft and the eight dead Americans were broadcast around the world. America's ability to use its military power successfully had reached a frustrating nadir. Later investigations of the operation revealed glaring problems. Every segment of the military was involved, each with its own communication system and chain of command. A rescue mission that could not get past the first step because of mechanical failure did not demonstrate a high level of contingency planning. Opinion polls showed that a large majority of Americans supported the attempted rescue. However, the attempt underscored the greatest weakness of the Carter presidency—no amount of good intentions could compensate for poor execution.

By 1980, the American nation was deeply scarred both in body and spirit. The previous two decades had been traumatic. The Vietnam War had divided the nation. Three prominent figures in American society, John F. Kennedy, his brother Robert, and Martin Luther King, Jr., were all assassinated during the 1960s. The Watergate scandal caused the first presidential resignation in American history. Trust in government had evaporated. Economic growth, which had been taken for granted in the sixties, stagnated in the seventies. The inflation fuse lit by Lyndon Johnson had exploded as two oil crises exposed America's economic vulnerability. The hostage crisis in Iran and the failed rescue attempt made the United States feel as if it were no longer in control of its own destiny. Americans were fed up. Change was needed. Tough choices had to be made. The presidential elections of 1980 were an opportunity for the nation to debate the long-term problems it faced—slower economic growth, inflation, foreign oil dependency, and a government that no longer seemed capable of governing.

Chapter 7

Living for the Moment:
America in the 1980s

During the 1980 presidential campaign, the United States needed to address a number of problems. Yet the campaign was determined not by the issues, but by the images, not by persuasion, but by promises. Indeed, the Republican candidate, former California Governor Ronald Reagan, promised much. The hostage crisis and the failed rescue attempt had shrunk America's military prestige. Reagan promised the largest peacetime defense buildup in the nation's history. Americans were fed up with higher taxes and bloated government. Reagan promised to cut taxes and reduce the size and scope of government. Americans were concerned about rising federal deficits. Reagan promised a balanced budget by 1984. Noticeably absent from Reagan's speeches was any recognition that effective governing requires making tough choices and unpopular decisions.

Throughout the campaign, Ronald Reagan projected optimism —just as Franklin Roosevelt had done forty-eight years before. As

Roosevelt skillfully used radio, Reagan used television. In his June 29, 1934, radio address, Roosevelt set the tone for the coming Congressional elections by asking the American people to judge the economic recovery by asking—"are you better off than you were last year?" In 1980, Reagan stung Carter by asking the American people during a national debate if they were better off than they were four years before. In both cases a simple question set the tone for an entire campaign. However, there was an important difference in the two presidential orators. Roosevelt used optimism as a tool to make easier the tough steps he knew he had to take to get America going again. For Reagan, optimism seemed to be an end in itself. Optimism meant popularity, and popularity meant political power.

The Reagan administration commenced with a flourish of patriotism and optimism. At his inauguration, Reagan repeated his campaign calls for lower taxes, lower inflation, more jobs, and a balanced budget. Within minutes after his inauguration, word came that Iran had released the American hostages. The American public rejoiced. But on March 30, 1981, a mere ten weeks after the inauguration, the national mood shifted abruptly. Reagan was shot by John W. Hinckley, Jr., and the event was recorded on television for all to see. The American people were stunned. Pessimism returned. Was it happening again? Would another American president be killed before fulfilling his mission? No, this time was different. Not only did he survive, but he survived in true Reagan style. As his concerned wife Nancy visited his hospital room, he told her simply, "Honey, I forgot to duck." Reagan's popularity soared.

After the shock of Kennedy's assassination, after the disillusionment of the Vietnam War, after the corruption of Watergate, and after the twin oil-shock recessions, Americans wanted to feel good about America again. As the cameras focused on President Reagan, what America saw was someone who projected strength, confidence, and optimism about the future. Ronald Reagan had spent his entire life in front of the camera playing a variety of roles. Now his role was president of the United States. Reagan's media operatives planned each television appearance in order to project the right image and carry the proper message. During the Reagan presidency, like no other before it, politics and media merged.

The Reagan Revolution

The policies of the new administration were billed as the "Reagan Revolution"—a new conservative approach to the twin problems of economic stagnation and big government. The American welfare state, created during the prosperous and idealistic sixties, had run headfirst into economic reality during the seventies. But economic stagnation did not stop the expansion of government. Taxes kept rising. Indeed, with high rates of inflation, individuals found themselves pushed into higher tax brackets, a process known as "bracket creep." Although there was no direct linkage between rising oil prices and expanding government, the coincidence of timing had a profound impact on American politics. Individuals were paying more in taxes, and they did not see their lives improving. Instead, they saw a slow, inefficient government bureaucracy that had a seemingly insatiable appetite for taxpayers' money. Voters wanted change.

Ronald Reagan offered a vision for the future. He carefully selected his campaign themes—lower taxes, more military spending, and a balanced federal budget—to capitalize on voter discontent. In his inaugural address, Reagan attacked the failures of big government: "In this present crisis, government is not the solution to our problem; government is the problem." No single sentence better describes Reagan's governing philosophy. When John Kennedy became president in 1961, Americans had faith in government and were idealistic about what government could accomplish. By 1980, that faith and idealism had disappeared. When Reagan argued that big government was the problem, the American people agreed.

Reagan's solution to the problem, however, was not better government but simply less government. Behind the well-chosen phrases and amusing anecdotes hid the truth: it was not a revolution of new ideas but of old ideas in a new package. The ideas were simply warmed-over laissez faire. The package was Reagan himself. The emphasis was on style not substance. His made-for-TV presidency accentuated the positives and minimized the negatives. At a time when Americans were desperately looking for a leader, they got an actor. Instead of solutions, they got soundbites. But while Reagan knew how to tap America's disenchantment with government, his presidency exposed significant problems with politics in the media age: the fuzzing of the lines between news and hype, between rhetoric and reality, and between wishful thinking and cold, hard facts.

Supply-Side Economics

Reagan inherited an economy in bad shape, still reeling from the aftershocks of OPEC oil price hikes. In 1980, the economy had stopped growing, the inflation rate was 13.5%, and unemployment had reached 7%. Federal Reserve Chairman Paul Volcker, appointed by Carter in 1979, adopted tight monetary policy (high interest rates) to combat inflation. After the 1980 election, Volcker continued to raise rates. By late December the Fed discount rate was 13% and the prime rate hit a record 21.5%.[1] It was the harsh medicine needed to curb the inflation that had plagued the American economy since the Johnson years.

Tight monetary policy, the generally accepted method of fighting inflation, lessened inflationary pressures by reducing business investment and consumer spending—two components of aggregate demand. The cost of tight monetary policy, however, was slower growth and higher unemployment. But a small group of economists thought they had a better idea—inflationary pressures could also be mitigated by increasing the aggregate supply of goods. Their prescription: cut marginal tax rates to increase the incentives to save, invest, and produce. Because it focused on aggregate supply, this approach was called supply-side economics.

Canadian economist Robert Mundell presented many of the supply-side ideas at an economics conference on international monetary problems held in Bologna, Italy, in April 1971. At the time, few economists thought there was a need for a new approach because the world's industrialized nations were enjoying strong economic growth. Critics of the supply-side approach pointed out that cutting taxes would cause a shortfall in tax revenue and increase budget deficits. But Mundell argued that the tax cuts would stimulate economic growth, which in turn would mitigate the loss in tax revenue. He also felt that a modest budget deficit was worth running to promote economic growth.[2]

The two oil crises in 1973 and 1979 caused similar economic cycles: inflation increased dramatically, interest rates rose, the economy went into a deep recession, and millions of Americans lost their jobs. The severity of the oil shocks and the importance of oil to the American economy guaranteed that the economy would have suffered no matter what fiscal and monetary policies were adopted. However, voters put pressure on politicians to do *something*. Politicians responded, not by adequately addressing America's oil dependency problem, but by seeking a new mix of fiscal and monetary policies. The economic problems of the seventies opened the door for supply-side economics.

In late 1974, economist Arthur Laffer helped the supply-side cause by creating a simple way of thinking about the relationship between tax rates and tax revenues. When put in graphical form, it became known as the Laffer curve, shown in Chart 7.

At point A, the tax rate is 0% and the government collects no tax revenue. At point D, the tax rate is 100%, nobody works, and again the government collects no tax revenue. In between these two endpoints, the amount of tax revenue is some value greater than zero. Laffer made the argument that there were two tax rates for a given level of tax receipts—for example, points B and C. At

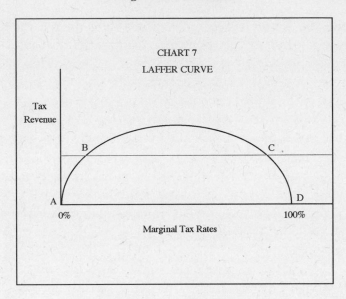

CHART 7
LAFFER CURVE

point B, taxes can still be raised in order to increase tax revenue. Point C, however, lies in the prohibitive zone—an area where tax rates are so high that an increase in taxes would actually produce less revenue. Conversely, a tax cut in this zone would actually *increase* government revenue.

While the Laffer curve brought a new perspective to examining the relationship between tax rates and tax revenue, it did not easily lend itself to implementation. An actual graph representing marginal income tax rates for the United States could *never* be drawn because the *exact* relationship between tax rates and tax revenue was not quantifiable. It was simply a conceptual graph. While supply-siders agreed on the need to cut taxes, they disagreed about the impact on revenues. Most agreed with Mundell that a tax cut, while spurring economic growth, would result in a loss of tax revenue. However, a more ardent group of supporters argued that cutting taxes would actually increase government tax revenue. This second group believed that income tax rates were in the prohibitive zone.

While the Laffer curve focused attention on the relationship between tax rates and tax revenues, it provided no useful insight into the location of tax rates on the curve. If a large income tax cut was passed and the economy rebounded, what would happen to revenue? While everyone had an opinion, no one knew for sure. An unknown variable is normally disconcerting in financial matters, but in the political realm an unknown variable was an attribute individuals could use to make up their own numbers. A politician could propose a tax cut which would be paid for not by a reduction in spending, but by an optimistic assumption about future tax revenue. *Supply-side theory was politically appealing, not as a new way to fight inflation, but as an economic cover for fiscal irresponsibility.*

Reagan's Supply-Side Approach

During his campaign, Reagan promised to increase defense spending, cut taxes, and balance the budget by 1984. But balancing the budget would be difficult. Reagan had inherited a budget from Carter with a $79 billion deficit in FY 1981. An increase in defense spending would increase the deficit. A cut in taxes would also increase the deficit. If Reagan followed through on his first two campaign promises, there was no way for him to make good on the third without *massive* cuts in domestic spending. When submitted to Congress, Reagan's first budget included higher military spending, an across-the-board income tax cut, and cuts in domestic spending. While substantial, the proposed spending cuts failed to offset the budgetary impact of defense increases and tax cuts, and made no dent in Carter's $79 billion deficit legacy.

On its way through Congress, Reagan's budget bumped into political reality. After an early victory in the Republican-controlled Senate, the budget met a different fate in the House of Representatives, where the Democratic majority had its own spending priorities. House members danced around the proposed cuts and designed a variety of accounting gimmicks to pay for pet projects.

In addition, powerful special interest groups launched an aggressive campaign to stop *any* budget cuts. In the end, the administration was forced to compromise on a variety of issues, eliminating most budgetary savings. If Reagan had thrown his popularity behind substantial spending cuts and had appealed to the American people for the need to sacrifice, the prospects for real cuts would have been much better. But the incentives for taking such an unpopular course simply did not exist.

Not surprisingly, cutting taxes proved much easier than cutting spending. Reagan's budget called for slashing both personal and business taxes. Included in the package was the Kemp-Roth tax cut—a twenty-five percent reduction in personal income taxes phased in over three years. In the absence of significant spending cuts, however, many members of Congress were concerned about the effect the tax cuts would have on the deficit. To generate support for the package, the administration handed out tax breaks to powerful interest groups. An irresponsible bidding war broke out between the White House and the Democrats in Congress. The weapons of choice, generous tax breaks, were crafted to increase dramatically in 1985, which just happened to be right after the next presidential election. The political momentum was unstoppable. Strong support by special interest groups and Reagan's personal lobbying helped to push the tax cuts through.

When Reagan signed the tax cuts in August 1981, supply-siders were ecstatic. They expected the bond and stock markets to react favorably to the news. The markets did not; both markets remained in a slump as the recession continued. The short-term health of the nation's economy was being set at the Federal Reserve, not in the halls of Congress. Tight monetary policy had deepened the recession, and only easier monetary policy would end it. When Volcker changed the Fed's monetary policy in the summer of 1982, the markets rebounded strongly and the economy soon followed. Once lower interest rates sparked an economic recovery, lower tax rates and higher military spending fueled the fire.

Although the economy embarked on a seven-year period of economic growth, supply-side economics did not work as advertised. According to supply-side theory, tax cuts would increase savings and investment, spurring economic growth. However, a comparison of the Reagan growth years (1983-88) with the stagnant seventies (1975-80) shows otherwise. While average annual real GDP growth increased (from 3.2% to 3.8%), personal savings fell (from 5.2% to 4.3% of GDP) and private domestic investment also declined (gross investment fell from 17.7% to 17% of GDP; net investment fell from 6.9% to 5.7%).[3]

For all of Reagan's rhetoric, the economic growth of the mid-eighties was fueled not by supply-side ideas, but by Keynesian economic principles—increased consumption financed through government borrowing.

One benefit of hiding behind supply-side theory was that it allowed Reagan to take credit for the economic expansion, blame Congress for the huge budget deficits, and never publicly admit to any relationship between the two. But the administration's own numbers tell a different story. After Congress passed a FY 1982 budget which contained small domestic spending cuts, large military spending increases, and a large cut in both individual and corporate taxes, the Reagan administration still claimed that the budget would be balanced by 1984. How was this possible? While not publicly endorsing the ardent supply-side theory that the tax cuts would pay for themselves, the Reagan administration adopted an economic forecast which yielded the same result. Critics aptly named it "rosy scenario."

Rosy Scenario

There was no economic foundation for "rosy scenario" other than the optimistic hopes of Reagan administration officials. In early 1981, Federal Reserve Chairman Paul Volcker was waging an unprecedented war on inflation by pushing interest rates to record levels. However, Murray Weidenbaum, the chairman of Reagan's Council of Economic Advisors and father of "rosy scenario," expected high inflation to continue. Instead of high interest rates causing a recession, the administration's supply-side supporters expected the tax cuts to cause strong economic growth. "Rosy scenario" was a combination of these two unlikely projections. Table 12 compares "rosy scenario" with what actually occurred.

The Reagan administration overestimated both economic growth and inflation. What was the impact on future revenue and spending projections? Table 13 shows that over three fiscal years (1982-84), federal tax receipts fell a whopping $558 billion short of projections. During the same period, the federal government actually spent $89 billion *less* than anticipated. The federal government ran huge budget deficits during this period not because of unanticipated spending increases, but because the administration had grossly overestimated future tax revenues. The ascendance of supply-side economics proved to be the triumph of politics over experience. The result was an unprecedented tide of red ink.

Table 12
ROSY SCENARIO
AND ACTUAL ECONOMIC PERFORMANCE

| | Real GNP Growth | | | |
	1981	1982	1983	1984
Rosy Scenario	0.9%	3.5%	3.5%	3.7%
Actual	1.9%	-2.5%	3.6%	6.8%

| | Inflation | | | |
	1981	1982	1983	1984
Rosy Scenario	12.5%	10.3%	8.7%	7.7%
Actual	10.3%	6.2%	3.2%	4.3%

Sources: *Economic Report of the President, 1991*, and *Budget of the United States Government, FY 1982*.

Table 13
REAGAN ADMINISTRATION'S BUDGET
PROJECTIONS VS. ACTUAL FINANCIALS
($ BILLIONS)

| | Federal Spending | | | |
	FY 1982	FY 1983	FY 1984	Total
Projected	757.6	832.6	905.0	*2,495.2*
Actual	745.8	808.4	851.8	*2,406.0*
Difference	-11.8	-24.2	-53.2	*-89.2*

| | Federal Receipts | | | |
	FY 1982	FY 1983	FY 1984	*Total*
Projected	711.8	809.2	922.3	*2,443.3*
Actual	617.8	600.6	666.5	*1,884.8*
Difference	-94.0	-208.6	-255.8	*-558.5*

| | Budget Surplus (Deficit) | | | |
	FY 1982	FY 1983	FY 1984	*Total*
Projected	-45.8	-23.4	17.3	*-51.9*
Actual	-128.0	-207.8	-185.4	*-521.2*
Difference	-82.2	-184.4	-202.7	*-469.3*

Note: Projected spending includes outlays for off-budget federal entities. Numbers may not add up due to rounding.

Sources: *Economic Report of the President, 1994*, and *Budget of the United States Government, FY 1982*.

During the 1980 presidential campaign, Reagan had lambasted Carter for running huge deficits. Once in office, Reagan's budget deficits made Carter's budgets look almost balanced in comparison. Reagan's lowest deficit was the $128 billion in FY 1982 and his highest was $221 billion in FY 1986. Over the eight Reagan fiscal years, 1982–89, the federal government ran eight budget deficits totalling $1,412 billion, an annual average of $177 billion.

It was a far cry from Reagan's promise of balanced budgets. Instead of eliminating large budget deficits, Reagan institutionalized them. He had simply replaced the tax-and-spend policies of the Democrats with his own borrow-and-spend policies.

In his first inaugural address, Ronald Reagan was quite clear about his view of budget deficits.

> But great as our tax burden is, it has not kept pace with public spending. For decades we have piled deficit upon deficit, mortgaging our future and our children's future for the temporary convenience of the present. To continue this long trend is to guarantee tremendous social, cultural, political and economic upheavals. You and I, as individuals, can, by borrowing, live beyond our means, but for only a short period of time. Why, then, should we think that collectively, as a nation, we're not bound by the same limitation? We must act today in order to preserve tomorrow. And let there be no misunderstanding. We are going to begin to act, beginning today.[4]

Reagan told the American people what they wanted to hear, and then he did just the opposite. What political price was Reagan forced to pay for his deficit deception? In 1984, he won a landslide re-election victory.

The Rebirth of Laissez Faire

America experienced more than just record budget deficits during the Reagan years. The nation also witnessed the re-emergence of laissez faire. It was not laissez faire in the strictest sense, for that had met its demise during the Great Depression. No, during the Reagan administration laissez faire became a guiding philosophy, a belief that, to the extent possible, economic decision making should be moved from the public to private sector.

Hidden behind this philosophy and the lofty rhetoric accompanying it were the interest groups that benefitted. Supply-side economics was sold as a way to increase savings, investment, and economic growth; it also resulted in a huge tax cut for the wealthiest Americans. Deregulating the savings and loan industry would allow market forces to spur growth; it also gave thrift owners wide access to federally insured deposits and few investment restrictions. Allowing a flood of mergers and acquisitions would improve corporate America's productivity; it also created a boom on Wall Street not seen since the 1920s.

In the late 1970s, Michael Milken, a young bond specialist at the firm Drexel Firestone, began spreading the good news about low-rated corporate bonds. Milken told investors that the yields on low-grade corporate bonds more than compensated for the risk of default. These bonds were typically issued by fallen angels: companies that were still profitable but had fallen on relatively hard times. Historical studies showed that Milken was correct in his analysis and he started to make large sums of money trading high-yield or "junk" bonds. He also found that many small and medium size companies were eager to issue high-yield bonds to finance their growth and expansion. In the past, these companies were shut out from the capital markets because of their size. Milken had found a profitable niche for himself, benefitting both issuers and investors.

If Milken had continued these practices, his financial legacy would have been overwhelmingly positive. He became, however, a victim of his own success. As the demand for high-yield bonds outstripped the supply, Milken sought other uses for his debt techniques. The vehicle of choice was the leveraged buyout (LBO)—the purchase of a company using a small equity investment and a large quantity of borrowed money. Milken had struck gold. Milken and his firm, now named Drexel Burnham Lambert, created a tidal wave of mergers, acquisitions, and corporate restructurings. Drexel made billions in fees, corporate raiders bought companies for relatively small investments, bond buyers got high yields, and shareholders benefitted from higher stock prices. There were profits for everyone, or so it seemed.

As is often the case under laissez faire, other important issues were being ignored. Corporations now looked at their businesses from an entirely different viewpoint. America's business managers, routinely criticized for ignoring long-term issues, became more short-term oriented. Instead of focusing on products and new technology, they focused on share price and corporate raiders. Plants were shut. Workers were fired.[5] Underperforming assets were sold off. Research and development spending—vital to America's future competitiveness—was slashed because it was a drain on cash. Billions of dollars in profits were made, not by growing companies, but by shrinking them; not by building products, but by shuffling paper; not by focusing on the future, but by living for the present.

Leveraged buyouts helped to spark another of the speculative waves that periodically engulf Wall Street. A corporation that became the target of a raider saw its stock soar. Holders of the stock stood to make a fortune if their company became a target. As takeover money flew fast and furious, investors wanted in. During the mid-1980s, as the economy grew and interest rates fell, stock prices rose strongly (the Dow Jones Industrial Average (DJIA) rose 27.7% in 1985 and 22.6% in 1986). In 1987, however, the speculative fever took hold. Between January 1 and August 25 of that year, the DJIA rose 43.6%.

But like all speculative periods, this one did not last. On October 19, 1987, the stock market crashed as the DJIA plunged 508 points. The next day, trading on the stock exchange nearly came to a standstill. Many people worried about a repeat of 1929. The structural flaws that caused the Great Depression, however, had been remedied. Federal deposit insurance, tighter securities regulation, and quick action by the Federal Reserve kept the stock market crash from precipitating an economic catastrophe. Nevertheless, a warning message had been sent. Reality had caught up with the market, and it would soon catch up with the major players.

The LBO craze had spawned a new type of stock trader, one who would trade on inside information. Trading on inside information is the financial equivalent of playing blackjack in Las Vegas with a marked deck—it doesn't take much skill to make large amounts of money. But the game was now ending. On May 12, 1986, Dennis Levine, an investment banker at Drexel, was arrested for insider trading. More significantly, he agreed to cooperate with the government. Soon other insiders were snared. On November 14, 1986, Ivan Boesky, who had been hailed as a financial genius, pleaded guilty to insider trading and agreed to cooperate with the government. The government's investigations created a path of indictments, finally leading to Michael Milken who was indicted on ninety-eight counts of fraud, racketeering, and illegal insider trading. On April 14, 1990, Milken consented to a plea bargain agreement. He pleaded guilty to six lesser counts, paid a fine of $600 million dollars, and was sentenced to ten years in jail, of which he subsequently served two years.

Michael Milken was a symbol of Wall Street in the 1980s. He dramatically changed America's corporate landscape, and he made fabulous sums doing so. Indeed, his 1987 compensation was $550 million—one individual, one year. But by the end of the decade the reality finally emerged. The junk bond craze left America's corporate landscape strewn with highly leveraged companies and the most prominent market player sitting in jail.

Ethical Lapses in Washington

During the eighties, greed and financial scandal were not restricted to Wall Street. The Reagan administration set records for ethical misconduct and rules violations. It was not only the number of violations that was appalling, but how high up they reached in the administration and how little was done to punish the offenders. Michael Deaver, a close Reagan political advisor, was convicted of perjury when he lied to a congressional subcommittee and a federal grand jury about his lobbying activities. He received a mere "slap on the wrist:" three years probation. A congressional committee asked Samuel Pierce, the secretary of the Department of Housing and Urban Development (HUD), about charges that HUD ignored its mandate of providing low income housing to the poor and instead focused on giving projects to developers with strong political connections in the administration. Pierce refused to answer questions by invoking his Fifth Amendment rights. A special prosecutor found that Edwin Meese, the Attorney General of the United States, the highest law enforcement officer in the country, had filed false income taxes. The prosecutor declined to recommend that Meese be indicted.[6] No amount of media hype could hide a simple fact: the Reagan administration was an ethical wasteland.

The corruption of the Reagan administration went far beyond individual acts of a self-serving nature. Congress, with the support of the American public, had first restricted and then banned aid to the Nicaraguan contras. In response, the administration created a government-sponsored operation outside the oversight reach of Congress. This secret initiative was funded, in part, by illegal arms sales to Iran. Contrary to Reagan's public statements, the weapons were sold in exchange for the release of American hostages held in Lebanon. When the two operations became public, the Reagan administration went on the offensive, destroying documents, creating false chronologies of events, and releasing half-truths to the news media. The Tower Commission was created to investigate the role of the administration and the allegations of linkage between the sale of arms and aid to the contras.

The Iran-contra scandal had all the makings of another Watergate. There were, however, important differences. Attempting to free American hostages and support Nicaraguan rebels were more politically appealing causes than undermining your opponent's campaign. Nixon's tape recordings led to his downfall, yet in the Iran-contra scandal there was no smoking gun. The popularity of Oliver North helped to diffuse the scandal, while the death of CIA chief William Casey provided a convenient scapegoat for the illegal acts. In addition, successful manipulation of the news media clouded the facts. The Tower Commission report established the view that it was Reagan's responsibility, not because he had authorized the actions, but because he had exercised poor oversight. Damage control was successful, but it did not change the facts. The Reagan administration, with Ronald Reagan's knowledge and consent, had broken the law.

When Ronald Reagan became president in 1981, the United States clearly needed a new direction. The Vietnam War and Watergate had devastated the public's confidence in their own government, two oil crises had ravaged the economy, the federal budget deficit was on the rise, and the Iranian hostage crisis had the nation feeling like a helpless giant. Reagan responded to these problems with optimism and lofty rhetoric. And while a severe recession finally choked off rampant inflation and Reagan's Keynesian economic policies, sold under the supply-side label, fueled seven years of economic growth, no amount of media manipulation could hide the widening gap between the rhetoric and the reality.

Reagan stated that he was against big government and would cut wasteful domestic spending. In reality, a few domestic cuts were passed in 1981, but domestic spending as a whole continued to increase every year. Reagan promised to balance the budget. Instead, America was left with the largest deficits in the nation's history. Reagan was a strong advocate of deregulation and a more limited role for government. But his deregulation policies sparked the LBO craze and the S&L crisis. America had gone to the polls in 1980 to elect a leader to solve the nation's problems. What it got instead was someone who masterfully kept them from public view. The fine art of political evasiveness had reached a new level.

Chapter 8

A Noticeable Lack of Substance

Nothing breeds imitation like success. Reagan's popular anti-government, anti-tax rhetoric proved wildly successful at the voting booth and bred imitation across the political spectrum. For eight years, Reagan successfully combined positive imagery with a debt-financed economic boom to obscure the reality—that his "less is better" philosophy of government did nothing to help solve the nation's most intractable problems. It is this difference, between the rhetoric and the reality, which is the most lasting and most devastating legacy of the Reagan years. For it demonstrated that problem avoidance, hidden behind empty rhetoric, need not be a political liability.

Political Campaigns

The lack of substance in American politics is a direct result of the nation's monetary democracy. The dynamics of modern election campaigns encourage candidates to attack each other rather than propose innovative solutions to the nation's problems. Indeed, negative campaigning has become a political art form. The mechanics are simple—find issues that produce a negative voter reaction about your opponent and repeat them over and over. All that is needed is a research staff, a large campaign war chest, and some slick television ads. Although negative campaigning does nothing to promote democracy, it does win elections.

As the Republican presidential candidate in 1988, George Bush became heir to the Reagan legacy. Eight years earlier, when he was challenging Reagan for the Republican nomination, Bush referred to Reagan's economic proposals as "voodoo economics." Bush was correct in his appraisal, but lost his bid for the nomination. As a candidate in 1988, Bush adopted Reagan's policies as his own. His main campaign motto, "read my lips, no new taxes," was an extension of Reagan's anti-tax stance.

Bush's Democratic challenger was Michael Dukakis, governor of Massachusetts. Initially, Dukakis held a sizable lead in the polls. But then Bush went on the offensive. Lee Atwater, Bush's campaign manager, and media consultant Roger Ailes found a number of issues with which to attack Dukakis. The most potent was the issue of prisoner furloughs. A black murder convict by the name of Willie Horton had been released on a weekend pass and had raped and stabbed a white woman. A well-crafted TV commercial—complete with its racially charged message—attacked Dukakis as being soft on crime.

The Dukakis campaign could have attacked the Bush campaign on a number of easy targets: huge budget deficits, the Iran-contra scandal, or the polarization of wealth. But, Dukakis did not attack. In fact, he failed even to respond to the "Willie Horton" attacks, which would not have been difficult. The Massachusetts furlough program had been established by Dukakis's Republican predecessor. In addition, Ronald Reagan had his own prisoner furlough program while governor of California.[1] All Dukakis had to do was to respond by admitting that it was a tragedy and that the program needed to be changed. But Dukakis failed to respond effectively to any of the Bush attacks. His failure to do so contributed heavily to his loss at the polls.

The 1992 United States Senate race in New York also made clear the effectiveness of negative campaigning. In the Democratic primary, State Attorney General Robert Abrams won after he and candidate Liz Holtzman bombarded front-running candidate Geraldine Ferraro with brutally negative ads. In the general election campaign, Abrams faced two-term Republican Senator Alfonse D'Amato, whose political reputation was in tatters as a result of a Senate ethics inquiry into his use of public office for personal gain. D'Amato's strengths were incumbency and a huge campaign war chest. On the day after the Democratic primary, a financially strapped Abrams began a new round of campaign fund-raising. On the same day, D'Amato began launching a series of highly negative commercials attacking *Abrams's ethics*—proving that in politics the best defense is a good offense.

D'Amato was able to keep Abrams on his heels throughout the campaign and, as a result, won a third term in the Senate. While D'Amato's tactics were successful, from the voters' perspective the race was less than satisfactory. The ubiquitous negative ads and the lack of substantive debate turned voters off to both candidates. In

So which candidate do you like for the U.S. Senate?

the general election, 6.9 million New Yorkers cast a vote for president of the United States, but 467,734 of those voters—one out of every fifteen—looked at the candidates running for the Senate and decided not to cast a vote for any of them.[†]

Decline in Mediating Institutions

The lack of substantive political discourse is not confined to campaigns, and America's monetary democracy is not the sole cause. Traditionally, the American people have had mediating institutions acting on their behalf, allowing individuals to convey their views to those in power. Over the last thirty years, as demographic change created a larger gulf between the governing and the governed, these mediating institutions have been substantially altered and no longer play an effective mediating role.

Political parties were once the main mediators for individual citizens wishing to express their political views. Parties provided voters with information and a place where individuals could go to become politically involved. Candidates for federal office were chosen by party leaders, not by party members. As a result, elected officials had an important allegiance to the party leadership and the policies espoused by the party.

Today, all of this has changed. Political parties focus less on issues and communication with average voters and more on raising money and winning elections. Individuals wishing to become politically active now turn to special interest groups, which seek to influence Congressional legislation on narrow issues. Candidates for federal office are now selected in primaries where financial resources are critical to victory. Parties help in this process, but

---

[†] In addition to Abrams and D'Amato, the U.S. Senate race included four minor party candidates who received a combined total of 3% of the vote. Final election statistics from *Congressional Quarterly*. Presidential results–January 23, 1993, p. 190. Senate results–April 17, 1993, p. 978.

candidates are substantially on their own. As a result, once candidates are elected they feel more of an allegiance to campaign contributors than to their own political party. America's two main political parties have become little more than clubs whose membership is required to hold federal office. The cohesion, so crucial to a smooth functioning political party, has been fractured by the realities of modern American politics.

The transformation of another important mediating institution —the national news media—has not been the result of demographic change, but of technological innovation. The print media has played an important role in politics since the founding of the republic more than two hundred years ago. Radio became a potent political medium during the long administration of Franklin D. Roosevelt, while television marked its emergence as the most important medium in the 1960 Kennedy-Nixon presidential debate. Surveys taken of voters after the debate proved interesting—those who had listened to the debate on the radio thought that Nixon had won, while those who had watched the debate on television thought Kennedy was the winner. The television age of media politics had begun, and its impact on American politics has been growing ever since.

During the sixties and seventies, the national news media flexed its political muscles. Media coverage of the Vietnam War exposed the hollowness of government optimism and helped to turn public opinion against the war. The persistent work of *Washington Post* reporters Carl Bernstein and Bob Woodward sparked the Congressional investigation of Watergate. As a result of its success in Vietnam and Watergate, the media took on a new role as public watchdog, critically analyzing the actions and statements of government officials.

While the national news media can proudly point to both Vietnam and Watergate as examples of a vital and successful role in informing the American public, since that time the public benefit of a growing media role has been decidedly mixed. On the positive side, by focusing public attention on issues, the media can elicit quick government action. The media focus on the starving people of Somalia was the main impetus for America sending troops to help the relief effort. Yet, the sheer volume of news stories tends to shorten the public's attention span. Stories of mismanagement, official misconduct, and government incompetence have become so commonplace, that an increasingly cynical public is no longer surprised or shocked. More importantly, the "image is everything" mentality that permeates modern American politics places excessive importance on media exposure and intensifies the emphasis on style over substance.

The strange irony is that the transformations that have taken place in both America's political parties and the news media have arguably made our public affairs more "democratic" while simultaneously harming American democracy. Primaries allow individuals to participate in selecting candidates, yet this democratic change has helped increase the power of campaign contributors at the expense of political parties. The national news media has been successful in bringing much of politics out of the back room and into the nation's living rooms. In response, special interests must make their case in public, so they hire media consultants, fund detailed reports from public policy foundations, and make endless presentations to Congressional committees. The final result is more political theater, but not a more responsive or effective democracy.

Perhaps the most vivid example of how media politics distorts American democracy is the political focus group. The mechanics of a focus group are quite simple. A group of homogeneous voters—typically all of the same gender, race, and economic class—is interviewed by a poll taker regarding their views and opinions of particular candidates. The object of the focus group is to get beyond the public opinion polls to understand why voters hold particular opinions and to find out what they actually feel about the candidates. While the exercise seems to promote democracy—ordinary voters expressing their political opinions—the information is used to tailor specific campaign messages and enhance a candidate's electoral chances by "packaging" him correctly. In a political age when perception is more important than reality, focus groups provide the ammunition to wage the war over who can manipulate the voting public most effectively.[2]

The character of present-day American politics—the empty campaigns, the mind-numbing rhetoric, and the limited opportunities for individual participation—has not occurred by accident. The political system has simply become an ongoing contest between various interest groups wealthy enough to play the game. Those well-funded and well-organized groups can push their agendas in the halls of Congress or in the backwaters of federal regulatory agencies. Those groups without organization or sufficient funds are systematically ignored. The appearance of a functioning government—where legislators pass laws enforced by the executive branch—belies the reality of an environment where everything is negotiable for those groups with political power.[3]

The American people look at the machinations in Washington and rightfully ask: "who is speaking for us?" Representatives in Congress must each represent more than half a million Americans—a ratio not conducive to frequent interaction. The traditional mediating institutions—political parties and the news media—no longer play a mediating role. There are a few public interest groups operating in Washington, yet they are outgunned both in terms of money and resources. The American public has been deprived of a voice either through the political parties, the Congressional hearings, or the campaign finance laws. When elections occur, voters are given limited choices of candidates who speak to a few "wedge" issues and attack their opponents. In such an environment, it is not hard to understand why Americans are fed up with politics as usual.

The third era of American political economy began in the wake of the Great Depression and thrived during the difficult circumstances of World War II. During the first two decades of the postwar era, a unique set of economic conditions and a fiscally conservative government set the stage for unprecedented prosperity. America's transition to a new era—when a structure of limited government would play a more activist, yet fiscally responsible role—seemed to have been completed successfully.

The last thirty years have demonstrated otherwise. As the unique conditions of the postwar era started to disappear, the federal government was confronted with complex and difficult issues—from Vietnam to economic stagnation to an exploding federal debt. Solving the problems that confront the United States today requires the development of a national consensus to make difficult decisions. Yet, no incentives exist for politicians to pursue such a path. America's political system, driven by demographic change and a warped system of campaign finance, has deteriorated into a free-for-all where powerful groups pursue their own short-term interests at the expense of the general public. Politicians have become adept at manipulating perception, but it is the reality with which Americans must live every day. And it is to the present reality of America's economic ills to which we now turn.

Part III

Economic Myopia

Chapter 9

Running on Empty:
America's Economic Problems

During World War II, massive government military expenditures transformed an economy that no longer seemed to work into an economy that worked better than ever. As we have seen, after the war, a baby boom, a growing consumer culture, little foreign competition, and a fiscally conservative government combined to foster two decades of strong economic growth. But America had gone from depression to prosperity as a result of circumstance, not of plan. When the unique postwar conditions began to disappear, a rapid series of events—the creation of the welfare state, the emergence of foreign economic competition, and the twin oil crises of the seventies—exposed America's economic shortcomings. The United States needed new economic policies. Faced with tough decisions, Ronald Reagan responded with optimistic rhetoric and an economic expansion fueled by profligate government borrowing. His economic legacy, however, does not end with a swollen national debt. For as we shall see, Reagan's policy of laissez faire and its international corollary—free trade—have left an indelible mark on America's economy.

Economic Productivity

Before we examine America's long-term economic trends, let's return for a moment to the world of economist Adam Smith. In the first chapter of *The Wealth of Nations*, Smith noted that while self-interest provides the motivation, the great engine of economic growth is the division of labor. As each individual seeks to improve his own situation, he specializes in a particular business. This specialization gives way to increased knowledge of the activity, an increase in innovation and machinery, and a division of specific tasks. Smith described the daily activity at a business that made pins:

> One man draws out the wire, another straights it, a third cuts it, a fourth points it, a fifth grinds it at the top for receiving the head; to make the head requires two or three distinct operations; to put it on, is a peculiar business, to whiten the pins is another; it is even a trade by itself to put them into the paper; and the important business of making a pin is, in this manner, divided into about eighteen distinct operations, which, in some manufactories, are all performed by distinct hands, though in others the same man will sometimes perform two or three of them. I have seen a small manufactory of this kind where ten men only were employed, and where some of them consequently performed two or three distinct operations. But though they were very poor, and therefore but indifferently accommodated with the necessary machinery, they could, when they exerted themselves, make among them about twelve pounds of pins in a day. There are in a pound upwards of four thousand pins of a middling size. Those ten persons, therefore, could make among them upwards of forty-eight thousand pins in a day. Each person, therefore, making a tenth part of forty-eight thousand pins, might be considered as making four thousand eight hundred pins in a day. But if they

had all wrought separately and independently, and without any of them having been educated to this peculiar business, they certainly could not each of them have made twenty, perhaps not one pin in a day; that is, certainly, not the two hundred and fortieth, perhaps not the four thousand eight hundredth part of what they are at present capable of performing, in consequence of a proper division and combination of their different operations.[1]

Smith observed that by working together, dividing up tasks, and using machinery, the workers at the pin factory dramatically increased their output per worker—which is the common measure of worker productivity. Assuming that one individual could make twenty pins in a day and ten workers working together could make forty-eight thousand, then the division of labor and use of machinery increased worker productivity 240 times. Improving productivity requires finding better, cheaper, or faster ways of producing the same, or higher quality, goods or services. Today, we refer to such improvements as advances in technology.

Chart 8 shows what I call the productivity/technology (PT) curve. The chart has been drawn to show *no specific mathematical relationship*, but to highlight the fundamental relationship between technology and productivity—worker productivity growth depends upon increases in technology. I am using the term *technology* in a broad sense, covering everything from worker training to improved manufacturing processes.

The graph is simply for conceptual purposes, but the concept is vitally important not only for businesses, but for individuals and entire nations. Businesses can increase productivity by improving service or quality, or by lowering costs. For example, spending on research can help develop new products, while new manufacturing processes can reduce costs while boosting output. Individuals can increase their own productivity by improving their personal skills, either through education, job training, or work experience. Because the productivity of an entire nation is simply equal to the sum of

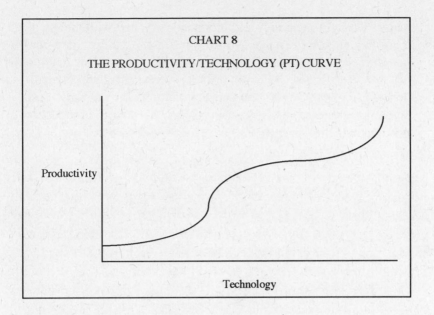

CHART 8

THE PRODUCTIVITY/TECHNOLOGY (PT) CURVE

Productivity

Technology

individual worker productivities, the best government economic policies are those which encourage investments in research and development, new plant and equipment, and education. Throughout the remainder of the book, I will refer to the PT curve when discussing policies designed to improve the productivity of workers, businesses, and entire nations.

Increasing productivity, however, is not a one-way street. Individuals, businesses, and governments must all face one of the great paradoxes of economics: increases in worker productivity are simultaneously a main source of economic growth and a major source of unemployment. For as worker productivity increases, fewer workers are needed. Excess labor is released to pursue other opportunities. What if other opportunities do not exist? Or what if workers are unable to take advantage of those opportunities? *If the growth of productivity outpaces the growth in job creation, then unemployment will rise and resistance to change will grow.* If a nation wants to increase its economic growth—in other words, to

move up the PT curve—then it must continue to improve its productivity *and* create jobs for those who are displaced. If it does not,
then a growing segment of the population will resist economic
change and when the resistance gets strong enough, the nation's
economy will stagnate. As we shall see later on, the United States
has failed to address the productivity paradox adequately.

Individual Time Horizons

There exists, in both politics and economics, a natural tension
between the present and the future. When the federal government
borrows money to increase current consumption, it has chosen to
increase today's standard of living at the expense of tomorrow's.
Individuals and corporations must make similar decisions. For
example, individuals must decide between savings and consumption, while corporations must decide between increasing dividends
and increasing investment. We have already seen how the federal
government's policies are focused on the present at the expense of
the future. Unfortunately, this dangerous myopia has spread to the
individual and corporate sectors of America's economy as well.

Let's begin with individuals. In the wake of the Great Depression, Americans avoided debt and saved a large portion of their
disposable income. After World War II, Americans continued to act
in a fiscally conservative fashion. But as economic prosperity
reduced concerns about another depression, American views began
to change. Advertising in newspapers, in magazines, on the radio,
and on television fostered the growth of America's consumer-ori-
ented society. Credit cards made it easy to borrow money for a
whole range of purposes—everything from vacations to VCRs—
for which an earlier generation of Americans would have never
borrowed money. As a result, individual consumption grew rapidly.

Table 14 shows a summary of personal debt, consumption, and
savings trends over the past three decades. Over this period, American consumers have been spending more, borrowing more, and

Table 14
SUMMARY OF PERSONAL CONSUMPTION, DEBT, AND SAVINGS TRENDS (PERCENTAGE OF GDP)

	Personal Consumption Expenditures	Consumer Debt	Mortgage Debt	Residential Personal Savings
1960s	63.3%	12.9%	30.0%	4.7%
1970s	63.9%	13.5%	31.7%	5.4%
1980s	66.1%	14.0%	39.3%	4.5%
1990-93	68.4%	13.4%	48.6%	3.4%

Source: Calculated from statistics in *Economic Report of the President, 1994.*

saving less. While consumer debt has increased steadily, residential mortgage debt has ballooned. Between 1984 and 1989, while consumer debt rose by $275 billion, residential mortgage debt, rose by $1.07 trillion. Over this period, the combined increase in consumer and residential mortgage debt exceeded the $1.3 trillion rise in the national debt.

Why did mortgage debt expand so rapidly in the late 1980s? The answer to that question can be found in sharply increasing housing prices. Between 1983 and 1988, while the consumer price index increased by 19%, the median sales price of existing single family homes rose by 27%. This national number, however, masks a wide disparity in regional price changes. In the Northeast, the median price rose by 98%, from $72,200 to $143,000.[†] As prices skyrocketed, people used the increase in their home equity to buy larger houses or finance other purchases. An overheated housing

---

[†] The median price on *new* single family homes in the Northeast also increased sharply during this five-year period, rising 81% from $82,200 to $149,000. Statistics from *Statistical Abstract of the United States*, 1992, p. 712.

market was making millions of Americans rich from asset inflation. When the 1990 recession hit, the residential mortgage market's speculative bubble broke. In areas of the country where
housing prices had not risen dramatically during the 1980s, the
impact was minimal. But in the areas with substantial price
increases, housing prices dropped precipitously. Many people saw
the equity in their homes, often their largest store of personal savings, plummet and in some cases disappear altogether.

Corporate Time Horizons

We turn next to corporate America. In emphasizing either the
present or the future, businesses face tradeoffs between short-term
and long-term profitability. Investments in new plant and equipment, research and development, and employee training programs
all help increase future profits, but depress short-term earnings.
Reducing these expenditures can dramatically cut costs and
increase short-term profits, but hurt long-term corporate growth
and competitiveness. During the eighties, the leveraged buyout
craze and the heavy use of stock options in executive compensation packages kept corporate eyes focused squarely on short-term
profits and short-term share price.

As companies pursued short-term strategies, business investment, as measured by net private domestic investment, declined
sharply, as shown in Table 15. The investment drop was a major
contributor to the successive declines in worker productivity
growth. In the early 1990s, productivity growth rebounded as corporate America intensified its downsizing efforts. Over the past
few years, this activity has painfully exposed the productivity
paradox. While corporations are becoming more productive and
profitable, millions of skilled workers are unemployed or underemployed. The low level of new business investment has greatly
aggravated America's growing employment problem.

Table 15
BUSINESS INVESTMENT
AND WORKER PRODUCTIVITY GROWTH

	Net Private Domestic Investment (% GDP)	Average Annual Worker Productivity Growth
1960s	7.4%	2.4%
1970s	7.3%	1.3%
1980s	5.4%	0.8%
1990-93	2.9%	1.6%

Note: Productivity measure is for all non-farm workers. Net private domestic investment equals total business investment minus replacement of worn out machinery.

Source: Calculated from statistics in *Economic Report of the President, 1994.*

America's economy has done a complete turnaround since World War II. At the end of the war, individuals had high levels of savings, businesses invested heavily in new plant and equipment, and the federal government followed fiscally conservative policies. Four decades later, consumers save less and borrow more, businesses invest less in new plant and equipment, and the federal government borrows excessively for consumption, not investment. These myopic activities have taken their collective toll on America's long-term economic growth rates, as shown in Table 16.

America's Foreign Trade

Since the end of World War II, the United States has been a strong advocate of free trade. In the early postwar era, when America's high standard of living was dependent upon a technological edge and manufacturing prowess, free trade was in the nation's best interest. But as America's technological edge began to shrink,

Table 16
AVERAGE ANNUAL GROWTH
OF THE U.S. ECONOMY

	Real GDP Growth
1950s	4.0%
1960s	4.1%
1970s	2.8%
1980s	2.5%
1990-93	1.5%

Source: Calculated from statistics in *Economic Report of the President, 1994.*

foreign competitors were able to compete with American companies on a price basis. To retain a strong manufacturing base under such circumstances, the United States should have modified its trade policies. But the nation did not. Today, America continues to cling to trade policies no longer in the national interest.

It was economist David Ricardo who, in 1817, set forth his theory of comparative advantage stating that countries should produce those products for which they have a relative advantage. If every nation did what they do best and practiced free trade, the theory goes, then world production would be maximized and everyone would be better off. The reality, of course, is somewhat different than the theory. Free trade is always in the best interest of the world's dominant economic power. If no barriers to trade existed, then the private companies of that nation would dominate world trade. Just as monopolies arise from unrestrained laissez faire, a single dominant economic power arises from unrestrained free trade.

Throughout history, nations have realized this and have adopted protective tariffs to help develop domestic industries. During the nineteenth century, Great Britain was the world's leading economic power and, not surprisingly, a strong proponent of free trade. The United States, wishing to develop its own industrial base, consistently adopted tariffs to protect American manufacturers from British competition. In the twentieth century, two events transformed the United States from a protectionist nation to the leading proponent of free trade. First, the disastrous Smoot-Hawley Tariff Act of 1930 triggered a trade war that deepened and lengthened the Great Depression. Second, and more importantly, after World War II the United States was the world's dominant economic power. With little foreign competition, free trade was now in America's best interest. That the United States could espouse its own self-interest as a principled stand on sound economic theory made free trade even more irresistible.

America's economic success during the fifties and sixties solidified free trade as the foundation of the nation's international economic policies. However, foreign governments, eager to develop domestic industries, made liberal use of trade barriers to protect selected markets from American manufacturers. As time passed and standardized, mass-production technologies became familiar to nations across the globe, foreign companies began exporting manufactured goods to the United States. Able to hire workers at substantially lower wages, foreign competitors held an important cost advantage. With protected domestic markets and aggressive exporting practices, foreign companies made large inroads into America's manufacturing base. A new age of global competition had dawned.

Japan proved adept at pursuing a national export strategy. Over the past three decades, Japanese companies, hiding behind domestic tariff barriers, have targeted various American industries with stunning success. For example, beginning in the late fifties and early sixties, Japanese manufacturers began exporting televisions to the United States at below cost in order to capture market share. Although a violation of American trade laws, the federal government failed to stop this monopolistic practice. Over time, all but one of America's television manufacturers either sold their companies or were driven out of business.[2]

Over the last twenty years, manufacturing companies in Japan, South Korea, Taiwan, Hong Kong, Singapore, and Thailand have all benefitted from America's free trade policies. In return, the American consumer has benefitted from low-cost, high-quality consumer goods. America's economic well-being, however, is not measured simply by low-cost consumer products or higher short-term corporate profits. The quantity and quality of jobs available in the United States has an important impact both in individual human terms and also in terms of aggregate purchasing power.

If a plant is closed down in the United States and moved overseas to take advantage of lower wages, then the drop in consumer prices must be weighed against the loss of wages at home. If the United States had a system of economic transition—where workers who lose their jobs are retrained and given higher-skilled, higher-paying jobs—then free trade would actually help the United States move up the PT curve. But the United States has no such system, and, as a result, workers who lose their high-paying manufacturing jobs tend not to be retrained and end up in lower-paying service jobs. This segment of the population is actually regressing—moving down the PT curve.

The American government's failure to adequately enforce existing trade laws and the lack of an efficient system of economic transition are just two of the glaring problems with the nation's current trading policies. Perhaps more disturbing, though certainly not surprising, is the lack of substance in the nation's trade debate. At one end of the debate is "free trade" and at the other end is "protectionism." In the middle lies reality; yet all too often the debate ignores everything but the two extremes. Politicians need to recognize that, while reducing barriers to trade is both desirable and achievable, truly free trade—with no government interference or barriers to trade—has never and will never exist. A balance needs to be sought between low trade barriers, low consumer prices, and the quality and quantity of jobs available to American workers. Unfortunately, in a monetary democracy it is a difficult balance to achieve.

America's trade policies, no matter how flawed, have a large constituency of individuals and corporations who benefit from them. The quotas and duties that the United States levies on thousands of different imported products are not the result of well constructed policy, but a reflection of special interest lobbying power. These groups exert powerful political influence to ensure that the United States remains a status quo economic power. In addition, a disorganized federal trade bureaucracy keeps America from developing a coordinated trade policy, and a revolving door between lobbyists and important trade positions ensures that special interests have their say. America's myopia, however, does not stop there. In keeping with the spirit of equal opportunity, the purchase of political influence in America's monetary democracy is open to all, foreigners included. Large foreign corporations, with deep pockets and a long-term orientation, take full advantage of this gift.

The political appeal of free trade is similar to the appeal of laissez faire—it requires the government to do nothing. But blind pursuit of free trade in a world where manufacturing technologies move freely results in economic competition based on low wages. And in the fastest growing high-tech industries, comparative advantage is no longer indigenous, it is created—by the economic and educational policies a nation pursues. America's free trade policy, wholly sound and appropriate when first adopted after the end of World War II, no longer reflects the world in which we live, and without a well-structured system of economic transition, free trade is no longer in the nation's best interest. But with a federal government that simply sits on the economic sidelines, it is America's strategy by default.

Consequences of America's Trade Deficits

America's myopic economic and fiscal policies have worsened the nation's trade problems. To finance business investment and keep economic growth strong, a high level of national savings is crucial. During the eighties, however, the United States did not save enough to meet its own investment needs. As a result, a gap emerged between national savings and national investment, as shown in Chart 9. The primary cause of this national savings gap was large federal deficits.

When America's gross savings falls below the level of gross private domestic investment, the difference must be borrowed from abroad. When national savings and investment began to diverge in 1983, foreign investors purchased dollars in order to buy dollar-denominated securities and benefit from high real interest rates in the United States. This large influx of foreign money caused the dollar to rise relative to other foreign currencies, as shown in Chart 10. Between 1980 and 1985, the value of the dollar increased by over 50% in foreign exchange markets.

As the dollar climbed, the price of imported goods fell, while the price of American exports rose. As a result, imports increased while exports plummeted. America's foreign trade deficit grew to record levels, as shown in Chart 11. The sharp rise in the dollar decimated America's export sector, eliminating manufacturing jobs

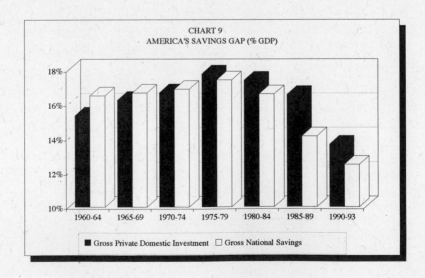

CHART 9
AMERICA'S SAVINGS GAP (% GDP)

■ Gross Private Domestic Investment   □ Gross National Savings

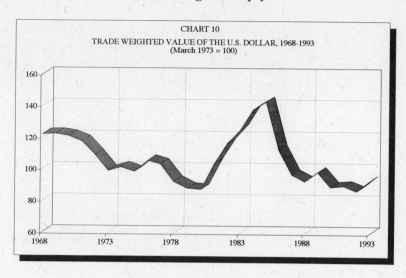

CHART 10
TRADE WEIGHTED VALUE OF THE U.S. DOLLAR, 1968-1993
(March 1973 = 100)

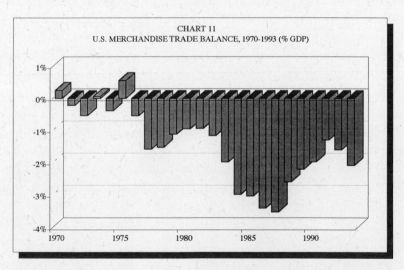

CHART 11
U.S. MERCHANDISE TRADE BALANCE, 1970-1993 (% GDP)

Note: Merchandise trade balance is equal to goods exported minus goods imported, excluding services. Between 1970 and 1988, the United States ran a small trade surplus in services (never exceeding 0.4% of GDP). Since 1989, America's trade surplus in services has been between 0.6% and 0.9% of GDP. While this trade growth is encouraging, America's trade surplus in services is still overwhelmed by its large merchandise trade deficit.

and driving many American companies out of business. Even as
the dollar has fallen in foreign exchange markets over the past few
years, these companies and jobs have not returned, and America's
large trade deficits continue.

Political commentators often fail to focus on the relationship
between budget deficits and trade deficits. One reason for this failure is that the Reagan administration, once it realized that big budget deficits were not going away anytime soon, argued that the
economic side effects of budget deficits were limited.[3] Nevertheless, the linkage between America's budget and trade deficits is
quite strong and easy to understand. By increasing the demand for
private sector savings, government budget deficits increase interest
rates and, subsequently, the value of the dollar in foreign exchange
markets. The dollar will also rise in value if foreign borrowing is
used to finance budget deficits (as during the 1980s). As we have
seen, a rising dollar can have a devastating impact on America's
merchandise trade deficit.

The international system of floating currency exchange rates
typically *moderates* merchandise trade imbalances. For example,
when Japan runs a large trade surplus, other nations must purchase
their goods in Japanese yen, causing the yen to rise in foreign
exchange markets. As a result of a higher yen, the price of Japanese exports rises, while Japan benefits from cheaper imports. A
higher yen should therefore tend to reduce Japan's trading surplus.
America's trade experience during the eighties, however, was an
aberration. The dollar was not bid up in the foreign exchange market because of a large American trade surplus, but because the
United States had a high demand for foreign savings to fund its
budget deficit. Instead of reducing a large trade surplus, a rising
dollar during the mid-1980s made a large trade deficit even worse.

Every year the flow of goods and currency leaving the United
States must equal the flow of goods and currency entering the
country. If the nation runs a trade deficit, then it must export dollars. Foreigners turn around and use these dollars to buy treasury

securities, bank certificates of deposit, shares of stock, and other investments. In order to finance the large trade deficits of the 1980s, foreign investment in the United States increased dramatically, resulting in a sharp decline in America's net investment position, as shown in Chart 12. *At the beginning of the 1980s, the United States was the world's largest creditor, while at the end of the decade it was the world's largest debtor.*

One of the most politically appealing, and least discussed, aspects of the Reagan policy of laissez faire was that it allowed the government to make unpopular decisions, but shroud them in the mystery of "the market." If the market was setting foreign exchange rates, then the administration would not have to take responsibility for the devastating impact its fiscal policies were having on the nation's export sector. In a political world where avoiding responsibility is a favorite pastime, adherence to laissez faire provides many benefits. But for a nation running large budget and trade deficits, it is one more step down the wrong path. The failure of the federal government to deal with the nation's foreign oil dependency makes this point abundantly clear.

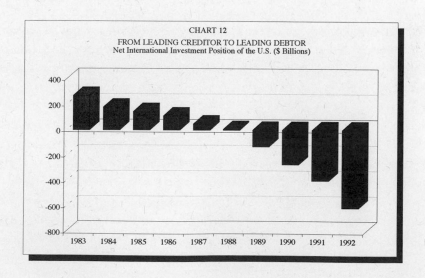

CHART 12

FROM LEADING CREDITOR TO LEADING DEBTOR
Net International Investment Position of the U.S. ($ Billions)

Mortgaging America's Future

America's Foreign Oil Addiction

Dependence on foreign oil was the major cause of the two most severe recessions in the postwar era. From 1973 to 1975, in the aftermath of the Arab oil embargo, the civilian unemployment rate rose from 4.9% to 8.5%, as 3.6 million Americans lost their jobs. From 1979 to 1982, in the wake of another oil shock, the civilian unemployment rate rose from 5.8% to 9.7%, as 4.5 million Americans lost their jobs. Oil imports are the single largest contributor to America's foreign trade deficit (59% of America's trade deficit since 1980)[4] and are a direct transfer of national wealth to foreign nations.

Economic concerns alone are important enough for America to reduce its dependence on foreign oil, but other strong reasons also exist. Burning fossil fuels increases air pollution, which not only contributes to global warming but also increases America's health care costs. The most compelling reason for reducing America's foreign oil dependency, however, was demonstrated in 1991, when the United States sent 500,000 troops halfway around the world to Kuwait. America's interests, contrary to Bush administration statements, were not to stop aggression or to promote democracy in Kuwait, but to make sure that Kuwait's vast oil reserves did not fall into the wrong hands. The cost of America's foreign oil dependency was the loss of American lives.

Continued reliance on foreign oil carries huge costs: more damage to the environment, higher national health costs, continued economic vulnerability, high trade deficits, and the potential of future wars over oil supplies. While the arguments for a national energy policy are overwhelming, the political will is weak. By continuing to pursue a laissez faire energy policy, the United States is courting economic disaster. As the decades pass, world oil supplies will continue to dwindle, oil prices will oscillate higher, and the United States will switch to other sources of energy. But the transition process will not be smooth. Future oil crises will cause severe recessions, high unemployment, and, potentially, other military conflicts. After two oil shock recessions in the seventies and a recent war in the Persian Gulf, it is scandalous that America has no national policy to reduce its foreign oil dependency.

A Change For The Worse

As we have seen, the United States emerged from World War II as the world's leading economic power. Over the next two decades, Americans enjoyed tremendous prosperity as standardized, mass-production techniques were utilized to create a wealth of consumer products. Economic success, however, bred complacency. Americans began to save and invest too little while consuming too much. Foreign companies copied American manufacturing techniques and then improved upon them, ushering in a new era of global competition. The twin oil-shock recessions of the seventies made painfully clear America's economic vulnerability. By 1980, the United States needed effective government policies to raise savings and investment, reduce the nation's foreign oil dependency, and provide training and jobs to workers left unemployed by foreign competition.

The United States got new policies, but not what was needed. By paying for tax cuts and large defense spending increases with borrowed money, the Reagan administration entered uncharted territory. The use of huge budget deficits failed to reverse the long-term decline in economic growth rates but did have many other effects: a sharp rise in the dollar, a decline in American exports, a bigger trade deficit, and a drop in national wealth. Reagan's laissez faire and free trade policies had the political benefit of allowing the administration to avoid responsibility by hiding behind the mystique of the marketplace, but the devastating impact on the economy emerged once the deficit-financed economic boom came to an end. In 1994, just as in 1980, the United States needs new economic policies, for the nation cannot hope to prosper in the future by pursuing the myopic policies of the past.

Chapter 10

The Foreign Challenge

World War II was an economic turning point not only for the United States, but also for Germany and Japan. After the war, America's two main wartime enemies faced difficult circumstances: their economies were in shambles, their industries devastated, their people exhausted, and their prospects bleak. The political and economic structures that emerged from postwar Germany and Japan were, by necessity, future-oriented. Unlike their counterparts in the United States, no German or Japanese politician could tell voters that things were fine and that no major changes were needed. *Emerging from the war, the United States was a status quo power, while Germany and Japan were forward-looking.*

To foster economic growth, both Germany and Japan adopted policies to encourage savings, increase business investment, constrain consumption, and assist developing industries. In both countries, government and business worked together to promote economic growth. Their future-oriented economic policies have

served them well. In the almost half century since the end of the
war, both nations have experienced tremendous economic
renewals. As its economy begins to suffer from myopic policies,
America has the opportunity to learn from the examples of Germany and Japan. If the United States fails to recognize that other
nations have *some* economic structures and policies that are superior, it does so at its own risk.

This chapter focuses on economic comparisons between the
United States and Japan. I have chosen Japan instead of Germany
because Japan has a larger trade surplus, more foreign investment, and the second largest economy in the world. In 1987,
Japan's per capita GDP exceeded that of the United States.
Despite Japan's current economic difficulties, if long-term
macroeconomic trends continue, Japan will become the world's
largest economic power sometime during the first decade of the
twenty-first century—an amazing feat considering Japan's population is half that of the United States. Japan has also orchestrated
its superb economic performance while possessing few of its own
natural resources other than the most important resource of all—
its people.

Comparing the Japanese and American Economies

A macroeconomic comparison underscores the different economic orientations of Japan and the United States. Chart 13 compares the economic growth rates of the two nations. During the
sixties, American economists attributed high Japanese growth rates
to Japan's lower starting point. The economists argued that once
Japan grew larger, its growth rates would slow significantly. While
this prognosis has proven correct, Japanese economic growth rates
have settled down to a level that is consistently higher than those
of the United States. Prior to 1990, the closest the United States
had come to the Japan during any five-year period was during the

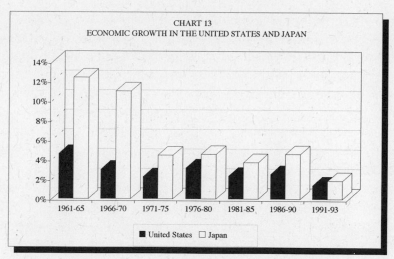

CHART 13
ECONOMIC GROWTH IN THE UNITED STATES AND JAPAN

■ United States □ Japan

Note: Chart shows average annual rate of real economic growth. Years 1961-1970 reflect GNP growth, while years 1971-1993 reflect GDP growth.

1981-85 period when America's GDP growth averaged 2.8%, while Japan's GDP growth averaged 3.7%.[†]

Over the 1991-95 time period, America's economic growth will probably exceed that of Japan because the United States economy is recovering from recession ahead of Japan and Europe (it must be pointed out that the United States also entered into recession before the other large industrialized nations). The focus of this section, however, is on a comparison of *long-term* economic trends. While the American economy may register higher economic growth over the next few years, over the long-term the Japanese economy will continue to register higher levels of growth because of stronger

[†] Unless otherwise noted, comparisons between the American and Japanese economies use statistics from The World Bank, *World Tables 1993* (Baltimore: John Hopkins University Press, 1993), pp. 348-51, 628-31. This source has been chosen to improve the comparability of the data. The World Bank's economic statistics for the United States differ slightly from those found in the *Economic Report of the President*, which is the source used elsewhere.

economic fundamentals. Indeed, if past trends continue, then early in the twenty-first century Japan will surpass the United States in total GDP. The exact timing will depend not only upon economic growth rates, but on the dollar/yen exchange rate.[†]

The reasons for Japan's consistently higher rates of economic growth are no great secret. At the macroeconomic level, Japan saves and invests a significantly higher portion of gross domestic product than does the United States. A comparison of savings and investment rates over the past two decades is shown in Table 17. Over the past two decades, Japan's rates of savings and investment have averaged almost twice those of the United States.

High rates of savings and investment, however, are only part of the story. The human side of the economic equation can be seen in Chart 14, which compares unemployment rates in the two

Table 17
COMPARISON OF SAVINGS AND INVESTMENT (PERCENTAGE OF GDP)

	Gross Domestic Savings		Gross Domestic Investment	
	U.S.	Japan	U.S.	Japan
1970s	19.7%	34.3%	20.1%	33.6%
1980s	17.2%	31.7%	19.4%	29.6%
1990-91	15.2%	33.8%	16.1%	32.5%

Source: Calculated from statistics in World Bank: *World Tables 1993*.

[†] A recently released study by the International Monetary Fund compares national economies on the basis of purchasing power of its own currency at home rather than on the value of the currency on international exchanges. See Steven Greenhouse, "New Tally of World's Economies Catapults China Into Third Place," *The New York Times*, May 20, 1993, p. A1. While under this measure it will take longer for Japan to become the world's largest economic power, it does not change the economic fundamentals that ensure such an outcome.

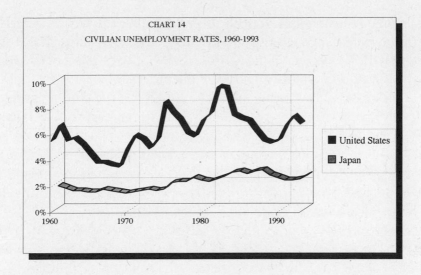

CHART 14

CIVILIAN UNEMPLOYMENT RATES, 1960-1993

countries. Unemployment has consistently been higher in the United States than in Japan. The nations' different approaches to employment are underscored by their disparate reactions to economic slowdowns. When the economy goes into a recession in the United States, companies fire workers to keep costs low and profits high. Unfortunately, if all companies react in the same way, unemployment increases and the recession worsens.

In Japan, even during periods of severe inflation or economic turbulence, companies typically do not fire workers. In order to keep employees, Japanese companies are willing to withstand extended periods of low or negative profits. As a result, Japan's unemployment rate remains relatively stable and recessions tend to be moderate.[†] By offering most workers lifetime employment,

---

[†] As the Japanese economy entered into a rare postwar recession in 1992, major companies began reviewing their no layoffs policy, and in a few cases even fired some workers. While such cases received wide press coverage in the United States, corporate firings are still the exception to the rule in Japan and it will probably remain that way for a long time to come. See Andrew Pollack, "Japan Finds Ways to Save Tradition of Lifetime Jobs," *The New York Times*, November 11, 1993, p. A 1.

Japanese companies have solved the productivity paradox. Japanese workers know that if they develop a new method of production that reduces the number of workers needed, they will not lose their jobs. Instead, they will be retrained and given jobs of equal or higher pay.

In response to the rising value of the yen, Japanese companies have moved many low-tech manufacturing jobs to other nations, such as Thailand, where wages are significantly lower. Both nations benefit from this transfer of jobs—Japanese companies benefit from lower labor costs while Thailand increases employment. In sharp contrast, moving domestic manufacturing jobs overseas is unpopular in the United States because most workers are not retrained and must struggle to find jobs that generally offer lower pay. While Japan moves up the PT curve, the United States has stagnated.

A Fiscal Comparison

Strong macroeconomic fundamentals are important not only to economic growth and job creation, but to moderating the impact of large government deficits. As we saw in the previous chapter, America's large budget deficits during the 1980s not only increased real interest rates, but also had a devastating impact on the nation's foreign trade balance.

Surprisingly, Japan actually ran larger budget deficits (as a percentage of GDP) during both the 1970s and the 1980s than did the United States, as shown in Table 18. But Japan's economy has not shown the fiscal strains of large deficits for two reasons. First, a significant portion of Japanese government spending was for capital investment. During the 1980s, Japan spent 16.7% of its federal budget on capital expenditures, while the United States spent only 6.3%.[1] Second, Japan had a sufficiently high rate of national savings to finance its own deficits. Indeed, as a percentage of gross domestic savings, it was the United States which ran significantly larger budget deficits during the 1980s.

Table 18
COMPARISON OF FEDERAL GOVERNMENT BUDGET DEFICITS IN THE UNITED STATES AND JAPAN

| | As a Percentage of Gross Domestic Product | | As a Percentage of Gross Domestic Savings | |
	U.S.	Japan	U.S.	Japan
1970s	2.1%	4.7%	10.7%	13.6%
1980s	3.9%	4.9%	22.9%	15.4%

Note: U.S. budget deficit as a percentage of GDP is slightly different from figures shown in table 8 due to different statistical source.

Source: Calculated from statistics in World Bank: *World Tables 1993*.

Japan's Trade Surplus

Over the last decade, Japan's trade surplus with the United States has become a contentious political issue. But while Japan has been running a merchandise trade surplus with the United States for over two decades, it was not until the 1980s that Japan began to run large *overall* trade surpluses, as shown in Chart 15.

The Reagan administration's fiscal policies gave Japanese exports a tremendous boost. As the dollar rose in the early eighties, American consumers bought up cheap foreign products and Japanese exports boomed. In 1980, Japan had a $10.4 billion trade surplus with the United States. By 1986, it's surplus with the United States had grown to $54.4 billion.[2] Japan's overall trade surplus during the 1980s was $437 billion, of which trade with the United States accounted for 82%.[3] In return for Japanese goods, the United States sold assets—ranging from treasury securities to golf courses to Rockefeller Center—to Japanese investors. As legendary investor Warren Buffet notes, America is "much like a wealthy family that annually sells acreage so that it can sustain a

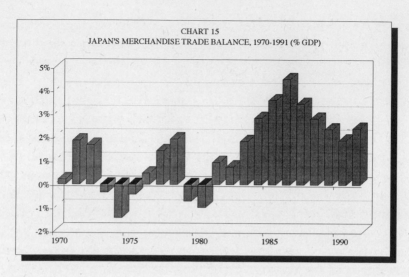

CHART 15
JAPAN'S MERCHANDISE TRADE BALANCE, 1970-1991 (% GDP)

lifestyle unwarranted by its current output. Until the plantation is gone, it's all pleasure and no pain. In the end, however, the family will have traded the life of an owner for the life of a tenant farmer."[4]

Japan's Approach to Manufacturing

Sound macroeconomic policies have played an important role in Japan's economic success, as has the nation's strong emphasis on education. But equally important is the long-term outlook that Japanese business leaders bring to their companies both in employment policies and in their relentless pursuit of product quality. At the end of World War II, the American and Japanese economies were on opposite sides of the economic spectrum—one thriving, the other devastated. Since that time, however, America's economy has grown resistant to change, while Japan's economy has openly embraced it.

The standardized, mass-production techniques espoused by Fredrick Winslow Taylor early in the twentieth century were a critical component in America's efforts to build the huge quantity of military equipment needed to fight World War II. After the war, the same mass-production techniques were used to produce consumer goods for the nation's rapidly expanding population. But while breaking down a manufacturing process into simple, discrete steps allowed production to be maximized, the imposition of strict work standards and rules made production processes resistant to change.

In 1942, another approach to manufacturing processes emerged in the United States. W. Edwards Deming, a statistician at the Census Bureau, began giving lectures on the use of statistical techniques to improve a manufacturing process. Expanding on the work of Bell Laboratories statistician Walter Shewhart, Deming explained how employees could monitor a manufacturing process to determine how long different operations took to perform, which operations caused product defects, and which operations caused breakdowns of the process. Once the information was compiled, it was easy to see where the process could be improved. Deming emphasized that improvements in the manufacturing process *not only improved quality but also reduced costs*. But Deming's ideas fell on deaf ears. Unprecedented economic success with mass-production techniques led America's corporate executives to view statistical charting as a waste of time, and, as a result, quality control remained synonymous with end-of-the-line inspection.

In 1950, Deming traveled to Japan to help with a national census and, at the same time, found corporate managers who were more receptive to new ideas. On June 19, 1950, in the first of a series of lectures, Deming explained to Japan's business leaders how statistical techniques could be used to improve industrial processes. The Japanese liked what they heard and began using Deming's ideas to improve quality while reducing costs. In 1951, in recognition of his work, Japan established the Deming prize to be given to those companies demonstrating the most success in the application of statistical techniques. Today, the Deming prize is the most prestigious award in Japanese industry and is presented in a nationally televised ceremony. Although he provided the Japanese with an important ingredient in their industrial success, Deming remained virtually unknown in the United States until the airing of a television documentary in June 1980.[5]

Japan's Recent Economic Slump

While it has strong macroeconomic fundamentals and low unemployment, Japan also has its share of economic problems. During the late eighties, the United States and other leading industrialized nations made a coordinated effort to push down the value of the dollar in foreign exchange markets. As the dollar fell and the yen rose, Japanese bureaucrats grew increasingly concerned about a recession. The Japanese central bank responded by pushing down interest rates. As a result, the Japanese economy boomed. But the central bank's easy money policies also sparked a wave of speculation.

In 1990, as the speculation continued, the Japanese central bank began to raise interest rates. The economy quickly slowed down, and the speculative bubble burst. Between 1990 and 1992, the Japanese stock market lost roughly half of its value, commercial real estate prices dropped sharply, and corporate bankruptcies skyrocketed. The Japanese economy entered a rare postwar recession. Although some critics argue that mighty Japan Inc. has been grounded, the nation has the strong fundamentals necessary to ride out its current slump and to continue its impressive record of postwar economic growth.

For the moment, a comparison of living standards between the United States and Japan still favors the United States. Consumer prices in Japan are much higher than they are in the United States and the average American worker has a higher income, a larger house or apartment, and a better overall standard of living than does the average Japanese worker. However, things are changing quickly. Forty-five years ago, it would have been ludicrous to even compare the standard of living of the average Japanese to that of the average American. Japan was devastated from the war and its greatest economic concern was making sure that its people did not starve. Since then, Japan has made great strides. If the United States fails to respond to the Japanese challenge, future living standard comparisons between Japanese and American workers will again be ludicrous—but for different reasons.

Replicating a Wartime Economy

Japan's economy is clearly oriented toward the long-term. Japanese companies focus on innovations, invest heavily in new plant and equipment, generously fund research and development, stress market share over short-term profits, and offer the vast majority of workers lifetime employment. The Japanese government pursues policies that encourage individuals to save a high portion of their incomes, while at the same time discouraging consumption by keeping consumer prices relatively high. Japanese industries are given subsidized loans while protectionist legislation keeps out foreign competition in many industries.

If the conditions Japan has created for its economy—high levels of savings and investment, constraints on consumption, and high levels of production—sound a little familiar, they should. *Japan has replicated the economic conditions of a wartime economy.* Instead of producing goods for war, Japan produces goods for export. The purpose of the production is different, but the economic effect is the same. Japan has harnessed the tremendous productive capacity of its capitalist economy and enjoys the benefits of strong economic growth and low levels of unemployment.

One of the great ironies of Japan's economic success is that the nation's political system is dominated by money politics. Political bribery is commonplace in Japan and financial scandals periodically rock the nation's political parties. Just as in the United States, the role of money in politics limits voter choice in Japan and gives the general population little voice in how the country is actually run. But in contrast to the United States, Japanese politicians know that their primary political objective is to pursue policies that are in the *long-term* best interest of Japanese businesses. As a result, Japan's farsighted orientation permeates every sector of society— from individuals who save a substantial portion of income, to businesses that invest heavily, to the government that pursues long-term policies. Japan has its faults, but chronic economic weakness is not one of them.

America's economic problems are of its own making. Near-sighted actions on the part of individuals and businesses have played a part, but it is disastrous government policies that have played the leading role. Japan's economy provides a striking case study in what the United States could do to improve its economic performance, yet America's political system is unable to respond. If the post-cold war era is to be marked by economic competition, then the United States faces some difficult hurdles if it wishes to be the world leader in the twenty-first century. *The greatest hurdle is the delusion that an economy that maximizes short-term corporate profits and blindly espouses laissez faire and free trade can, in the long run, outperform an economy that maximizes savings, investment, and employment.*

Part IV

Setting a New Course

Chapter 11

Back to Basics:
What Role for Government?

More than two hundred years have passed since the founding fathers established a strong foundation of *limited* government. Since that time, America's population has grown from three million to 250 million, while the nation's agrarian economy has evolved into a diversified economy that focuses on industrial production, information technology, and a wide range of services. However, the high levels of specialization that have made economic growth possible carry a price—economic interdependency. Today, a smooth running industrial economy requires not just productive companies, but efficient infrastructure, a quality education system, and plentiful investment capital. As a result, government policies have a crucial impact on a nation's economic success. In the United States, however, the evolution from limited to expansive government has been haphazard, driven not by design, but first by circumstance and then by political expediency. As government grew, interest groups took advantage of campaign finance laws to shape government policies to their own benefit. In this effort, they have been highly successful. But as a result, the United States has adopted myopic policies and lost the ability to act in the national, rather than the special, interest.

The Economic Fracturing of America

The great promise of America has always been the ideal that an individual, of any race, gender, or economic class, could, through hard work and determination, achieve financial and personal success. It is referred to as "the American dream." Over the last twenty years, however, the dream has been vanishing for an ever-increasing number of Americans, and, as a result, the United States risks developing the highly skewed, and completely undesirable, income and wealth distributions characteristic of a developing nation.

The United States still has the world's largest and most productive economy, the best system of higher education, and the highest quality medical care. Yet at the same time, the United States has a rising level of poverty, thirty-seven million people with no health insurance, and the most violent, crime-ridden society in the industrialized world. This sharp dichotomy mirrors a more fundamental split taking place along economic lines. As America's middle class is squeezed by higher taxes, stagnant real wages, and vanishing manufacturing jobs, the gap between the rich and the poor is expanding. Wealthy Americans have access to good education, housing, health care, and careers. In contrast, low-income Americans typically attend problem-ridden public schools, live in dilapidated housing, have no health insurance, and work at dead-end jobs. The government's myopic economic and fiscal policies are accelerating the transformation of America into a nation of the haves and the have-nots.

The primary cause of the economic fracturing of America is an absence of opportunity. As a case in point, take the future prospects

Table 19
PUBLIC AID EXPENDITURES -
FISCAL YEARS ($ BILLIONS)

	1960s	1970s	1980s	1990-93
Medicaid	7	69	227	237
Unemployment Compensation	28	92	181	117
Food and Nutrition Assistance	4	57	178	120
Public Assistance	45	115	251	167
Housing Assistance	2	21	104	73
Total	*85*	*354*	*941*	*714*
Total (% GDP)	*1.3%*	*2.3%*	*2.5%*	*3.1%*

Note: Numbers may not add up due to rounding.

Source: Calculated from statistics in *Budget of the United States Government, FY 1995, Historical Tables*.

of a young girl who grows up in a poor inner-city neighborhood. Often living in a one-parent family, she is exposed to high levels of crime and drugs. The school she attends has large classes, high dropout rates, and difficulty attracting good teachers. She may beat the odds, graduate from high school, find a job, and become a productive member of society. But the odds are that she will end up in a dead-end job, on welfare, in jail, or even dead. In the worst areas, a cycle of poverty has developed that is excluding whole generations from participating in the mainstream of American life.

At the height of American prosperity, Lyndon Johnson sought to use the nation's wealth to help the less fortunate members of society. It was a worthy goal, but the means he chose were suspect. His approach—using large federal spending programs to eradicate the nation's social problems —failed for two reasons. First, once the postwar restraints on government growth were removed, politicians couldn't create new programs fast enough. As never before, special interest groups descended on Washington to get their share of federal spending. Second, the government's large spending programs attempted to help those in need, not by including them in the economic mainstream, but simply by raising their incomes. Instead of focusing on the causes, government programs treated the symptoms. The result was an explosion of dependency.

Although patterned after the New Deal, Johnson's Great Society failed to differentiate between handouts and opportunity. In contrast, Franklin Roosevelt made the distinction abundantly clear in 1935:

> A large proportion of these unemployed and their dependents have been forced on the relief rolls. The burden on the Federal Government has grown with great rapidity. We have here a human as well as an economic problem. When humane considerations are concerned, Americans give them precedence. The lessons of history, confirmed by the evidence immediately before me, show conclusively that continued dependence upon relief induces a spiritual and moral disintegration fundamentally destructive to the national fiber. To dole out relief in this way is to administer a narcotic, a subtle destroyer of the human spirit. It is inimical to the dictates of sound policy. It is in violation of the traditions of America. Work must be found for able-bodied but destitute workers.[1]

The American welfare state was established to provide a safety net for those in need, but for too many Americans dependency has become a way of life. Table 19 shows that federal public aid expenditures have been on a steep upward climb since the 1960s. While the financial costs of public aid have been staggering, the human costs, in terms of opportunities denied, have been much greater.

Government's Role

For too long, America's policymaking has been bogged down by empty rhetoric and rigid ideology. As a result, simple, basic, yet vitally important questions do not get asked, such as—what is it we want government to do? Because America's postwar expansion of government has been driven by narrow interest groups, the federal government has become thoroughly involved in American life, yet thousands of programs, tax loopholes, and subsidies cannot hide the lack of coherent government policies. For example, is it the responsibility of government to ensure that every American has a job? If so, then government policies should seek to maximize employment. If not, then the government should have no jobs programs or unemployment insurance. By not asking the basic questions, the government is not coming up with the right answers, and, as a result, lacks the coherent policies the nation needs.

The economic stagnation of the seventies should have provoked a soul-searching national debate over both economic policy and government's role. It did not. Instead, Ronald Reagan responded with strong anti-government rhetoric and laissez faire. Instead of having a national debate over when and how the government should intervene in the economy, Reagan adopted a "less is more" philosophy, which meant returning as much decision making as possible to the private sector.

The private sector is efficient at many tasks, such as determining prices, allocating resources, rewarding success, and punishing failure. If private companies do not pay competitive wages, they will not be able to hire enough workers. If they price their products too high, customers will not buy them. If their products are of poor quality, competitors will produce better products and take away market share. A healthy, competitive private sector is the best way to ensure high employment and strong economic growth.

However, private companies on their own will not build highways or fund public education. Unregulated markets may encourage entrepreneurial activity, but they also lead to socially indefensible excesses, such as monopolies, child labor, and skewed distributions of wealth and income. The Great Depression made clear the need not only for securities regulation and federal deposit insurance, but also for government spending programs to extricate the economy from prolonged slumps.

Ronald Reagan's political success with his anti-government rhetoric deflected attention from the central issue in the private/public debate. The core of Reagan's argument was that economic decision making should be left to the private sector because the private sector is more efficient. Efficiency, however, was not, and is not, the issue. Indeed, there can be little disagreement that a private company, which has strong financial incentives to offer the best product or service at the lowest cost, is more efficient than a public bureaucracy, where such financial incentives do not exist. No, the challenge to those in power is to determine what government's economic role should be and how best to carry it out. It is a challenge that both the Reagan and Bush administrations ignored.

Debate over Industrial Policy

The clash between political rhetoric and economic reality is nowhere so effective at subverting honest debate than in the area of industrial policy. In conservative political circles, the term *industrial policy* evokes thoughts of a Soviet-style, centrally planned economy with a few bureaucrats making decisions on every aspect of economic life. As a result, the thought of an American industrial policy is rejected out of hand. Other critics of industrial policy argue that government should not "pick winners and losers," that government is too ineffective to make good decisions, and that government intervention simply results in wasteful pork barrel projects. To these critics, industrial policy is simply a euphemism for more big government.

The reality is that the United States already has an industrial policy, though elected officials are loathe to admit it. Federal intervention in the economy, however, is not the result of conscious planning, but driven by political expediency and historical precedent. Tax breaks, favorable regulatory rulings, and pork barrel

Let me emphatically state for the record,
that the United States does not have, has never had,
and will never have an industrial policy.

projects are the currency of exchange in America's monetary
democracy. Historical precedent has validated other economic pursuits of government. The New Deal validated federal public works
projects and established social security; the cold war necessitated a
permanent defense industry; and the Great Society established the
welfare state. Other attempts at economic intervention, however,
such as providing subsidized loans or making direct equity investments, are politically unacceptable except in times of crisis.
Indeed, the extensive package of federal loan guarantees made to
the Chrysler Corporation in the early eighties was politically possible only because the company was on the brink of bankruptcy.

The lack of a coherent national industrial policy often results in
farcical policy decisions. For example, in 1992—an election
year—Congress approved funding for a Seawolf nuclear submarine. Defense experts readily admitted that the United States did
not need any more nuclear submarines, but cancellation of the
program would have caused the Electric Boat Corporation to lay
off thousands of workers at its Groton, Connecticut, plant. In an

election year, Congress was unwilling to entertain such a thought.
The lack of a coordinated national industrial policy means that
instead of using defense savings for new projects, such as high-
speed trains, the United States purchases weapon systems it
doesn't need in order to keep workers employed. In other words,
part of the defense budget has become an expensive make-work
program.

The time has come for the United States to bring logic and reason into its haphazard approach to economic intervention. The economic success of Japan has clearly demonstrated that the most
effective relationship between government and business is one of
cooperation. In contrast, the relationship between business and
government in the United States oscillates between indifference
and confrontation. *If the United States government fails to create a*
coordinated national industrial policy because of ideological rigid-
ity, then in the long run it will have chosen winners and losers. In
many cases, the corporate winners will be foreign and the losers
American.

The United States is faced with a basic choice—it can help
people once they have fallen out of the mainstream or it can improve the educational and economic structures in society so that
fewer people fall out. It is a choice between treating the symptoms
or the causes. For too many years the government has focused on the
former rather than the latter. The time has come for a new approach.

Part IV of this book details policy proposals to treat America's
social and economic ills. The chapters that follow deal with the
budget deficit, the economy, tax policy, and education. The proposals offered are fundamental, rather than incremental, in nature.
As a result, their viability is dependent upon structural political
reform, which, for the sake of emphasis, will be discussed in
Part V. The reader should note that the proposals offered are by no
means the only ones available, but are examples of what could be
done to solve America's problems if the federal government had
the ability to act in the general, rather than the special, interest.

Chapter 12

Avoiding the Abyss

If the United States continues down its current fiscal path, unable to reconcile the demands for spending with the voters' willingness to be taxed, then the result will be continuing budget deficits, a rising national debt, and, eventually, financial disaster. It is a legacy that no individual American wishes to leave behind, but it is the legacy that we, collectively, are leaving the next generation. In order to regain its fiscal health, America must do three things: reform social security, adopt a well-structured system of universal health care, and pursue economic policies that maximize employment and long-term growth. If the United States fails in any one of these three areas, then the nation will not be able to avoid falling into the fiscal abyss.

Budget Accounting Reform

The federal government should begin by reforming its deceptive accounting practices so that current operating surpluses in social security and government retirement funds can no longer be used to reduce the size of reported budget deficits. One way to

180

accomplish this is to split the federal budget into three separate budgets: a trust fund budget, a current budget, and a capital budget. The trust fund budget would include social security, medicare, and all federal employee retirement funds. Each year, the trust fund budget would report both on an operating basis—income and expenses for the current year—and on a balance sheet basis—showing long-term liabilities and total trust fund assets. The current budget would show all consumption expenditures—everything from defense spending to interest on the national debt. Because it deals only with the current year, the current budget would have only an income statement, not a balance sheet. The capital budget would show all federal capital investments, which would be amortized over the expected life of the asset (as is done in the private sector). As a result, the capital budget would have both an income statement (for the current year) and a balance sheet (showing assets and long-term liabilities).

Each year, the government would report a budget surplus or deficit for each of its three budgets, and it would report on the government's total balance sheet—showing all assets and liabilities. This new structure of budget accounting would be more accurate and would no longer allow the government to hide from public view the huge unfunded liabilities of federal retirement funds, social security, and medicare. In addition, the ability to depreciate capital spending over time would encourage government to reorient spending away from current consumption and toward investment.

The federal government should also stop the practice of automatically investing trust fund assets in treasury securities. One alternative would be for the federal government to create two types of government-sponsored investment funds—a fixed-income investment fund (which invested only in treasury securities, corporate bonds, and mortgage securities) and a growth investment fund (which invested in both debt and equity securities).

The federal government could hold a dutch auction, an example of which is given in Table 20, to select thirty fixed-income

Table 20
EXAMPLE OF A DUTCH AUCTION

A dutch auction process selects multiple winners, with each winner paying the same price. For example, let's assume a city wishes to privatize its garbage collection services, which currently cost $4 million a year. The city decides to select three winners, each responsible for garbage collection in one-third of the city. Each winner will receive an annual fee of $1.3 million for the life of the five-year contract. The city will save $100,000 per year and whatever up-front fees it receives in auctioning the contracts. Below are listed six companies and their hypothetical bids. The three winning bids are marked with a "W" and those three companies would all pay the price of the third highest bidder, which in this case is $320,000. The dutch auction process is an effective auction method because bidders will submit the highest price that they are willing to pay, knowing that if they win they will pay either the price they bid or a lower price.

Bidder	Bid	
Company A	$250,000	
Company B	$320,000	W
Company C	$170,000	
Company D	$420,000	W
Company E	$360,000	W
Company F	$240,000	

investment fund managers and a similar number of growth investment fund managers. The fixed-income investment funds would pay interest on a monthly basis, while the growth funds would reinvest all interest and dividends. The federal government would retain an equity investment in each of the funds, and the fund managers would receive a management fee equal to a fixed percentage of total assets. The government would move money from its social security trust funds and other retirement trust funds into the new investment funds. Later in the book, other proposed structures will also invest money in the government-sponsored fixed-income and growth funds.

Social Security Reform

As a percentage of gross domestic product, social security expenditures increased from 1.2% in the 1950s, to 2.7% in the 1960s, to 4.1% in the 1970s, to 4.7% in the 1980s.[1] In fiscal year 1993, social security became the single largest budget category (surpassing national defense for the first time), accounting for 21.6% of all federal spending. Without reform, the demographics of the baby boom generation will eventually bankrupt the social security system, sparking an intergenerational political battle never before seen in American history. To avoid such an undesirable situation, the federal government must begin reducing the huge gap between social security assets and long-term liabilities.

The underlying cause of the gap is social security's "pay-as-you-go" funding mechanism, which means that benefits for current retirees are paid for by current workers. The first social security recipients benefitted tremendously from this structure. For instance, Mrs. Ida Fuller, who received the first social security check in 1940, paid a total of $22 in payroll taxes, but received more than $20,000 in benefits.[2] While this is an extreme example, today's social security recipients receive multiples of what their tax contributions warrant. The danger of the pay-as-you-go funding system is that when the baby boom generation begins to retire, the ratio of retirees per worker will climb so dramatically that it will quickly reach a point where promised benefit levels will no longer be able to be supported. In order to avoid this demographic dilemma, the federal government must reduce the massive gap between trust fund assets and long-term liabilities. This will require both increases in social security taxes and reductions in the growth of social security benefits.

In 1993, the social security payroll tax (which is matched by the employer) was 6.2% of the first $57,900 of income. As Table 21 shows, the payroll tax is highly regressive (a lower percentage of income as income rises).

Table 21
SOCIAL SECURITY TAXES
AS A PERCENTAGE OF INCOME (1993)

Earned Income	Employee Taxes	Percentage of Income
$10,000	$620	6.2%
$30,000	$1,860	6.2%
$50,000	$3,100	6.2%
$100,000	$3,590	3.6%
$250,000	$3,590	1.4%
$1,000,000	$3,590	0.4%

One way to make the social security tax more progressive, and raise additional revenue, would be to drop the rate from 6.2% to 5% and remove the cap on income. This would result in a social security tax increase for those Americans earning more than $71,796 (in 1993) and a tax cut for everyone else. If this social security tax had been in place in 1993, it would have raised an additional $20 billion in tax revenue. An additional tax change would be to make all social security payments taxable. Under current law, 85% of social security benefits are taxable for incomes exceeding $25,000 for individuals and $32,000 for couples.[3] Additional tax reforms discussed in Chapter 15 would minimize the impact of this change on low-income social security recipients (by eliminating income taxes on the first $10,000 of an individual's income).

One way for the federal government to reduce the growth of benefit payments over time would be to reduce the cost of living adjustments (COLAs) for the most wealthy recipients. Current law provides for an annual COLA equal to the prior year's change in the consumer price index (CPI). To reduce long-term expenditures, the government could establish a monthly benefit cap equal to the

highest current monthly benefit payment. As long as the future liabilities of the social security trust fund exceed current assets
(which will be for the foreseeable future), the cap would increase
by one percent annually and those individuals receiving at least
three-quarters of the cap amount would have an annual COLA of
CPI minus one percent (until hitting the cap). Initially, the savings
from a cap would be small, but over twenty or thirty years, as more
recipients bumped into the cap, the savings would increase dramatically (those bumping into the cap would be the wealthiest social
security recipients). Such a mechanism would reduce long-term
social security expenditures without unduly harming current recipients. Additional changes in the way America saves for retirement
will be discussed in Chapter 13.

Health Care Reform

The other entitlement program in desperate need of reform is
health care. In 1991, America's overall health care spending
totalled 13.4% of GDP. In contrast, total health care spending in
Japan, Germany, Canada, Great Britain, and France ranged from
6.8% to 10% of GDP.[4] What does the United States get for spending at least an additional 3.4% of GDP—$195 billion in 1991 dol-
lars—on its health care? It gets the best medical facilities and
doctors in the entire world. At the same time, however, thirty-seven
million Americans have no health insurance, and the United States
ranks eighteenth in infant mortality.[5]

How can a health care system that is so expensive fail to adequately provide basic health care to so many? America's health
care system reflects the dangers of partial government intervention
and unrestrained market forces. In the current system, there are
huge incentives for participants to run up costs, but few incentives
to keep costs under control. Doctors, worried about potential malpractice suits, often overprescribe tests and procedures—an expensive phenomenon known as "defensive medicine." That such

actions generate additional income for some doctors only com-
pounds the problem. Instead of looking for ways to reduce costs,
insurance companies typically just pass cost increases on to consumers. With thousands of health insurers using different forms
and offering different coverage, administrative costs have skyrocketed. Because they are required to pay only a small portion of
medical costs with out-of-pocket dollars when sick, Americans
with health coverage (whether through medicare, medicaid, or private insurance) seek out the best—and frequently the most expensive—medical care available. Those individuals without health
insurance often wait until their medical condition has reached an
acute stage before showing up in a hospital emergency room. Local
and state governments and, by default, the American taxpayer,
must pick up the tab for these expensive emergency room services.

With so many forces pushing costs higher, it is not surprising
that the nation's health care costs have exploded over the past two
decades—from 7% of GDP in 1970 to over 14.5% in 1993.[6] Federal spending on medicaid and medicare rose from 1.3% of GDP in
the 1970s to 2.2% in the 1980s to 3.3% in FY 1993.[7] While consumers are frequently shielded from large out-of-pocket costs, the
full cost of medical care is passed back to the consumers by the
government, in the form of higher taxes and larger deficits, and by
private industry, in the form of higher prices for consumer goods
and higher insurance premiums. The United States, for reasons of
social equity and economic competitiveness, desperately needs a
comprehensive, well-structured system of universal health care.

*America's new health care system must, at a minimum, contain
two things: a basic core package of health care for all Americans
and a cap on total government health care spending.* The cap is
necessary to ensure that a universal health care system does not
significantly worsen America's fiscal problems.

At the heart of America's health care debate is the reality that
achieving the twin goals of universal coverage and cost containment will require some form of health care rationing. The rapid

advancement of medical technology has provided doctors with more tools to save lives, but there are limits to what the nation can afford. Just because new, expensive medical technology is available does not mean it should be used at each and every opportunity to prolong life. For example, the average cost of attempting to save the life of a severely underweight crack-addicted baby easily exceeds $100,000. Statistics show that the baby's chance of survival correlates strongly with its birth weight. Should doctors attempt to save the child's life when the chance of survival is thirty percent? What if the chances are only ten percent? And who should make the decision? Should it be the drug-addicted mother, who pays none of the cost? Or should it be society, which will have to pick up the bill?

These are difficult questions, but they are questions that require well-thought-out answers. By failing to construct an adequate decision-making framework, the United States encourages doctors to make all efforts to prolong life, regardless of the cost or chance of success. Quality of life issues are also routinely ignored. Statistics show that twenty-one percent of all medicare expenses are reimbursed in the last 180 days of life.[8] In fiscal year 1993, those expenditures totalled $27 billion. By shielding individuals from high out-of-pocket expenses, medicare encourages individuals to make some health care consumption decisions whose benefits do not justify their cost.

The Clinton Plan

On September 22, 1993, President Clinton, in a nationally televised speech to Congress, outlined his sweeping health care proposal entitled "The American Health Security Act." Six weeks later, Clinton submitted the formal 1,342-page document to Congress. The Clinton proposal seeks to provide every American with a package of core health care benefits that includes a broad range of medical services and free preventive care. Individuals would have the option of choosing one of three types of medical plans: a health maintenance organization (HMO) plan, a fee-for-service plan, or a combination plan. These plans would be offered by regional entities called "Health Alliances" or by large employers (those with over 5,000 employees that choose to do so). All employers would be required to pay eighty percent of the average premium for their employees. Individuals and families would pay the difference between the employer contribution and the cost of the plan they select. Out-of-pocket expenses would be capped annually at $1,500 for each person and $3,000 per family. A National Health Board would be created to oversee the system and attempt to limit cost increases. States could begin implementing the plan on January 1, 1995, and would be required to do so by January 1, 1998.

The Clinton plan addresses the issue of rationing by encouraging people to join health maintenance organizations, a trend already well under way. Indeed, between 1987 and 1992, the number of Americans enrolled in HMOs grew from 29.3 million to 41.4 million.[9] HMOs offer individuals ready access to primary care physicians, but restrict access to specialists and to expensive or experimental therapies. This approach reduces costs, but also reduces the quality of care and consumer choice.

For all its sweeping rhetoric, the Clinton plan fails to address a number of important issues. In return for slightly higher premiums, the Clinton plan offers medicare recipients new prescription drug and long-term care benefits. These changes will be insufficient to stop the rapid rise in medicare costs. The health care systems for veterans, workman's compensation, and automobile accidents are all in need of substantial reform. The Clinton plan leaves them intact. The plan also offers no malpractice insurance reform. Instead of creating Health Alliances, states are given the option of adopting a single-payer system (the government would collect all premiums and pays all medical bills), an action that would result in state-run socialized medicine.

The Clinton administration deserves credit for attempting to tackle America's health care problems. However, the nation's health care debate and the legislation that results will again expose all the shortcomings of America's monetary democracy. The powerful interest groups involved in the health care debate will fight hard for incremental changes to the current system. America's health care system, however, needs a fundamental overhaul.[†] Universal coverage and cost containment will require health care rationing. The issue of rationing is at the core of the debate, but America's politicians are loathe to discuss the issue. As a result, whatever health care reform legislation that emerges will have a difficult time reining in the nation's runaway health care costs.

A Different Approach

With all the focus on health care reform and the changes that should be made regarding the role of doctors, insurance companies, hospitals, health care providers, and government, scant attention is being paid to preventive care. America's health care system is designed to treat illnesses once they occur instead of trying to prevent illnesses from occurring. It is another example of American society treating the symptoms rather than the causes. To reduce costs, health care reform should include powerful incentives for Americans to change their unhealthy habits, from the fatty diets that cause heart disease to the cigarettes that cause lung cancer. In a recent study, researchers at Brandeis University estimated that the economic cost of smoking, drinking, and illegal drugs totalled $238 billion in 1990 alone.[10]

An alternative approach to health care reform would be to provide every American with health care insurance offered by one of

---

[†] A *Newsweek* poll conducted on September 23-24, 1993, showed that 32% of the public felt that America's health care system needed fundamental changes, while 47% thought that the system needs to be completely rebuilt. *Newsweek*, October 4, 1993, p. 34.

twenty or so designated health insurers.[†] The insurance package would include free preventive care and a core package of health care benefits. Individuals would choose between a primary care physician and a HMO. Those individuals who selected an HMO would pay only a small per visit fee when receiving core benefits, while those individuals who selected a primary care physician would pay twenty percent of core benefit costs.

Every American would have an individual health account (IHA) and a health security card. The health security card would act like a credit card to purchase health care services. All medical services not included in the core package would be available to individuals under a sliding scale of reimbursement (high cost medical procedures with a low success rate would have a low level of reimbursement). The costs not reimbursed would be charged to the individual's health account. The individual would receive a monthly statement, similar to a credit card bill, showing the account balance and minimum payment due (if any). Caps would be set on the maximum monthly out-of-pocket costs and insurers would be given more influence in the decision-making process when the balance in an individual's health account exceeded some maximum level.

Once the system was set up, the federal government's primary role would be funding. The federal government would eliminate the current medicare payroll tax (1.45% of income) and replace it with a payroll tax, matched by employers. One percent of the payroll tax (matched by employers) would be placed directly into the worker's IHA. The remaining payroll tax would be combined with higher alcohol and cigarette taxes and used to make a monthly

---

[†] The designated health insurers would be selected by a dutch auction process with the federal government retaining an equity stake. These new corporate entities would focus exclusively on health care. In addition to offering the same core package of health benefits, the designated insurers would all use the same filing forms and procedure codes to reduce administrative costs.

benefit payment based upon each person's age (in recognition of the natural correlation between increasing age and higher health care consumption). The age-based benefit would be sufficient to cover the monthly premium for the core benefits package, and any additional amount would accrue in the account and be available to purchase medical services outside the core benefits package.

In setting up this structure, the federal government must decide what is to be included in the core health care package and what the reimbursement rate should be for those services not covered. Higher cigarette and alcohol taxes could easily generate $30 billion annually. A five percent payroll tax, matched by employers, would bring in roughly $350 billion in 1994 dollars. Combining these revenues could purchase an average of $1,450 in health benefits for every American. Is this the "right" level of benefits? Should it be higher, or maybe lower? The difficulty is that there is no "right" level. As a nation, America must decide how much of the nation's health care costs should be shared by society and how much should be borne by the individual. It is a difficult decision to make. But governing requires making difficult decisions, and not making a choice condemns the nation to a dangerous fiscal path.

There are many benefits to be obtained from a system similar to the one sketched here. Because they would receive a monthly cash flow based on the age of the individuals insured, the designated health insurers would have strong incentives to reduce health care costs by focusing on promoting good nutrition and preventive care, while discouraging cigarette, alcohol, and drug use. By all using the same forms, administrative costs would be drastically reduced. Designated insurers would also act as a consumer information center for individuals in their choices of managed health care programs, primary care physicians, and a host of medical specialists. Once a new system of universal health care was in place, medicaid and medicare would no longer exist. In addition, the federal government would no longer have an open-ended funding commitment for health care.

The plan also keeps government role limited while focusing on the importance of personal responsibility. Between 1960 and 1991, the percentage of health care costs paid out-of-pocket by patients has declined from 56% to 22%.[11] As patients paid less out-of-pocket costs, their consumption of health care increased. As we have seen, rationing is crucial to health care reform. Rationing, however, need not be a "yes or no" decision. By requiring individuals to bear more of the economic consequences of their health care decisions, the United States can begin to create an appropriate decision-making framework. Patient-outcomes research can provide valuable information regarding the success rates of various medical treatments. Armed with this information, an individual, in consultation with a physician, can make a cost/benefit analysis of a proposed treatment and make an informed decision. Equally important, individuals would have strong financial incentives to lead healthier lives—a development that could actually begin to *reduce* the nation's total health care bill.

An additional comment needs to be made about how a system of universal health care should be financed. America's current health care system is a descendent of the corporate paternalism that emerged after World War II when health costs were low and easily borne by large, profitable corporations. Today, with health costs high and the majority of new jobs being created in small and medium size companies, it is imperative that the federal government not create an employer-financed system of universal health care that places an onerous burden on the job-creating sector of America's economy. Therefore, a payroll tax is preferable to a government regulation requiring employers to purchase health care for employees.

America's current health care system shows the dangers of unrestrained market forces. In today's health care market, doctors have incentives to overcharge and overprescribe, insurers simply pass on higher costs, and most consumers are shielded from the direct financial burden of their personal health care decisions. The result is high quality, but exorbitantly expensive medical care that is not universally available. A comprehensive universal health care system, like the one outlined here, could expand health care coverage, while using market forces to improve quality and reduce costs.

In order to avoid the fiscal abyss, the federal government must reform both its social security and health care systems. Health care reform must occur soon. The Clinton administration has made health care reform a high priority, but the political battle will be intense. America's politicians would much rather not make the difficult decisions regarding health care rationing that must be part of any true reform package. Reforming social security will be equally difficult, for social security's current operating surplus is a convenient argument for not doing anything, even though demographics and deceptive accounting ensure a future financial disaster if current policies remain unchanged.

However difficult it will be, reforming entitlement programs is only half the battle. In the long term, the only true guarantee against fiscal catastrophe is an economy growing faster than the national debt. To achieve that end, the United States must begin pursuing macroeconomic policies that maximize employment and long-term growth. A high level of employment is important not only because it increases tax receipts and decreases government "safety net" expenditures, but also because it has a strong impact on an individual's self-worth and ability to pursue one's dreams. The political acceptance of the status quo would be somewhat more palpable if it were clear that the economy was structured to maximize employment. The American experience during World War II and Japan's postwar experience, however, clearly demonstrate that this is not the case. To the issue of economic policy we now turn.

Chapter 13

Revitalizing America's Economy

By saving and investing too little while borrowing and consuming too much, the American economy suffers from declining long-term growth rates, a persistent trade imbalance, and a burgeoning national debt. More troubling than these trends, however, is the absence of a political consensus that a major change in course is needed. Many politicians still spout incessantly about the benefits of laissez faire because railing against the failures of government is still a winner at the polls. Once elected, however, support for laissez faire translates into gridlock and a perpetuation of the status quo. As a result, the perverse incentives of America's monetary democracy have not only resulted in myopic policies, but have poisoned the nation's political and economic debates. Locked in an economic marathon with Germany and Japan, the United States continues to pursue policies that guarantee only defeat.

If it is to reverse its long-term economic trends, America's focus must shift from what sells politically to what works economically. And there is no great secret about what works. To tap its economic potential, the United States should imitate the conditions of a wartime economy—saving, investing, and producing more while consuming less. The proposals in this chapter offer a variety of ways to do this. A consistent theme of all the reforms is a willingness to make short-term sacrifices for long-term gains. And it is this tradeoff which America's monetary democracy is loathe to make.

Reducing Unemployment

Atop the long list of America's economic problems is a glaring lack of job creation. Chart 16 shows the civilian unemployment from 1988 through the end of 1993. The civilian unemployment rate hit a *sixteen-year low* of 5.1% in March 1989, but 6.3 million Americans were still looking for work and could not find a job. In addition, this number failed to account for underemployed workers (those working part-time but looking for full-time work) and discouraged workers (those who are no longer actively seeking employment).

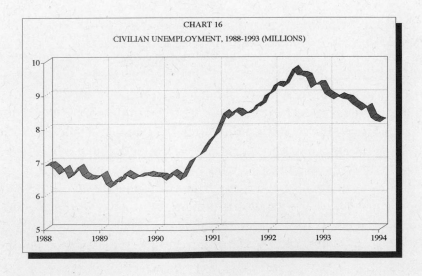

CHART 16

CIVILIAN UNEMPLOYMENT, 1988-1993 (MILLIONS)

The economic recession beginning in June 1990 exposed the depth of America's employment problem. Technically, the recession ended in March 1991 (recessions technically end when the next two quarters register positive GDP growth). Over the next few months, as is typical during the early stages of a recovery, the ranks of the unemployed grew—from 8.5 million in March to nine million in December. The ranks of the unemployed, however, did not peak until June 1992, when 9.8 million Americans were out of work. The economic recovery was so anemic at job creation that in December 1992, twenty-one months after the recovery began, the number of unemployed Americans was still 800,000 higher than when the recession technically ended.

There are a number of important reasons why the recent economic recovery has fared so poorly at job creation. High levels of individual, corporate, and government debt have inhibited the expansion. The commercial real estate market, typically a major engine of both economic and employment growth, will not completely recover from the overbuilding of the eighties until early in the twenty-first century. With the cold war over, federal defense spending and, as a result, defense industry employment, have both fallen. But perhaps the most important factor is that corporations, facing a slow growth environment, have sought to increase profits by cutting costs, principally by reducing employment. Many of America's largest corporations, such as IBM and General Motors, have either eliminated or announced plans to eliminate hundreds of thousands of high-paying jobs. Even companies reporting record profits are downsizing to improve both productivity and profits.

In early 1994, the economy is showing clear signs of moving forward. The driving force behind this progress is the substantial drop in interest rates, which began in January 1991. Why did it take so long for lower interest rates to stimulate the economy? From 1990 to 1993, the American economy suffered from a familiar ailment—a lack of sufficient aggregate demand. Consumers, worried about their jobs and still paying off their debts, were in no hurry to increase consumption. Businesses, worried about the economy and busy cutting costs, were hesitant about increasing investment. With interest rates at twenty-year lows, sufficient funds existed for an increase in investment, but the investment was not happening. The brightening of America's economic picture in 1994 will improve the job outlook, but will not solve America's employment problem.

It makes good *economic* sense for the United States to increase government spending to create jobs, instead of spending additional billions on unemployment compensation and other safety net expenditures. There exist, however, formidable obstacles to such a path. First, after more than a decade of ignoring sharply rising federal deficits, Ross Perot brought deficit reduction back into the political discussion in 1992. With a $255 billion budget deficit in FY 1993 and a $4.35 trillion national debt, the American people have had enough of wasteful government spending. But the danger of this new deficit-reduction focus is that it will distort the debate in the opposite direction—making it conventional wisdom that government deficits, for any reason, are inherently bad. In a political world dominated by simplistic rhetoric, this argument is frequently made and, too often, readily accepted.

A second obstacle is that when it seeks to stimulate the economy, the federal government has questionable priorities and inadequate delivery systems. Changes in tax and fiscal policies are not dominated by an overriding legislative desire to do what is in the nation's best interest, but by special interest groups seeking short-term advantage. The ubiquitous stories of federal waste have made the logrolling and pork barrel nature of federal spending programs all too familiar to the voting public. As a result, the majority of Americans would probably agree with humorist P. J. O'Rourke when he says that "giving money and power to government is like giving whiskey and car keys to teenage boys."[1] The sad truth is that the American public simply does not trust its own government to efficiently spend or invest its tax dollars. It is this deep feeling of distrust, not sound economic arguments, which provides support for laissez faire and free trade. But a lack of trust is a strong argument for government reform, not inaction.

Inefficient Macroeconomic Tools

The federal government is further handicapped by imprecise macroeconomic tools. For example, in order to fight inflation, Congress can cut spending or raise taxes. Because both actions are politically unpopular, fighting inflation has become the sole responsibility of the Federal Reserve Bank. Yet high interest rates are a blunt instrument with which to clobber the economy. Indeed, history has clearly shown that high interest rates are effective at curbing inflation, but the cost, in terms of employment and economic growth, is severe.

Stimulating the economy is a much easier task politically, requiring Congress to either increase spending or cut taxes. Both actions, however, take time to debate and pass, and a lag time exists between passage and economic impact. By the time Congress acts, the economic stimulus may no longer be needed. In addition, stimulative actions increase the budget deficit, pushing interest rates higher, and subsequently dampening economic activity. The Federal Reserve Bank, with its ability to set short-term interest rates, can act faster to stimulate the economy, and lower short-term rates have the added benefit of reducing interest costs on the national debt, thereby reducing the federal budget deficit. Nevertheless, a lag still exists between lower rates and higher economic activity, and it is long-term rates, over which the Federal Reserve Bank has little control, that influence activity in the crucial housing industry.

Deficit concerns, a lack of trust in government, and imprecise macroeconomic tools combine to support the argument that the best thing for government to do to stimulate the economy is to reduce the deficit, causing inflation and interest rates to fall, business investment to pick up, and economic growth to increase. Lower interest rates alone, however, do not ensure increased economic activity. The Bush administration responded to the 1990-91 recession by waiting for the Federal Reserve Bank to lower short-term interest rates. The Fed aggressively began doing so in December 1990, reducing the discount rate from 7% to 3.5% over the next year.[†] With long-term rates stubbornly high and businesses hesitant to increase investment, lower short-term rates were insufficient to bring America's economy quickly out of recession. Underestimating the depth of the nation's economic problems and overestimating the benefits of lower short-term interest rates, the Bush administration decided to take no additional actions to stimulate economic activity—a decision that contributed heavily to Bush's loss in the 1992 election.

Today, lower interest rates are finally propelling the economy forward, reducing pressure on politicians to act on the economic front. But America's employment problem continues. It still makes little sense for the government to spend so many billions of dollars for safety net programs instead of spending additional money to create jobs. The government should increase public investment to

---

[†] When the economy failed to react strongly after short-term interest rates had fallen significantly, many Republicans argued that the Federal Reserve Bank was negligent by not lowering interest rates sooner. This argument conveniently forgets about the impact Iraq's invasion of Kuwait had on world oil prices. On August 1, 1990, the day before the invasion, the spot price of Brent North Sea crude oil was $20.20 a barrel. A week later it was $26 a barrel; two weeks after that it was over $30 a barrel. From late August 1990 to mid-January 1991, the "war premium" in the oil market averaged about $10 a barrel. Given America's dependence on foreign oil, inflation jumped from 4.8% (annual rate Jan. 1990–July 1990) to 6.5% (July 1990–Jan. 1991). With such a sharp rise in inflation, due entirely to a sharp rise in oil prices, it would have been irresponsible for the Federal Reserve Bank to begin lowering short-term interest rates before oil prices fell. On January 17, 1991, the day after the United States started to bomb Iraq, the spot price of Brent crude oil did fall— by a record $9.20 a barrel.

create jobs and bolster economic growth, but legitimate concerns about inflation and wasteful federal spending must be addressed. To reduce the impact of increased government spending on inflation and interest rates, the federal government should create better macroeconomic tools. To assuage the public's fears about wasteful government spending, the federal government should develop better delivery systems for government spending and investment. Making government economic intervention more efficient and more politically acceptable is an integral part of the following proposals.

Proposals to Increase Savings

The first step in imitating a wartime economy is to increase America's dismal rate of national savings. Reducing the size of future federal budget deficits would increase national savings (or, more precisely, reduce government dissavings), but additional changes are also needed. Lowering the capital gains tax, discussed in Chapter 15, would encourage corporations to retain a higher portion of earnings, thus increasing corporate savings. Another way to increase corporate savings is for the federal government to create a structure that links employee compensation with corporate performance. Many companies have established stock option programs for this purpose, but option programs are frequently available only to top executives and the time horizons are too short. If the goal is to encourage long-term growth—and that should be the goal—then executive and employee compensation should be linked to long-term stock price changes.

To achieve this end, the government could prohibit corporate stock option plans and instead create a program of equity compensation accounts. Instead of paying worker's salaries completely in cash, companies would have the option to pay a certain percentage of employee compensation in corporate stock (a maximum percentage would be set that would increase as salary increases). The stock would be deposited in an individual equity account at a local federally insured bank. Employees would not be able to sell the stock for a minimum of five years after receiving it, and income taxes would be deferred until the stock was sold. Corporations would not be required to pay payroll taxes on equity compensation and, as a result, would have strong financial incentives to pay a certain portion of compensation in stock form. A nationwide system of individual equity accounts would not only increase national savings, but also lengthen corporate time horizons.

The federal government should also reform the nation's pension system. As currently structured, America's private and public pension plans have a number of serious drawbacks. First, an individual's pension payments depend upon his salary and length of employment. As industry life cycles grow shorter and as employee-for-life arrangements disappear, the average American worker is changing jobs with much greater frequency than he did twenty years ago. As a result, the percentage of workers qualifying for pensions has fallen—indeed, sixty percent of all working Americans are *not* covered by a pension plan.[2] Second, the most common pension plan structure is the defined-benefit plan, which means the plan sponsor is responsible for setting aside enough money to make promised benefit payments in the future.[3] This structure allows plan sponsors in both the private and public arenas to underfund pensions when financial difficulties arise. Third, the Pension Benefit Guaranty Corporation (PBGC), the government fund that insures private pensions, is currently $2.7 billion in the red, and the government recently estimated its long-term liabilities to be $45 billion.[4] Without reform, another costly taxpayer bailout is a real possibility. Fourth, pension fund managers' compensation is based on their quarterly performance. As a result, retirement savings, which should be one of America's greatest sources of long-term capital, is invested based on short-term market moves.

In November 1993, the PBGC released its annual top fifty list of underfunded defined-benefit pension plans. The fifty companies had combined pension liabilities exceeding $120 billion and unfunded liabilities of $38 billion, of which $31.7 billion was guaranteed by the PBGC.[5] Just five companies on the list, however, account for over seventy percent of the pension underfunding, as shown in Table 22.

It is the defined-benefit pension structure that allows plan sponsors to practice selective underfunding, and it is not only the private sector that is engaging in the practice. Public workers' pension funds are being systematically raided by elected officials looking for short-term fixes to budgetary problems. Indeed, the practice is widespread. Greenwich Associates, a Connecticut-based consulting firm, estimated in 1991 that state and local government pension funds had unfunded pension liabilities totalling $180 billion.[6]

In order to increase savings and avert a future taxpayer bailout, the United States needs to eliminate the glaring flaws of the nation's current pension system. One way to do this would be to create a nationwide system of individual retirement funds (IRFs), whose goal would be to create a single, efficient structure

Table 22
COMPANIES WITH THE LARGEST UNFUNDED PENSION LIABILITY ($ BILLIONS)

| | Unfunded Liability | |
	PBGC-Guaranteed	Total
General Motors	17.2	20.2
Bethlehem Steel	2.1	2.4
LTV Steel	1.9	2.1
Chrysler	0.9	1.4
Westinghouse Electric	1.0	1.3
Total	*23.1*	*27.4*

Source: Pension Benefit Guaranty Corporation.

of retirement savings for all Americans. Every worker would be *required* to have an individual retirement fund established at a local federally insured bank. Under the IRF program, a payroll tax of three percent would be withheld, matched by the employer, and automatically deposited in the IRF. The bank would act as an intermediary, sending the money on a monthly basis to one of the government-sponsored growth investment funds (see Chapter 12) selected by the individual worker. The individual would be allowed to change funds once every few years. Because fund managers would receive a management fee equal to a fixed percentage of assets, those funds consistently earning the highest returns would attract the largest quantity of funds and earn the highest profits.

Each year, individuals would be allowed to select the percentage of income to be placed in their IRF. They would select a withholding percentage, matched by employers, between the minimum (initially three percent) and the maximum (initially six percent). The contribution percentages would be increased annually until reaching a preset limit, say ten and twenty percent respectively. Between January 1 and April 15, every individual would also be allowed to make an additional lump sum contribution (also tax-deductible) for the preceding year, up to a total dollar maximum (initially $10,000 raised slowly over time to $30,000). Employers would not be required to match lump sum contributions.

At retirement, an individual would be required to use the money from her IRF to purchase an annuity from one of many designated insurance companies (again, a fixed number determined by dutch auction). Corporations would slowly phase out contributions to existing corporate pension funds, and once the companies were contributing ten percent into the IRFs for all employees, the government would establish strict guidelines for the transfer of money from corporate pension funds into IRFs. The government would also establish guidelines for transferring assets from existing individual retirement accounts (IRAs) and Keogh retirement plans into the nation's IRFs. Moving pension funds from corporate auspices to IRFs would require those companies that have underfunded their pension plans to come up with the financial resources they have promised their employees. Once the transfer was completed, corporations would no longer have the responsibility of managing pension funds and would instead focus on their business concerns. The IRF structure could also be broadened to allow tax-free savings for two other purposes—college tuition payments and the down payment on a first home.

To be effective, pension reform must also apply to the public sector. Defined-benefit plans have allowed government, particularly the federal government, to be long on promises and short on funding. As we have seen, state and local governments have underfunded pension plans to the tune of $180 billion. Yet this number is relatively small compared to the civil service retirement system, which in 1991 was estimated to be underfunded by $409 billion, and the military retirement system, which was estimated to be underfunded by $393 billion.[7] The federal government should switch these plans from "defined benefit" to "defined contribution." The practice of making promises of future benefits without paying for them should stop.

The creation of a universal system of IRFs would not only increase national savings, but also provide the federal government with an opportunity to create a powerful macroeconomic tool. Once the minimum percentage reached its ten percent target level, the president of the United States could be given the power to move the minimum percentage within a band (say seven to thirteen percent). If the economy starts to overheat, then instead of having the Federal Reserve Board raise interest rates, the president could increase the minimum contribution percentage, which would immediately reduce aggregate demand and lessen inflationary pressures. It would be a much better approach to fighting inflation than high interest rates, recession, and high unemployment. Conversely, when the economy was slowing down, the president could lower the minimum contribution percentage, thereby raising workers' take-home pay and causing a subsequent increase in aggregate demand and economic activity.

America's low level of national savings is a result of decades of government policies that emphasize the present at the expense of the future. To increase national savings substantially, the government must create new structures that either encourage or require more savings. A system of IRFs, phased in slowly, would require little sacrifice, create a huge pool of needed savings, and help avoid a costly taxpayer bailout of the Pension Benefit Guaranty Corporation. Over the long run, IRFs could replace social security as the primary source of retirement income. The IRFs would also allow the federal government to create a new macroeconomic tool to quickly impact economic activity.

Proposals to Increase Investment

Savings facilitates, but does not ensure, investment. Businesses make investment decisions based not only on interest rates, but tax rates, economic activity, and expectations for future growth. During the Great Depression, low interest rates and low corporate tax rates were insufficient encouragement for businesses to increase investment. As John Maynard Keynes noted, the failure of the private sector to maintain a constantly high level of investment is at the heart of the economic problem. In recessionary periods when businesses are reluctant to increase investment, the federal government should increase investment spending to keep economic growth strong and unemployment low. To this end, the government needs a coherent investment policy.

As we have seen, the stumbling blocks to increasing federal investment are the budget deficit, the lack of public trust, and the absence of an efficient delivery system. To be effective, any proposed reform must address these related issues. If the United States were to create a well-designed delivery system, which the public approved of, then the federal government could use its countercyclical spending ability to increase public investment when needed. One way to accomplish this would be for the federal government to create a national investment corporation (NIC) which would seek to increase public investment in three areas: human capital (discussed in Chapter 14), strategic industries, and physical resources. The NIC would be run by a board of directors chosen from private industry. A board member would serve a single fifteen-year term, be paid a private-sector salary, and be given a lifetime consulting or teaching position after her term expired in order to minimize outside influence.

To help develop strategic industries, the NIC would provide equity capital and subsidized long-term loans to corporations in vital industries. The federal government already has a somewhat analogous program in the defense department called the Defense Advanced Research Projects Agency (DARPA).[†] DARPA has played an integral role in making America's military the best in the world. A NIC could have a similar impact on the American economy. Conservatives argue that if sufficient demand for a product existed, then the market would respond by creating it. If, however, a potential market has social and economic benefits that the marketplace ignores, then government action and investment may be required for the new industry to emerge and thrive.

Electric-powered automobiles provide a good example. The main stumbling blocks to a vast electric car industry are current limitations on battery technology (existing cars go approximately 100 miles between recharges) and the simple fact that the infrastructure for a gasoline car industry already exists. As previously discussed, however, America's dependence on petroleum products carries with it certain negative externalities—such as pollution, larger trade deficits, and vulnerability to price shocks—whose

---

[†] The Clinton administration has renamed the agency the Advanced Research Projects Agency (ARPA) to de-emphasize its orientation toward defense spending.

costs are not borne by private companies, but by society as a whole. Until the price of oil rises significantly above alternative sources of producing electricity, market forces alone will not be sufficient to create a vibrant electric car industry.

Let's assume that the federal government decided to promote the development and production of electric cars in order to reduce pollution, shrink the nation's trade deficit, and lessen America's foreign oil dependence. There exist many steps for government to promote such a policy. A large gasoline tax phased in over many years would make electric cars more cost competitive with gasoline-powered automobiles. A law requiring all government agencies to purchase only electric cars after a particular date would guarantee demand for the new product, spurring commercial production. A new annual federal registration fee for gasoline-powered cars, set at a low initial level but gradually increased over a long period of time, would also increase demand for electric cars.

All of these policy changes are currently available to the federal government and would help to create a market for electric cars. A NIC could accelerate the development of the new market by providing companies with equity investments and long-term, low-interest loans to increase spending on new plant and equipment and funding for research and development. These funds would be especially crucial for entrepreneurial companies like Solectria, a small firm with eighteen employees and a twenty-six year old president whose electric car designs have set numerous records.[8] The NIC's role would be to increase funds available for private investment, while leaving day-to-day business decisions to corporate management, where such decision making belongs.

The creation of a new market would also allow the government to ensure that the jobs would be created in the United States. The federal government could prohibit the importation of electric cars for some fixed period of time (say ten years). After that date, the percentage of imports allowed would be slowly increased from zero to some low fixed percentage (say 25%). The government could also require that electric cars made domestically contain 100% American-made parts. Foreign competitors would still be able to compete in the American market, but they would have to build their facilities in the United States and hire American workers.

There are other promising areas where the NIC could play a crucial role in developing new domestic industries. Germany has developed magnetic levitation (mag-lev) trains that can carry passengers at speeds up to 300 miles per hour. Developing a high-speed rail network in densely populated areas (such as the Northeast corridor and Southern California) would reduce congestion both on highways and at airports. The federal government could again require that the production of high-speed railroad cars be done primarily, or exclusively, in the United States.

Another promising area is in the energy sector. Advances in wind power and solar energy technology have dramatically dropped the cost of these two sources of renewable energy to the point where they are roughly equivalent to electricity generated from coal-burning plants.[9] The major obstacle to developing these renewable energy sources quickly is that the infrastructure for coal-burning plants already exists. If the federal government wished to encourage the production of renewable energy, it could require utilities to generate an annually increasing percentage of their electricity from renewable sources. In addition, a NIC could make long-term, low-interest loans to utilities and companies that specialize in generating renewable energy.

Domestic Production Rules

Domestic production rules can play an important role in increasing the quality and quantity of American jobs while simultaneously reducing America's persistent merchandise trade deficit. In 1992, America's merchandise trade deficit was $96.1 billion. In the same year, America spent $51.6 billion on imported oil and had a

$50.5 billion trade deficit with Japan.[10] If America wishes to reduce its trade deficit, the nation must do two things: reduce its dependence on foreign oil and reduce its imports from Japan.

Many economists argue that a higher yen and a lower dollar will solve America's trade deficit with Japan. But it will not. Exchange rates will improve the balance of trade significantly only when domestic substitutes exist for foreign imports. For many goods imported into the United States—everything from oil to VCRs to Nintendo games—domestic substitutes simply do not exist. As the dollar falls in value, prices for these goods rise and consumers have the choice of paying higher prices or not buying the item at all.

To reduce the nation's trade deficit, the federal government could phase in domestic production rules for a small number of industries. The rules would require foreign companies whose imports exceed a certain dollar value to produce a portion of goods in the United States. The domestic production requirement could be increased annually from zero to some fixed percentage (say thirty or forty percent). Domestic production rules should be used with consumer goods, not producer goods. For example, while it is important that the United States retain a certain steel-making capacity, it is not a good idea for the United States to require all, or even most, steel production to be done domestically because higher steel prices would raise the cost and reduce the competitiveness of all American products made with steel.

Consumer products, however, are another matter. The United States has the largest consumer market in the world and is in a sufficiently strong bargaining position to require more domestic production of consumer products such as televisions, microwave ovens, VCRs, and refrigerators. With the yen high and the dollar low, it would be cost effective for Japanese companies to move some of their production jobs from Japan to the United States. The Japanese will not do so on their own, however, because if they do decide to move jobs overseas they will send them to the nation with the lowest labor costs. Domestic production rules could change this and bring more manufacturing jobs to the United States. As a result of domestic production rules, consumers would probably pay slightly higher prices, but it would in essence be a consumption tax that automatically created domestic jobs while reducing the nation's trade deficit.

Proposals to Expand Production

A sizable increase in savings and investment would allow America to expand production dramatically. But production of what? During World War II, the United States increased production for the purposes of waging war. During the postwar era, Japan increased production of consumer goods for export purposes. If the United States dramatically increased production in the 1990s, what would it produce? Luckily, America is not at war. Export growth could provide an outlet for some production increases, but only a small portion. Developing new industries, such as electric cars and renewable energy, and the adoption of domestic production rules could also play a part. The production of consumer goods cannot increase dramatically, however, because higher levels of personal savings will cause a corresponding drop in consumer consumption. There exists only one clear outlet for massive increases in production—a national rebuilding program focusing on the building of highways, bridges, mass transportation systems, water and sewer systems, and affordable housing. This would be the focus of the NIC's physical resources division.

The nationwide program would have three main goals: increasing employment, improving the infrastructure, and encouraging mass transportation. In a world where global competition is radically altering the job market, infrastructure spending has the desirable characteristic of creating jobs in the United States. By focusing on mass transportation systems, especially high-speed trains, the United States can simultaneously create a new domestic industry while reducing pollution and oil consumption.

How much should the federal government spend on a nation-wide infrastructure program? In fiscal year 1993, the federal government spent $50 billion on non-defense physical capital investment, of which $31 billion were grants provided to state and local governments.[11] To increase employment and rebuild the nation's infrastructure, substantially higher sums would be required. As part of a nationwide rebuilding program, the federal government should increase spending by roughly $25 billion each year until reaching a target level between $150 and $200 billion of annual infrastructure spending.

Any such large increase in public investment must be preceded by actions designed to assuage public fears regarding wasteful government spending. It is with good reason that pork barrel spending has fallen into disrepute. For example, it is not by accident that the largest per capita highway expenditures in the United States occur in the home district of the House committee chairman who oversees such expenditures. If a large-scale rebuilding program is to be undertaken, then steps must be taken to minimize pork barrel politics.

One way to do this would be for Congress to pass an overall level of spending for infrastructure projects and overall guidelines for spending in particular categories (for example, twenty percent of all infrastructure spending in large urban areas must be for mass transit). The details for the projects should be drawn up locally and approved by the NIC. For the three areas it covers—physical capital, human capital, and strategic industries—the NIC could divide the United States into roughly twenty different geographic regions. In each region and in each of the three spending areas, the NIC would seek to spend money on an equal per capita basis. Within each region, expenditures would be concentrated in those areas with the greatest need (i.e. education expenditures where the schools are the worst, mass transportation systems where there is the most traffic congestion, and affordable housing where none is available).

An additional way to assuage the public's fears that an increase in government spending will automatically result in a pork barrel feeding frenzy is to create private/public partnerships to improve the efficiency of public investment expenditures. The federal government could create twenty or so private/public partnerships (again, selected by dutch auction with the federal government retaining an equity stake). Winning companies would put up half of the equity in the new partnership and the NIC would put up the other half. After five or ten years of operation, the private/public partnerships would sell some stock to the public. A stock issuance would not only provide the government and the parent company with a market value for their investment, but also allow employees to purchase a stake in the company and receive equity compensation.

Once the new partnerships were created, the NIC would play an active role in the awarding of investments. The new companies would focus on rebuilding the nation's infrastructure and providing many public services, such as garbage collection and operating mass transit lines, currently performed by state and local government. A nationwide infrastructure program could become the driving force in making privatization of government services the rule rather than the exception.[12]

In order to emphasize quality, bidding for infrastructure projects should not be determined solely on a price basis. Some type of point system, where each private/public partnership received equal bidding points and additional points were awarded based on the quality of work completed, could be integrated with the lowest price bidding system. Because the federal government would retain an equity stake in the partnerships, the emphasis should be on creating a system where the most efficient and highest quality partnerships thrive, while the inefficient ones go out of business. The primary goal of creating private/public partnerships would be to bring market efficiencies to public services.

Funding for the NIC would come from general tax revenues and from a new tax on gasoline. Instead of phasing in a gasoline tax in over some fixed period, the federal government could increase the gasoline tax by five cents per gallon per year, indefinitely. This structure would raise the gasoline tax one dollar every twenty years. A long-term program of gasoline tax increases would send a clear message to all market participants that the United States is serious about reducing its oil addiction. Each year, a five-cent tax increase would increase gasoline tax revenues by roughly five billion dollars. This tax revenue increase could help to pay for America's national rebuilding program. In addition, a slow, steady increase in the price of gasoline would encourage individuals to use mass transit, conserve energy, and purchase more fuel efficient, and eventually electric, cars.

Revitalizing the American Economy

The United States faces a familiar economic dilemma in the 1990s. Individual consumption and business investment are insufficient to foster the strong rates of growth required to reduce stubbornly high levels of unemployment. The economic solution is for the federal government to increase spending and investment. However, significant hurdles exist to such a course of action. Atop the list are an already huge federal deficit and wide public distrust of government's ability to spend taxpayers' dollars effectively. If it wishes to increase both employment and economic growth, the United States should imitate the conditions of a wartime economy—saving, investing, and producing more, while consuming less. At the same time, the government must address the public's lack of faith in the nation's current delivery systems.

The creation of a nationwide system of IRFs would increase national savings while providing the federal government with an important macroeconomic tool to stimulate a lackluster economy or cool an overheated one. The creation of a national investment company, insulated from the daily distractions of popular politics, would allow the nation to have an active investment policy and launch a national rebuilding program. Domestic production rules could be adopted to increase domestic manufacturing jobs and reduce the nation's trade deficit.

During the first few years, government borrowing for a national investment corporation and a national rebuilding program would cause an increase in the federal budget deficit, but the fiscal impact would be minimal for a number of reasons. First, the nation's IRFs would increase national savings, and by funding its own budget deficits with national savings, America would suffer no adverse impact on interest rates, dollar exchange rates, or foreign trade. Second, the increase in employment would reduce government expenditures on unemployment insurance and "safety net" programs. Third, the infrastructure program would spur economic growth and increase federal tax revenues.

While it is vitally important for the nation to get its fiscal problems under control, the United States must simultaneously fix its structural economic problems—low levels of savings and investment and high levels of unemployment. If, in the short-term, additional borrowing is needed, then the borrowing should be undertaken. Fiscal responsibility should not be equated with a deficit of zero, but with an economy that is growing faster than the national debt. Spending huge sums for public assistance programs, but insufficient sums to increase investment and employment, is not the right formula to solve America's economic and fiscal ills.

Chapter 14

Taxes: The Necessary Evil

Taxes are the lifeblood of government; yet America's federal tax policy has been poisoned by popular politics. Reagan's political success with his anti-tax stand reduced the nation's tax debate to a simplistic premise—fewer taxes are good, more taxes are bad. Missing, of course, are such important issues as what kinds of taxes are imposed, who is paying them, and what macroeconomic goals are being encouraged. Instead of focusing on whether to raise or lower taxes incrementally, the government should seek ways to improve the efficiency and effectiveness of the tax code. For there are many ways America's tax code could be greatly improved, both in terms of fairness and positive economic impact, without a dramatic increase in overall taxes.

A look at a few popular tax concepts reveals some of the hurdles to tax reform. One political favorite is the idea of everyone paying his "fair share" of taxes. Paying your "fair share" has a nice ring to it, but raises an important question: who gets to determine what is your fair share? While politically useful when arguing for higher or lower taxes, the concept of "fair share" is not a practical

guide for tax policy. Other frequently used concepts in tax debate
are progressivity and regressivity. Progressive taxes take a higher
percentage of income as income rises, while regressive taxes take a
smaller percentage of income as income rises. The progressivity
issue has been the main argument for having higher income taxes
and lower taxes on consumption (i.e. sales taxes). Income taxes,
however, have their own drawbacks, for income tax withholding—
taking a percentage of worker's income before she ever receives
it—reduces individual choice. In contrast, sales taxes are collected
only when an individual has made a choice to purchase a particular
item. In addition, sales taxes are the most effective means of reducing consumer consumption. If tax fairness is the goal, then a balance needs to be struck between the issues of progressivity,
individual choice, and promoting important macroeconomic goals
such as savings, investment, and employment.

Unfortunately, America's politicians do not seek such a balance. Instead of promoting macroeconomic goals, the tax code is
primarily used to placate special interest groups. Members of Congress have three primary methods of helping out constituents and
special interest groups: spending programs, favorable regulations,
and tax breaks. Changes in the tax code are popular because they
attract less attention than pork barrel spending programs. As a
result, America's tax code is full of loopholes, exemptions, and tax
credits that please special interest groups, frustrate ordinary citizens, and create lots of jobs for accountants and lawyers. Fostering
long-term macroeconomic goals is not even a blip on the political
radar screen.

Tax reform should embody a number of changes. First, the tax
code should promote macro, rather than micro, economic goals.
Second, in levying taxes, the government should focus more on
taxing activities it wishes to discourage instead of providing tax
breaks for activities it wishes to encourage. Third, to increase public support the government should increase the use of linkage
taxes—taxes where all the revenue goes to a specific purpose, such

as gasoline taxes for infrastructure spending. Fourth, to simplify both compliance and collection, duplication of effort by federal, state, and local tax officials should be eliminated. Most taxes should be collected at the federal level, with block grants given to state and local governments. In the pages that follow, these are the general guidelines used for proposed tax reforms.

Tax Reform Proposals

Every spring, Americans look for all of their receipts, W-2 forms, bank statements, and a whole series of other financial records necessary for filling out their federal and, in most cases, state tax forms. The tax forms are highly detailed, and the instruction booklets are long and frequently ambiguous. In theory, America's income tax raises government revenue while promoting fairness. Congressional attempts to help out special interest groups, however, have destroyed both the perception and the reality of fairness.

One way to return fairness and simplicity to the tax code would be for the federal government to replace the current personal income tax with a flat tax. Flat tax proposals are not new. Economist Milton Friedman proposed one in his 1962 book *Capitalism and Freedom*. Early in the Reagan administration, the idea of a flat tax spawned numerous congressional proposals, but the idea soon disappeared from public view.[1] It resurfaced in 1992 as a proposal of Democratic presidential candidate Jerry Brown. But his proposal—a 13% tax on all individual and corporate income—placed too large a tax burden on low income workers.

There are two main benefits to a flat tax system. First, by simplifying the tax code, compliance is easier and cheaper, while fairness is increased. Second, by taxing all income once, tax rates can be lowered. One substitute for the current individual income tax would be a flat tax of twenty percent levied on all individual income. Short-term capital gains (holding period less than three years) would be treated as regular income, while long-term capital gains (holding period more than three years) would not be taxed.[†] Individuals would have only two deductions: a $10,000 personal deduction and a $5,000 deduction for each dependent. Under this system, a married couple with two children would pay no income tax on the first $30,000 of income and would pay twenty cents for each dollar of income over $30,000. For most Americans, filing taxes would require nothing more than taking earned income, subtracting deductions, and taking twenty percent of that figure.

America's corporate income tax code suffers from the same maladies as the individual tax code—needless complexity, countless loopholes and exemptions, and a clear bias toward politically powerful special interests.[2] Corporate tax reform could be achieved through one of two ways, either a flat corporate tax of twenty percent or a value-added tax (VAT) of ten percent, both of which would raise roughly the same revenue. Under a flat corporate tax, a company would calculate its taxes by starting with gross sales revenues and subtracting purchases of goods and services, employee compensation, interest expense, and capital expenditures. Fringe benefits for employees and travel and entertainment expenses would not be deductible. Under a value-added tax, a company would subtract the cost of goods purchased from gross sales revenues to arrive at the taxable amount. VATs are popular in Europe because they are an easy and efficient way of collecting corporate tax revenues. Unlike the current corporate tax code, either a VAT or a flat corporate tax would allow business to fully deduct capital investment in the year it occurs, a strong incentive for companies to increase business investment. Revenues from a VAT have the additional appeal of not falling significantly during recessions.

[†] Capital gains taxes should also be applied to short-term trading gains of retirement accounts and pension funds in order to encourage investors to lengthen their time horizons.

Using statistics from 1990, Table 23 shows the estimated impact of tax proposals on government revenue. By lowering individual income taxes and raising corporate income taxes, the federal government would cause consumer prices to rise, thereby discouraging consumption and encouraging savings. Increasing taxes by $140 billion in a single year would have a devastating impact on economic activity, but most of this increase is simply cost switching. Instead of paying directly for employee health care, businesses would pay a payroll tax. Likewise, individuals would have lower health care expenses, but would also have to pay a health care payroll tax.

Table 23
IMPACT OF TAX PROPOSALS ON FEDERAL TAX REVENUES - ESTIMATES FOR FY 1990 ($ BILLIONS)

	Actual Revenues from Current Tax Law	Estimated Revenues from Tax Proposals
Individual Income Taxes - Federal	466.9	347
Individual Income Taxes - State and Local	105.6	—
Corporate Income Taxes - Federal	93.5	230
Corporate Income Taxes - State and Local	23.6	—
Medicare Taxes	68.6	—
Universal Health Care Tax	—	304
Social Security Taxes	281.6	304
Total	*1,039.8*	*1,185*

Sources: Estimates are calculated using information from *Economic Report of the President, 1993*; *Budget of the United States Government, FY 1995*; U.S. Bureau of the Census, *Statistical Abstract of the United States, 1993*; Internal Revenue Service, Statistics of Income Division, *Corporate and Individual Income Tax Returns 1989*.

Countercyclical Government Expenditures

Eliminating the duplication of tax collection efforts would allow the federal government to collect all individual and corporate income taxes (or VATs) and apportion a set percentage to state and local governments on a monthly basis. The apportionment of individual income taxes could be based on where each individual lives and works. If an individual lives and works in different states, then the state apportionment would be split equally between the two states. Corporate taxes could be apportioned on a population basis.

State and local governments typically spend whatever tax revenues they take in—spending more during good economic times and less during bad, a spending pattern which exacerbates the business cycle. Having the federal government collect all individual and corporate income taxes would provide the opportunity to create a new macroeconomic tool for moderating the business cycle. To accomplish this goal, the federal government would fix the apportionment for each state and local government to the average monthly apportionment of the first year. As the economy grows, tax revenues increase, but instead of sending the incremental increases in revenue directly to the state and local governments, the federal government would place the funds in a government endowment fund (GEF). A GEF would be established at a federally insured bank for each state and municipal government in the country. Money in the GEF would be invested in one of the thirty government-sponsored fixed income funds.

A large percentage of the interest from the fund (say three-quarters) would be reinvested, and the remaining percentage would be sent monthly to the state or local government. Over time, the state or local government would receive a constantly increasing monthly apportionment. In tough times, when unemployment exceeded some threshold level, all, or most, of the interest would be sent monthly to the state or local government. By adopting this system, the government would increase national savings, provide state and local governments with steadily increasing tax revenues, and create a mechanism for moderating the business cycle.

Fundamental reform of the tax code will not be easy because every tax break on the books has a constituency ready and willing to fight for its survival. Many groups, such as charitable organizations, can make a strong case for federal tax subsidies. However, the main purpose of the tax code is to raise federal revenues. If the federal government wishes to subsidize worthwhile efforts, it can do so on the spending side of the federal ledger.

For too long America's tax code has been the captive of special interest groups seeking favored status. Comprehensive tax reform would not only increase compliance and efficiency, but also encourage important macroeconomic goals. In addition, collecting taxes at the federal level and apportioning money to state and local governments would allow the creation of another countercyclical tool to moderate recessions. Tax policy is one of the most powerful weapons in the government's policy arsenal, but America's monetary democracy has rendered the weapon impotent. The time has come for this to change.

Chapter 15

Investing in Human Capital

The most important resource any nation has is its people. Japan's postwar economic success made this point clear. If it wishes to be truly competitive in the twenty-first century, then the United States must do more than just adopt new macroeconomic policies. While the country's colleges and universities are arguably the finest in the world, America's primary and secondary schools are lagging dangerously behind. Large public schools, handicapped by inadequate funding and weighed down by bureaucracy, are failing in their task of educating America's youth for the challenges that lie ahead.

It is difficult to overstate the importance of a good education. While academic success provides the skills necessary for a productive working career, academic failure reduces an individual's self-esteem, job prospects, and ability to become a productive member of society. The cycle of poverty is not being fed by high school graduates, but by high school dropouts. Many of those who fail do so not by choice, but because the quality of education is inadequate. Shattering the cycle of poverty requires a double-barrelled approach: access to both a quality education and a good job. Failure to provide all Americans with both will leave the United States stalled on the productivity/technology curve.

Proposals for Education Reform

The most significant problem with America's primary and secondary public schools is that they are government-run monopolies that have developed many familiar bureaucratic characteristics, such as high cost, low quality, low morale, and resistance to change. To improve American education, members of the National Education Association, the leading teachers' union, argue that more money is desperately needed. The main issue facing America's schools, however, is structural and not financial. Providing adequate funding, especially to inner-city schools, is an important ingredient to educational reform, but throwing more money at the current system is simply a waste.

In order to reinvigorate America's schools, the public school monopoly must come to an end. A comprehensive, well-structured program of school choice would interject competition and create incentives to reduce costs, improve quality, and innovate. Those schools that successfully met the needs of both parents and children would thrive, while those that did not would go out of business.

The Bush administration backed a plan calling for federally funded vouchers to be used by students to pay for education costs at any school of their choice—public or private. But, because the proposed program only covered a small portion of private school tuition, it would have had the practical effect of being a federal subsidy for individuals who were going to send their children to private school anyway. To be successful, school choice must be available to all students and cover the full cost of their education. How the program is structured is vitally important.

One way for the federal government to create a nationwide program of school choice would be to establish twenty or so private-
public partnerships to develop a new generation of public schools.
The partnerships would be run by a board of directors chosen from
government, private business, and the nation's colleges and universities. The federal government, through the national investment
company, would provide subsidized loans for building the new
schools. The schools would be smaller in size and would hire more
teachers to significantly lower the student-teacher ratio. Experi-
mentation with both curriculum and teaching methods would be
encouraged.

A new system of partnership schools would require significant
federal funding, because America's current system of school funding is a disaster. Every year school boards around the country must
come up with an annual school budget for their districts. In years
when the economy is growing and tax revenues are high, the local
school district benefits from increased education spending. When
the economy turns sour and the tax revenues fall, however, the
school district must lay off some workers and cut expenditures.
This expansion/contraction method of finance is bad enough when
used for normal government programs, but it is a catastrophe when
used for school funding.

One remedy to this problem would be to establish a nationwide
system of general tuition funds (GTFs). A GTF would be an
endowment fund established for the sole purpose of funding primary and secondary public education. Each county in every state
would be required to establish one. The funds would be invested in
one of the government-sponsored fixed income investment funds.
Each month, half of the income from the fund would be sent to the
county to help cover public education costs. The other half of the
fund's income would be reinvested in the fund. Within a set period
of time (say three to five years), the county would be required to
convert to a comprehensive voucher program. Under the program,
every child of school age would receive a voucher from the county

to cover tuition at any public or partnership school in the county. All educational resources—income from the GTF, local property taxes, and state educational expenditures—would be funnelled through the voucher program instead of being paid directly to the school districts.

Initially, as new partnership schools were just being built, the change to a comprehensive voucher system would simply equate educational resources within a county and provide for a system of public school choice. Over time, as more new schools for all grades were completed, choice would increase and the forces of competition would slowly transform America's schools. The federal government would play a significant role in funding the nation's GTFs. Table 24 shows that the federal government's current role in funding primary and secondary education—just 6.4% in 1992—has ample room for expansion.

A significant federal funding program—of say $50 billion in the first year and an additional $10 billion each succeeding year until the federal government was spending $100 billion annually—would facilitate the transition to a new generation of schools. The money would be split between loans to the partnerships for new

Table 24
SOURCES OF FUNDING FOR PUBLIC PRIMARY
AND SECONDARY SCHOOLS - 1992 ($ BILLIONS)

	Education Spending	Percent of Total
Federal Government	15.1	6.4%
State Governments	112.5	47.9%
Local Governments	107.5	45.7%
Total	*235.1*	*100.0%*

Source: U.S. Bureau of the Census, *Statistical Abstract of the United States: 1993.*

school construction, direct contributions to the nation's GTFs, and increased loans to college students. A generous portion of federal funds would be directed to those inner cities and rural areas where educational needs are acute. Besides receiving federal money, the nation's GTFs would also solicit individual and corporate donations. Because only the funds' interest was going to current expenses, private contributions would be helping to fund the education not only of today's students, but also of future generations of Americans.

Having created a new structure of primary and secondary schools and providing them with adequate funding, the government should also make changes to improve scholastic achievement. State governments should tighten entrance requirements into public colleges and universities, many of which are required to accept any applicant with a high school diploma. One potential way to raise the achievement level of applicants is to slowly reduce the number of entrance slots available. In addition, tuition for public colleges and universities should be raised over time to reflect educational costs more accurately. In 1991, public higher education cost $93 billion. State governments contributed $38 billion, or 41% of total spending, while tuition and fees raised $15 billion, or 16%. In contrast, at private colleges and universities, tuition and fees covered 42% of total costs.[1]

If tuition and fees at public colleges and universities were raised to cover 30% of total expenses, then an additional $12.6 billion would be available for states to spend on primary and secondary education in educationally needy areas. As a result of these changes, some individuals who currently go on to community college or state universities would be forced to enter the work force. America's national rebuilding program would ensure that jobs are available. Those individuals could always return to college after working for a few years. An increase in tuition at public universities, however, may place school out of the financial reach of some students. *While students can be screened out due to poor academic*

*performance, no student should be denied access to college
because of economic hardship.*

If states increase tuition, then other financial resources must be
made available to students. The federal government should establish a nationwide college loan program making low-cost loans
available to any student who meets the entrance requirements. Students would have two ways to pay off their loans—over a ten-year
period or by working a few years in a federally financed national
education corps (NEC). The NEC would provide graduates with
jobs in teaching or public service. This structure would provide a
constant flow of young, educated workers in the public service and
teaching fields. These individuals would be an important resource
as the nation's primary and secondary schools move from the public to the private sector. President Bill Clinton offered a similar
proposal during his 1992 campaign and passed a limited version in
his first budget.

The NEC concept could also be used at the graduate level.
Many state universities have medical schools and law schools that
are also heavily subsidized. These schools could raise their tuition
and institute a scholarship program that provided financial aid in
return for a few years of work after graduation. Law students could
perform work in the public defender's office, while medical students could work at managed care providers in the inner cities or in
rural areas. A limited program for medical schools already exists,
but the federal government should expand it dramatically. The
NEC is a structured way for the federal and state governments to
get more out of their education tax dollar, while giving an energetic
group of young people the opportunity to help improve vital areas
of American society.

Continuing Education Centers

Creating a new generation of schools will dramatically improve
America's economic competitiveness, but the United States also

needs to find an effective solution to the productivity paradox. As the pace of economic change and globalization continues to accelerate, America's workers will be switching jobs and learning new skills with increasing frequency. Today, the federal government's largest form of direct aid to workers is unemployment insurance, which does nothing to improve workers' skills or find them a new job. In fiscal year 1993, the government spent $37.8 billion on unemployment compensation, while only $6.7 billion on hundreds of different job training programs.[2]

It is a natural part of capitalist economies for new companies and industries to emerge and replace old and inefficient predecessors. It is, in essence, a natural process of creation and destruction. The challenge to America's political economy is to create an economic structure that facilitates the process while at the same time reducing the economic pain involved. One way to accomplish this would be for the government to create a nationwide system of continuing education centers (CECs) at the nation's colleges and universities. The CECs would act as the heart of a system of worker transition and training. The government would require every company with over ten workers to select a local CEC, to which the company would make monthly payments equal to one percent of payroll—half a percent to cover current expenses and half a percent placed in an endowment fund. The CEC would be run by a board of directors elected by businesses participating in the program. The CEC would survey area businesses as to their current and future hiring needs and develop programs to teach relevant business skills. In addition, businesses would be encouraged to switch some of their in-house training to their local CEC.

The CECs would be available for both workers who lose their jobs and employed workers seeking to improve their skills. The CECs, in essence, would act as a centralized location for both job training and placement. When a company fired a worker, the company would be required to pay ten percent of the worker's annual salary to the local CEC's endowment fund. Instead of paying unemployment insurance directly to workers, the federal government would require workers to enroll at a CEC of their choice and to take classes to improve their skills. The unemployed workers would receive a stipend and assistance with food and housing needs. The nation already has an untapped resource available that the CECs could tap—the millions of Americans who have taken early retirement in recent years as part of corporate cost-cutting programs. With their years of work experience and practical knowledge, these individuals would make excellent instructors.

In combination with a good job, a quality education can be America's most significant weapon against the cycle of poverty afflicting the nation's large cities. In addition, an educated work force is crucial to America's future economic competitiveness. It is imperative, therefore, that the United States reinvigorate its antiquated, bureaucratic public school system by adopting a comprehensive system of public school choice. Creating a nationwide network of CECs would help relieve the stress and anxiety associated with unemployment and create a much needed system of employee training. The combination of a national investment company, a national rebuilding program, and a system of economic transition would not only reduce unemployment, but would provide a powerful response to the productivity paradox. Without an effective system of economic transition, the United States will fail to adjust adequately to a rapidly changing world economy.

The United States faces a momentous challenge. To be economically competitive in the next century, the nation must adopt new macroeconomic policies while reversing dangerous fiscal trends. At the same time, the United States must also make profound changes to its tax policies and its health care and education systems. However, with America's current political structure these tasks are not just difficult, but politically impossible. America's first step, therefore, must be structural political reform. For if politicians have strong incentives to place the general interest ahead of the special interests, then the federal government can take a long-term view and adopt policies that encourage businesses and individuals to do the same—thus ensuring that the twentieth century was not the zenith of American prosperity. To the issue of political reform we now turn.

Part V

Fixing the Foundation

Chapter 16

A New Era of Political Economy

The third era of America's political economy began when the Great Depression made clear that government's role could no longer be limited. While the New Deal stopped the nation's economic slide, it was massive government spending during World War II that tapped the nation's economic potential as never before. The transition from limited to expanded government, a transition borne of necessity rather than plan, seemed to have been completed successfully. Indeed, more than two decades of postwar prosperity reinforced this view.

America's economic success during the fifties and sixties, however, was the result of unique postwar conditions and fiscally conservative government. When the unique conditions disappeared and the doors to the federal treasury were swung open, America's political flaws were revealed. As we have seen, by placing special interests ahead of the general interest, America's monetary democracy encourages myopic policies and fiscally irresponsible government. The United States desperately needs a fourth era of political economy, where the political structure reflects the expanded role that government plays and, more importantly, places the general interest ahead of the special interest.

Reclaiming America's Representative Democracy

The time has come for America to reclaim its representative democracy so that votes, not money, can again be the source of political power. To accomplish this, the financial umbilical cord between campaign donors and elected politicians must be severed and replaced with a comprehensive system of public funding for all federal elections. Public funding should also be used at the state and local level too, but it must start at the top.

Today, the American taxpayer is required to pay taxes to support the entire array of government services—from national defense to social security to highway construction. There is one item, however, that Americans do not have to pay for—the cost of election campaigns. No, this cost is gladly picked up by wealthy individuals and special interest groups because campaign finance is where political power resides in a monetary democracy. *The average American taxpayer gets stuck with all the bills except the one bill that could lower the cost of all the others.* It is time that the American taxpayer covers the cost of federal elections and reaps the benefits of a government no longer handicapped by a warped system of campaign finance.

Proposals for public funding of elections are not new. Indeed, President Theodore Roosevelt addressed the topic in 1907:

> It is well to provide that corporations shall not contribute to Presidential or National campaigns, and furthermore to provide for the publication of both contributions and expenditures. There is, however, always a danger in laws of this kind, which from their very nature are difficult of enforcement; the danger being lest they be obeyed only by the honest, and disobeyed by the unscrupulous, so as to act only as a penalty upon honest men. Moreover, no such law would hamper an unscrupulous man of

unlimited means from buying his own way into office. There is a
very radical measure which would, I believe, work a substantial
improvement in our system of conducting a campaign, although I
am well aware that it will take some time for people so to famil-
iarize themselves with such a proposal as to be willing to con-
sider its adoption. The need for collecting large campaign funds
would vanish if Congress provided an appropriation for the
proper and legitimate expenses of each of the great national parties, an appropriation ample enough to meet the necessity for
thorough organization and machinery, which requires a large
expenditure of money.[1]

More than eighty years have passed since Roosevelt's proposal—
more than ample time for the public to become familiar with such a
plan.

The United States currently provides public funds for presidential campaigns, but the structure is riddled with flaws. To qualify
for public matching funds during the primary season, candidates
must still raise substantial sums from private sources. During the
1992 presidential primaries, candidates received $42 million in
public matching funds—a substantial amount, but just one-third of
total primary campaign expenditures.[2] Once the two main parties
held their nominating conventions, an additional $110 million in
public funds was split between the Bush and Clinton campaigns.
By accepting these funds, the two major party candidates were
restricted from spending additional privately raised funds. Under
this system, over seventy percent of public funds during the 1992
presidential campaign were handed out after the two nominees
were already selected—too late to increase competition during primaries or lessen the influence of campaign contributors. If the
United States adopts a system of comprehensive public financing
for all federal campaigns, it should not use the current system of
presidential matching funds as a model.

The United States currently provides public funds for presiden-
    There are two main arguments against adopting a comprehen-
sive system of public funding for all federal elections. The first is

cost. In 1990, House and Senate elections cost approximately $446 million. The 1988 presidential campaign cost more than $303 million.[3] In the most costly year—a presidential election year—a comprehensive system of public financing could easily exceed $750 million. Quite a large sum of money. But by increasing the tax on gasoline by one cent, the government could raise $1 billion annually, more than enough to pay for a system of public financing. Now there is an interesting choice for the American people. Are they willing to pay an extra penny at the pump to remove the corrupt role of money in federal politics? They should be.

The second argument against public funding is that it is unconstitutional. The basis for this argument is the 1976 United States Supreme Court decision *Buckley v. Valeo*, which was a test of the Federal Election Campaign Act of 1971, amended in 1974. In its decision, the Court upheld the constitutionality of disclosure requirements, limits on campaign contributions, and public matching funds for presidential elections. However, the Court overturned mandatory spending limits for campaigns and spending limits on both individuals and independent groups. The majority's argument was that caps on expenditures were unconstitutional because such caps were a violation of free speech.

The Supreme Court's *Buckley v. Valeo* ruling has provided politicians with a convenient excuse not to enact public funding for federal elections. The issue, however, is too important to be settled by default. America must decide whether it is more important for each individual to have an equal opportunity to participate in elections both as voters and candidates, or more important that individuals have the opportunity to express their political support through campaign contributions. This question is at the heart of America's political dilemma. If Americans truly believe in the equal rights of all individuals, the current system of campaign finance must be replaced by a system of public financing; even if such a system requires a Constitutional amendment.

Solving America's Demographic Dilemma

The original cause of America's monetary democracy was not money, but demographic change. And America's demographic problem also needs to be solved, for it will only worsen with the passage of time. The Founding Fathers sought to have one representative for every 30,000 people, yet in 1990 there was one representative for every 571,747 people. With 435 members in the House of Representatives, however, the House has difficulty functioning effectively. America has, through the passage of time and political inaction, the worst of both worlds—too many representatives who are too far removed from the electorate.

As a historical aside, during the first Congress James Madison sought to remedy the Constitution's failure to set a floor on the number of representatives in the House. Fulfilling a campaign promise, Madison reviewed the amendments proposed by the various states during the Constitution's ratification process and drafted nine amendments, which he presented to the House on June 8, 1789. Eleven weeks later, the House passed a total of seventeen amendments. The Senate combined some of them to reduce the number to twelve, which were revised further by a joint Congressional committee before being passed by both houses of Congress.[4]

Amendments three through twelve were ratified by three-quarters of the states and became the Bill of Rights. Amendment two prohibited a Congressional pay raise from taking effect until after an intervening election. After being passed by a few states, the amendment went into hibernation, only to be awakened by the political disenchantment of the last decade. On May 7, 1992, Michigan became the thirty-eighth state to ratify what then became the 27th Amendment to the Constitution.

What about amendment one? It dealt with establishing a floor on the number of representatives in the House as the population grew. By 1791, ten out of fourteen states (Vermont became the fourteenth state in 1791) had ratified the amendment, leaving only

one more for the required three-quarters. But no more states ratified the proposed amendment. Would it have made a difference? If
the amendment had passed, it would have required Congress to set
the size of the current House of Representatives between 200 and
4,974 members. If Madison's original version had passed, the
House would be required to have between 4,974 and 8,290 members. A House of Representatives with thousands of members
would be absurd, but Madison's original amendment would have
forced Congress to come to grips with the structural changes
caused by population growth.

Although districts were common for state legislatures at the
time, the Constitution did not provide for the creation of Congressional districts. During the elections for the first Congress, five
states elected their representatives at-large. In 1840, six states were
still doing so. Another feature of early Congressional elections was
the multi-member district. For example, in 1838 New York had one
district electing four representatives and four districts electing two
representatives each. Congress finally passed districting legislation in 1842, and by 1848 all the states were electing their representatives by single-member district.[†]

Today, the issue of Congressional districting is again being
addressed in the federal courts. Under current election laws, a
political party with a plurality of support is able to control a

---

[†] A more problematic feature of Congressional elections was malapportion-
ment—huge population disparities between districts. For example, in 1962 the
largest district in Maryland had 711,045 people, while the smallest had
243,570. This problem was not fixed until the February 17, 1964 Supreme
Court decision *Wesberry v. Sanders*, in which the Court ruled that "as nearly as
practicable, one man's vote in a Congressional election is to be worth as much
as another's." See Congressional Quarterly, *Guide to Congress* (Washington,
D.C.: Congressional Quarterly, Inc., 1982), p. 695 and Congressional Quarterly, *Guide to U.S. Elections* (Washington, D.C.: Congressional Quarterly,
Inc., 1975), p. 520.

majority in Congress. Theoretically, a political party receiving
fifty-one percent of the votes could win all the seats. In response to
this structure, racial minorities have fought, both in the legislatures
and in the courts, for redistricting plans that create Congressional
districts where racial minorities make up a majority. On June 28,
1993, the Supreme Court ruled in *Shaw v. Reno*, a case questioning
the constitutionality of North Carolina's 12th District, that while
race-conscious redistricting is not per se unconstitutional, districts
drawn solely on the basis of race amount to "racial gerrymander-
ing" and violate the Equal Protection Clause of the Constitution.
One solution that has been proposed to address the issue of
minority representation is a return to multi-member districts.[5]

As we saw in Chapter 1, America's Congressional elections are
uncompetitive. The ability of state legislatures to carve up districts
along political lines contributes to this lack of competition. The
current districting debate offers the opportunity to inject competition into Congressional races and to encourage the creation of new
political parties. One way to accomplish this and address the problem of simultaneously having too many and too few representatives would be to create a new structure of government to deal
more directly with the American public.

Instead of having 435 Congressional districts, the nation could
be divided into twenty geographic regions, with each region having
roughly 250 districts, each containing an average of 50,000 people.
Each of the nation's 5,000 districts would elect a district representative who would respond directly to constituents. A department of
constituent service would be established in Washington and would
work closely with each of the district representatives. Voters would
elect a district representative and would also elect five regional
representatives, who would represent the region in Congress and
would focus on regional and national issues. As a result, the size of
the House of Representatives would be reduced from 435 members
to 100 members. Multi-member regions would ensure adequate
representation of all political parties. Voters would be given five

votes and would able to cast all their votes for one candidate or spread their votes among different candidates.[†]

Multi-member regions would dramatically reduce the tactic of negative campaigning. A successful candidate would have to work closely with the four other electoral winners and would quickly discover that negative ads have lost their utility. Instead of trying to make the other candidates unacceptable to voters (there would be too many for this approach to work), a candidate would have to convince voters why they should vote for her. Rules for Senate elections could be changed so that each state elects its two senators at the same time (where the two highest vote recipients win seats). Doing so would greatly reduce, though not eliminate, the use of negative campaigning in Senate races.

This new structure would allow for additional reforms. Each month, members of Congress would return to their region and meet with their district representatives. A week before the regional meetings, Congress would send out copies of the bills it was considering. At the meetings, members of Congress would be allowed to speak for or against the particular legislation, and district representatives would be allowed to ask questions and debate the issues. At the end of the public debate, the district representatives would vote on the proposed legislation. The results of the vote would *not* be binding. Members of Congress would then return to Washington and vote on the proposed legislation.

Why should Congress have to present bills for public debate in the various regions of the country? Because current Congressional legislation is excessively long and technical, resulting in the disturbing fact that many members do not even get a chance to read an entire bill before voting on it. Requiring Congress to present legislative bills for public discussion would mean that, at a bare

---

[†] This voting structure—multiple candidates on a single ballot for all the seats— is referred to as proportional representation. In this instance, the five highest vote getters in a particular region would win a seat in Congress.

minimum, every member would have to read every bill on which they vote. This requirement would encourage Congress to write shorter legislation, focusing on clear goals. The prevalence of pork barrel projects and special exemptions for favored interest groups would not long survive such close public scrutiny.

In addition, each region could be required to establish a national research center at a major college or university in the region. The research center would be run by a board of directors, nominated by the region's members in Congress and elected by the district representatives. The board of directors, in turn, would appoint a research director for the center. The center would conduct research on both regional and national issues in all areas. The center would act as an information source for all district representatives and the region's members in Congress. Instead of relying on the work of foundations funded by private interests, members of Congress would have access to publicly funded research compiled by some of their own constituents.

Public Financing for Federal Campaigns

With a new structure of government, creating a workable structure of public financing would be made easier. Such a system could work as follows. Three months prior to election day, those individuals wishing to run for Congress would be required to register and pay $10,000 (or a similar sum to discourage insincere candidates) to run for office. Each candidate would submit a one-page sheet containing: biographical information, a picture of the candidate, and his views on three or four major issues of the day (all candidates would be required to discuss the same three of four issues). These candidate sheets would be placed in random order and sent in a package, along with a ballot, to all the registered voters in a region or state. The voters would be able to select five candidates for the House (and one for the Senate if Senate elections were being held in that state). The fifteen highest vote recipients for

House seats and the eight highest vote recipients for Senate seats would qualify for the primary. The surviving candidates would then all receive the same amount of public funds (plus an additional $10,000 to cover the initial expenditure) and would be given a three or four-week period in which to campaign. A second primary would be held six weeks before the election, and the top ten House candidates and the top four Senate candidates would be placed on the general election ballot and given an additional amount of public funding.

The structure of presidential campaigns should also be changed. The current primary system is a horrifying ordeal that brutalizes presidential candidates. In addition, many voters never have an opportunity to help select the two major party candidates who run in November. The two most populous states in the country, California and New York, rarely have much choice left when their primary dates finally arrive.[†] The current process simply says to many voters: "It's November, time to select a president, here are your two choices, take it or leave it." Ross Perot's strong independent showing in the 1992 presidential race reflected Americans' disgust with the current exclusionary primary system.

With regions and public financing, presidential elections could be shortened and voter choice could be improved. On an established date, say six months before the election, candidates would be required to register and make a deposit. A one-page sheet with biographical information and views would be submitted, and the compiled package would be sent to all registered voters in the country. Individuals would be able to select three candidates, and any candidate who won at least two percent of the vote would qualify for the first primary and receive public financing. There would be twenty primaries—one in each region—spaced a week

---

[†] California has passed legislation to move its 1996 primary from June to March. With its winner-take-all format, the state's Republican primary will probably be decisive in selecting the party's 1996 presidential candidate.

apart, with four weeks between the time the original candidates are selected and the first primary. The primary season would then last twenty-three weeks, or about five months.

Every four years a different region would have the first primary, so that every region in the country would be equally involved in selecting presidential candidates. During the primary process, the field of candidates would slowly be reduced by higher minimum vote hurdles. After the primary season was concluded, there would be a nationwide primary of the remaining candidates. The top two finishers in the national primary would run in the general election. The two candidates would be given additional campaign funds and would have one more month of campaigning prior to the election.

Additional Reforms

Congressional elections should be held once every four years instead of every two, and Congressional terms should be limited. By holding Congressional elections every four years instead of every two, the cost of House campaigns is cut directly in half, while House members would be less obsessed with having to run for reelection. Term limits address a glaring problem—the unwillingness of elected officials to make difficult decisions because such decisions could risk their political futures. While 43.4% of the members of Congress have been in office less than six years, 15.5% have been in office over twenty years. It is this latter group that wields the power in Congress, and it is this group being targeted by term limit legislation. If members of Congress know that their time in office is limited, they will focus more on getting things done than on avoiding problems and responsibility.

Term limits is an idea whose time has clearly arrived. In 1990, voters in Colorado approved an initiative limiting the number of terms its members in Congress could serve. In 1992, fourteen states placed term limitation initiatives on the ballot. Every single one passed. While term limits have become a lightning rod for voter discontent with the political status quo, they need to apply to all states to have the desired effect. The Federal District Court in Seattle recently ruled that the Washington State law restricting Congressional terms is unconstitutional because it makes "qualified persons ineligible to serve."[6] Unless the ruling is overturned on appeal, a Constitutional amendment will be required for congressional term limits to be imposed.

Amending the Constitution

As the cornerstone upon which the nation's government rests, the Constitution should not be tampered with frequently or in a capricious manner. Nevertheless, America's high regard for the work of the founding fathers should not impede the adoption of amendments that are required to repair America's political flaws. In 1816, Thomas Jefferson addressed the issue of amending the Constitution:

> Some men look at Constitutions with sanctimonious reverence, and deem them, like the ark of the covenant, too sacred to be touched. They ascribe to the men of the preceding age a wisdom more than human, and suppose what they did to be beyond amendment. I knew that age well; I belonged to and labored with it. It deserved well of its country. It was very like the present, but without the experience of the present; and forty years of experience is worth a century of book reading; and this they would say themselves, were they to rise from the dead. I am certainly not an advocate for frequent and untried changes in laws and Constitutions. I think moderate imperfections had better to be borne with; because, when once known, we accommodate ourselves to them, and find practical means of correcting their ill effects. But I know, also, that laws and institutions must go hand on hand with the progress of the human mind. As that becomes more developed, more enlightened, as new discoveries are made, new truths disclosed, and manners of opinions change with the change of circumstances, institutions must advance also and keep pace with the times.[7]

Americans have had enough experience over the past two hundred years, and, in particular, with the past thirty years, to know that there are some serious structural problems that need to be fixed. If in order to fix America's broken system of government the Constitution must be amended, then it should be amended.

Amending the Constitution can take place in one of two ways. First, both houses of Congress, by a two-thirds majority, pass an amendment and it is then ratified by three-quarters of the state legislatures. Second, two-thirds of the state legislatures petition for the calling of a constitutional convention to propose amendments. Any proposed amendments would still require passage by three-quarters of the state legislatures. All of the twenty-seven amendments to the Constitution have passed by the first method. Through over two hundred years, the second method has gone unused. Now is a good time for that to change.

To facilitate reform, President Clinton could bypass Congress and ask the state legislatures to call for the convening of a constitutional convention. Delegates to the convention would be selected under clearly established rules and would meet for two or three weeks to discuss and debate proposals for amending the Constitution. Any proposals would then be presented to the states for ratification. Among the amendments discussed should be an amendment calling for a periodic constitutional convention to be held, say once every decade, in order to discuss proposed amendments.

Another route to political reform would be the creation of a well-funded and well-organized third party. To appeal to the voting public, the party would be fiscally conservative and socially liberal. It would develop a clear, concise blueprint for structural change, which included Constitutional amendments. To be successful, the new party would have to run candidates for president and for all congressional districts. America's current two-party system survives today, not because of its popularity or success, but because it possesses a tremendous capacity to withstand change.

As population growth has widened the distance between the governing and the governed, and those institutions which historically have played a mediating role no longer do so, individual Americans have lost the ability to make their voices heard above the special interest lobbyists in Washington. As a result, the sound structure of limited government established by the founding fathers has been co–opted by narrow interests seeking their own short-term advantage at the expense of the national interest. And a nation whose government is little more than a compilation of special interest groups loses sight of what it means to be a nation.

America urgently needs a fourth era of political economy, where the political structure encourages government officials to act in the long-term interests of the entire nation, not in response to the short-term desires of powerful interest groups. Adopting a comprehensive system of public financing for federal campaigns is vital to this effort. The political impact of demographic change is also an issue that needs to be addressed. Fixing these and other political flaws will require amending the Constitution, but America must not shrink from the task, for it is the nation's future which hangs in the balance.

Chapter 17

The Challenge of History

In many ways, America is a victim of its own success. Because the nation's political economy has worked in the past, the assumption is made that, for all its apparent faults, it can work again in the future. But this assumption is erroneous. America's political system has developed serious flaws rendering it structurally incapable of solving its long-term problems. But while the warning signs clearly exist, we, as a nation, do not see them. If America's political system is not fixed, disaster will be the result. Unfortunately, a disaster may be required to develop the consensus needed for fundamental change.

Only once before in American history has the nation's structure of government so completely failed to address the nation's problems. The difference, however, was that in the summer of 1787, when fifty-five delegates met in Philadelphia to propose changes to the Articles of Confederation, there was near unanimous agreement as to the nature and magnitude of the problem. The challenge then was concisely described in a letter from the Virginia state

246

legislature which was presented by the Virginia delegation on the first day of the Convention:

> The Crisis is arrived at which the good People of America are to decide the solemn question whether they will by wise and magnanimous Efforts reap the just fruits of that Independence which they have so gloriously acquired and of that Union which they have cemented with so much of their common Blood, or whether by giving way to unmanly Jealousies and Prejudices or to partial and transitory Interests they will renounce the auspicious blessings prepared for them by the Revolution, and furnish to its Enemies an eventual Triumph over those by whose virtue and valor it has been accomplished.[1]

The Articles of Confederation failed because they organized the nation as a loose association of sovereign states. America's current structure of government is failing because it treats the nation as a simple summation of disparate interest groups. And while it is widely acknowledged today that political problems exist, there is no consensus as to their depth or significance. The perverse incentives of a monetary democracy and the emergence of a politics of empty rhetoric and false choices combine to obscure America's political dilemma. In the absence of a consensus, American politicians will continue to make small, incremental changes to the status quo. Meanwhile, serious long-term problems simmer below the surface, like a volcano waiting to erupt.

In 1994, after more than three years of economic recession and stagnation, the nation's economy is finally moving forward. In the absence of a major oil shock, both the American and world economies are poised to enjoy a period of economic growth that should last for the remainder of the decade. While this is good news, it will divert public attention away from America's structural economic problems—low rates of savings and investment, high budget and trade deficits, and anemic job creation. Politicians need few excuses to avoid difficult decisions, and the economic expansion of the mid-1990s will give them all the political cover they need.

The recent collapse of communism demonstrated the superiority of democratic forms of government, but the United States should not forget the two other lessons of this historic event. The first is that the major cause of the Soviet Union's disintegration was the implosion of its *economic* system. The country had the ability to destroy the world and place men in orbit, but could not provide its people with an acceptable standard of living. The second lesson is that history does not wait for countries to make up for their past mistakes. To move forward, a nation must be ready, willing, and able to change. When it no longer can, whether by choice or by default, history passes the nation by.

To avoid that verdict of history, America must make structural changes to its political and economic systems. In the economic arena, it must reorient its economy away from consumption and short-term corporate profits towards an economy that maximizes employment and long-term growth. An active national investment policy and a sound system of economic transition would ensure that the United States moves up the productivity/technology curve. In order to avoid the fiscal abyss, the nation must curb entitlement spending and reform health care. Before any of these changes,

however, the nation must first reclaim its representative democracy by adopting a comprehensive system of public financing for campaigns.

America's monetary democracy, with its strong emphasis on the status quo, will not go silently into the pages of history. The tragedy of Vietnam demonstrated the government's ability to cling tenaciously to failed policies, even when the human and social costs are frighteningly high. More recently, Ronald Reagan's political success, based on large deficits and unrestrained optimism, set a dangerous precedent. Instead of engaging in substantive debate, politicians seek ways to avoid responsibility and lay blame at someone else's doorstep. The national news media, with its influential role in politics, has done its part by blurring the difference between perception and reality. As long as America's monetary democracy remains intact, as long as special interests are placed ahead of the general interest, as long as politicians can enjoy electoral success by ignoring problems and avoiding difficult decisions, then America's decline will continue.

The United States faces a critical choice—it can continue down its current path, allow problems to worsen and disaster to strike, or it can, by exercising foresight and courage, act today and make the small sacrifices required to ensure the health and prosperity of future generations. America's current structure of government will not, in the absence of a major crisis, make the changes required. But waiting for disaster to strike is a poor substitute for preventive action.

Only the American people can stop the nation from continuing down the dangerous path it now treads. It is all too easy, when seeing the corrupt flow of money in politics, when listening to the mind-numbing rhetoric and empty debate, and when given few choices at the voting booth, to decide that politics doesn't matter; that it is hopelessly dysfunctional; and that as an individual there is little you can do to change things. Indeed, if enough people feel this way, then America's fate is sealed.

But this need not be the case. America's political system can still be fixed. There are organizations working today for political reform, organizations needing help and support. Information about some of these groups has been included in Appendix B. If enough people view America's political problems as a call to action rather than an excuse for apathy, then political reform has a fighting chance. What is required of the current generation is little in comparison to what previous generations of Americans have sacrificed for the good of their country. The little time and effort, however, are vitally important. The greatest danger of the disease infecting American democracy is that it will continue to grow, avoiding detection until it has reached the advanced stages of illness.

The United States is still a wealthy nation and has the resources to address its problems. With each passing year, however, the problems worsen, the nation grows relatively poorer, and the amount of sacrifice required increases. The United States, by reason of its past accomplishments, is not immune from the laws of economics nor the verdict of history. The nation is, for the moment, the master of its own destiny, but it will not be this way for long. The American people must seize the moment while it exists. If the nation fails in this effort, then future generations will condemn our selfishness and collective myopia.

Appendix A

Debt and Deficit Projections

Accurately projecting future budget deficits is a difficult task. Government spending and tax policies, the rate of inflation, the level of interest rates, and the rate of economic growth all have an impact on the government's finances. Congress also has the ability to push certain costs into the future (as it frequently did with the S&L crisis) or reduce the size of reported deficits through various accounting devices (as it does with social security). With all of these moving parts, it should come as no surprise that the federal government has displayed a dismal lack of success in its efforts to forecast future budget deficits.

Past Government Projections

While the variables mentioned above are a major reason for the government's poor forecasting record, an equally important reason, discussed in Chapter 7, is that government officials have strong incentives to adopt overly optimistic budget forecasts. By making future budget deficits smaller or nonexistent, politicians do not have to take the difficult steps—raising taxes, cutting spending, or both—needed to reduce future deficits. In 1981, the Reagan administration's "rosy scenario" not only provided the cover needed to push through a huge cut in both individual and corporate income taxes, but also established a precedent for disingenuous budget forecasting. A closer look at the government's forecasting record since that time reveals a strong bias towards unfounded optimism.

Table 25 shows the government's deficit projections beginning with Ronald Reagan's first budget (fiscal year 1982). Table 25 should be examined in conjunction with Table 26, which shows the government's accuracy, or lack thereof. For example, in Reagan's first budget (fiscal year 1982), the administration projected a year

Table 25
ADMINISTRATION PROJECTIONS OF
FUTURE BUDGET SURPLUSES (DEFICITS) – $ BILLIONS

		Administration Projections				
FY	President	Year 1	Year 2	Year 3	Year 4	Year 5
1982	Reagan (1)	-46	-23	17		
1983	Reagan (2)	-107	-97	-83		
1984	Reagan (3)	-203	-205	-157		
1985	Reagan (4)	-195	-186	-188	-160	-128
1986	Reagan (5)	-178	-168	-149	-113	-89
1987	Reagan (6)	-144	-94	-68	-36	1
1988	Reagan (7)	-108	-93	-60	-21	12
1989	Reagan (8)	-130	-104	-79	-51	-23
1990	Bush (1)	-93	-67	-32	2	33
1991	Bush (2)	-63	-25	6	11	9
1992	Bush (3)	-281	-202	-62	-3	20
1993	Bush (4)	-350	-212	-194	-181	-188
1994	Clinton (1)	-255	-230	-188	-181	-202

Source: *Budget of the United States Government, Fiscal Years 1982-1994.*

1 (FY 1982) deficit of $46 billion and a year 3 (FY 1984) surplus of $17 billion. Table 26 shows that the actual deficits for FY 1982 and FY 1984 were $128 billion and $185 billion respectively. The Reagan administration underestimated the size of the budget deficit by $82 billion in FY 1982 and $203 billion in FY 1984. These two numbers are shown in the first row of Table 30 under years 1 and 3. Of the forty-four projections examined in Table 26, the government underestimated the size of future budget deficits thirty-nine times (89%). The bottom of Table 26 shows that, on average, the government's inaccuracy increases the further out it attempts to forecast.

Table 26
ACCURACY OF FEDERAL GOVERNMENT
BUDGET PROJECTIONS ($ BILLIONS)

Fiscal Year	Actual Deficit	President	Difference Between Projection and Actual				
			Year 1	Year 2	Year 3	Year 4	Year 5
1982	128	Reagan (1)	-82	-184	-203		
1983	208	Reagan (2)	-101	-88	-130		
1984	185	Reagan (3)	17	-8	-64		
1985	212	Reagan (4)	-17	-35	38	4	-24
1986	221	Reagan (5)	-43	18	-6	-40	-132
1987	150	Reagan (6)	-6	-62	-85	-186	-271
1988	155	Reagan (7)	-47	-60	-162	-248	-302
1989	152	Reagan (8)	-23	-117	-190	-239	-231
1990	221	Bush (1)	-129	-203	-258	-257	
1991	270	Bush (2)	-206	-265	-260		
1992	290	Bush (3)	-10	-53			
1993	255	Bush (4)	95				
		Average	*-46*	*-96*	*-132*	*-161*	*-192*

Note: The difference between projection and actual yields a negative number if the future deficit was underestimated; a positive number if it was overestimated.

Source: *Budget of the United States Government, Fiscal Years 1982-1994.*

Current Government Projections

Table 27 shows the Clinton administration's projections for future budget deficits, national debt, and GDP, as published in the fiscal year 1995 budget. The administration predicts that over the next six fiscal years (1994-1999), budget deficits will total $1.127 trillion, while the national debt will increase by $1.954 trillion. Treasury securities purchased by the social security and other trust funds account for the $827 billion difference between the projected deficits and the increase in the national debt.

If the Clinton administration were to meet its deficit goals, it would be a step in the right direction. However, as Chart 18 shows, the national debt would still be growing faster than the economy; in addition, no structural changes would have been made to start preparing for the retirement of the baby boom generation in the year 2010. The strong political incentives for optimistic budget forecasting have not disappeared. As a result, the Clinton administration's budget projections may prove to be, like their recent

Table 27
CLINTON ADMINISTRATION'S
BUDGET PROJECTIONS ($ BILLIONS)

	FY 1994	FY 1995	FY 1996	FY 1997	FY 1998	FY 1999
Deficit	235	165	170	186	190	181
National Debt	4,676	4,960	5,267	5,601	5,953	6,305
GDP	6,641	7,022	7,419	7,842	8,285	8,750
Deficit (% GDP)	3.5%	2.4%	2.3%	2.4%	2.3%	2.1%
Debt (% GDP)	70.4%	70.6%	71.0%	71.4%	71.9%	72.1%

Source: *Budget of the United States Government, FY 1995.*

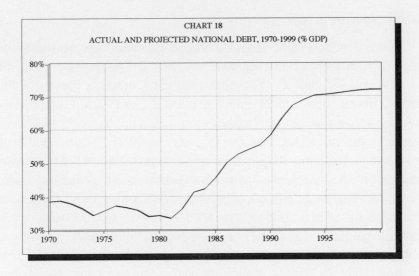

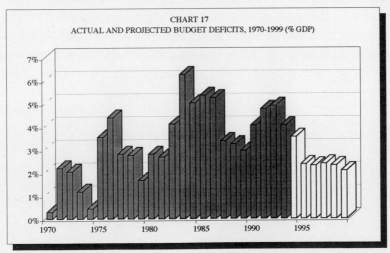

predecessors, woefully off the mark. But even if the projections are more accurate than those of the recent past, the dangerous long-term trends continue. America is still headed toward the fiscal abyss.

Author's Projections

In spite of the government's recent track record, budget fore-casting is still important because the United States must, in some way, be able to quantify the future implications of its current fiscal course. In the course of writing this book, I constructed a computer model to forecast future budget deficits. The two primary eco-nomic assumptions of budget forecasting models are economic growth and inflation. Other assumptions are required for interest rates, population growth, mortality rates, health care inflation, social security benefits, taxes, and government spending growth. The wide range of variables involved in forecasting makes it clear that any single forecast of future budget deficits should be viewed with a highly suspicious eye. In an attempt to compensate for this limitation, I have run a variety of different scenarios to create a matrix of possible outcomes. Table 28 shows snapshots of nine dif-ferent scenarios for the fiscal years 2000, 2010, and 2020.

The projections in Table 28 reinforce two important points: economic growth is vital to America's fiscal health and the nation's demographic wave begins hitting between the years 2010 and 2020. With strong economic growth, under any inflation scenario, America's debt and deficit, as a percentage of GDP, are still at manageable levels in the year 2020. In sharp contrast, weak eco-nomic growth spells fiscal disaster within the next quarter century. But even under the low growth scenarios, America's fiscal situa-tion is not acute in the year 2010. It is the decade between 2010 and 2020 that will test the nation's fiscal strength.

Politicians have strong incentives to ignore the nation's fiscal problems and simply hope for the best. But the chances are strong that a fiscal crisis is coming, a crisis that is best avoided.

Table 28

AUTHOR'S DEBT AND DEFICIT PROJECTIONS - FISCAL YEARS 2000, 2010, AND 2020 ($ BILLIONS)

| | | Years & Economic Growth | | | | | | | | |
| | | 2000 | | | 2010 | | | 2020 | | |
Inflation		Low	Mod.	High	Low	Mod.	High	Low	Mod.	High
	GDP	8,484	9,114	9,782	11,968	14,845	18,362	16,882	24,181	34,468
	National Debt	7,082	7,128	7,177	13,810	12,928	13,228	41,274	26,031	22,823
Low	Budget Deficit	369	310	248	919	553	158	3,202	1,794	257
	Debt (% GDP)	83%	78%	73%	115%	87%	72%	244%	108%	66%
	Deficit (% GDP)	4%	3%	3%	8%	4%	1%	19%	7%	1%
	GDP	9,157	9,828	10,541	15,641	19,333	23,832	26,718	38,031	53,884
	National Debt	7,338	7,387	7,439	16,410	15,551	15,931	61,649	37,441	32,874
Moderate	Budget Deficit	418	354	287	1,349	839	288	5,861	3,278	589
	Debt (% GDP)	80%	75%	71%	105%	80%	67%	231%	98%	61%
	Deficit (% GDP)	5%	4%	3%	9%	4%	1%	22%	9%	1%
	GDP	9,874	10,589	11,348	20,540	25,298	31,078	46,440	65,617	92,301
	National Debt	7,605	7,657	7,713	19,637	18,775	19,257	100,843	57,460	50,927
High	Budget Deficit	471	401	328	1,926	1,223	460	11,999	6,616	1,354
	Debt (% GDP)	77%	72%	68%	96%	74%	62%	217%	88%	55%
	Deficit (% GDP)	5%	4%	3%	9%	5%	1%	26%	10%	1%

Table 28 (continued)
AUTHOR'S DEBT AND DEFICIT PROJECTIONS -
FISCAL YEARS 2000, 2010, AND 2020 ($ BILLIONS)

Economic Assumptions (annual rates):

	Growth			Inflation		
	Low	Moderate	High	Low	Moderate	High
1994-1999	2.0%	3.0%	4.0%	2.5%	3.5%	4.5%
2000-2009	1.5%	3.0%	4.5%	2.0%	4.0%	6.0%
2010-2020	1.5%	3.0%	4.5%	2.0%	4.0%	7.0%

Historical:	Growth	Inflation
1950s	4.0%	2.0%
1960s	4.1%	2.3%
1970s	2.8%	7.1%
1980s	2.5%	5.5%
1990-93	1.5%	3.9%

Note: Inflation refers to Consumer Price Index (CPI). Debt statistics reflect end of fiscal year. In addition to growth and inflation, assumptions have also been made about demographics (see footnote 5, Chapter 3), real interest rates, tax receipts, and the growth of discretionary federal spending. It is also assumed that health care cost increases are brought in line with the CPI over the next decade.

Appendix B

Public Interest Groups

Over the past three decades, one of the fastest growing American industries has been the business of lobbying the federal government. Today, Washington is awash in lobbyists. Every large American company has some type of lobbying presence in Washington (either through a trade association, a law firm, or some other conduit). Major foreign companies and foreign governments also have a lobbying presence, as do groups representing the interests of business, labor, civil rights, the environment, and a host of other issues and ideological viewpoints.

Defenders of the political status quo argue that the current proliferation of lobbying groups is simply democracy in action— individual Americans forming groups to exercise their democratic right to be represented. In this argument I can find no fault. Interest groups are a vital component of any democracy. For example, it would be a poor business decision for a large American corporation not to have some lobbying presence in Washington, because what goes on in the halls of Congress can have a direct impact on the bottom line.

The crux of America's political dilemma is not that interest groups exist, but that a flawed system of campaign finance has endowed them with too much political power. When the positions of a narrow interest group and the general public are in direct conflict, then the issue should be resolved in favor of the general public. The notable exception to this rule is in cases dealing with the basic individual rights set forth in the Constitution. But in America's monetary democracy, well-financed interest groups are consistently able to protect their interests at the expense of the general public. Here is where change is desperately needed.

As discussed in Chapter 16, campaign finance reform is crucial to solving America's political dilemma. There are public interest groups that are currently working to reform the nation's campaign finance system. Five of these groups are listed below, along with information about how to contact them. As I have hopefully made clear in the previous pages, the need for individual action is great. Indeed, the nation's future depends upon it.

Information about the public interest groups listed in this section has been obtained from the groups themselves, from their publications, or from the Foundation for Public Affairs, *Public Interest Profiles, 1992-1993* (Washington, D.C.: Congressional Quarterly, Inc., 1992).

CENTER FOR RESPONSIVE POLITICS
1320 Nineteenth Street, N.W.
Washington, D.C. 20036
(202) 857-0044

Founded: 1983
Executive Director: Ellen S. Miller

General Information: The Center for Responsive Politics is a nonprofit, non-partisan research group founded to undertake research and public education to improve the quality of governance and to focus attention on the problems and possibilities for change in the nation's political system. The Center's work is aimed at creating a more involved citizenry and more responsive political institutions and systems. Through its publications, conferences, computer-generated analyses, technical assistance, and public outreach programs, the Center is recognized as an increasingly valuable institution—a reliable source of information for journalists, educators, grassroots organizers, and the public at large. The Center is a leader nationwide in public education activities on the American electoral system and the role of money in politics.

Since its founding, the Center has published authoritative books and monographs revealing the trends in campaign finance in federal campaigns; conducted major studies on the problems facing Congress as an institution, on voter registration and on political foundation activities; and explored through monographs and press releases a wide range of ethics issues. In addition, the Center has also undertaken a series of working conferences for media and citizens on the issues of money in politics. Its 1991 merger with another non-profit organization, now called the National Library on Money & Politics, enabled it to considerably improve direct access to databases on campaign contributions for educators, journalists and activists. The Center believes that an understanding of the issues concerning the quality of governance can be a critical link reconnecting citizens to the political system and ultimately to solving the many problems facing this nation.

COMMON CAUSE
2030 M Street, N.W.
Washington, D.C. 20036
(202) 833-1200

Founded: 1970
Executive Director: Fred Wertheimer

General Information: Common Cause was founded in 1970 by
John Gardner, former Secretary of Health, Education, and Welfare,
as a non-partisan citizens' lobbying group. His idea was to bring
together individuals from across the nation in an effort to lobby
elected officials on national issues of mutual concern. Common
Cause was to be financed by the dues and contributions of the individuals who joined as members. And its effectiveness was to be
drawn from the focused and concerted grassroots lobbying activities of its members around the country, combined with professional
lobbying on Capitol Hill. Within a year, more than 100,000 citizens
joined Common Cause, and its agenda quickly grew to include
ending U.S. involvement in the war in Vietnam, reforming the
campaign finance system, and pressing for civil rights, ethics,
financial and lobby disclosure, and open meeting laws. In recognition of the need for fundamental reform at the state level as well,
Common Cause soon began organizing parallel lobbying efforts in
the states and establishing Common Cause state organizations.

Today, Common Cause has over 275,000 members nationwide.
A 60-member National Governing Board elected by members sets
issue priorities and policy for Common Cause. Board members use
in-depth surveys of random samples of members, an annual issues
poll of the entire membership and staff recommendations in deciding priorities and policy. Since its founding, Common Cause has
helped achieve national and state reforms in the areas of campaign
finance, open meetings, lobby disclosure, government ethics, civil
rights, the federal budget process, and arms control. Members are

kept informed on national issues through the group's award-winning political journal *Common Cause Magazine*, which features investigative articles, in-depth interviews, legislative updates, and Action Alerts explaining issues and suggesting lobbying actions that members might take.

PUBLIC CITIZEN'S CONGRESS WATCH
215 Pennsylvania Avenue, S.E.
Washington, D.C. 20003
(202) 546-4996

Founded: 1971
Director: Pamela Gilbert

General Information: Congress Watch is the legislative advocacy arm of Public Citizen, a non-profit consumer organization with over 150,000 members nationwide, founded in 1971 by Ralph Nader. Congress Watch represents the interests of consumers in legislative battles over health care, trade policy, banking and credit practices, and the civil justice system. Because of its central role in all of these substantive areas, campaign finance reform is at the top of Congress Watch's legislative agenda.

To reduce the influence of corporate and special interest money and level the playing field between incumbents and challengers, Congress Watch supports voluntary spending limits on congressional campaigns accompanied by partial public funding for participating candidates. Congress Watch also supports placing limits on the amount that PACs can contribute to campaigns and plugging the soft money and bundling loopholes through which special interest money continues to corrupt the political process.

In support of its campaign finance reform and related good government efforts, Congress Watch has published reports and studies such as: "Cashroots Campaigns," an analysis of large donor contributions in the 1992 elections; "Contributing to Death: The Influence of Tobacco Money on the U.S. Congress;" "Government Service for Sale," an exposé of the revolving door between Congress and private lobbying firms; and "On the Road Again," a report on privately funded travel by Senators.

Congress Watch involves its members in the campaign finance reform effort through special action alerts before crucial votes and regular updates contained in the Public Citizen bi-monthly magazine.

THE LEAGUE OF WOMEN VOTERS
OF THE UNITED STATES
1730 M Street, N.W.
Washington, D.C. 20036
(202) 429-1965

Founded: 1920
Executive Director: Gracia Hillman

The League of Women Voters seeks to encourage the informed and active participation of citizens in government and to influence public policy through education and advocacy. Among the group's current concerns are voter participation, national health care, and campaign finance reform. Since 1976, the 100,000-member League has been the primary sponsor of presidential debates.

UNITED WE STAND AMERICA
P.O. Box 6
Dallas, TX 75221
(214) 960-9100

Founded: 1992
Executive Director: V.B. Corn

United We Stand America was founded by Ross Perot in the aftermath of his 1992 presidential campaign. United We Stand America is an educational, non-partisan, non-profit citizens' action group designed to inform members on critical issues facing the nation.

NOTES

Chapter 1

Democracy in Disrepair

1. Alexander Hamilton, James Madison, and John Jay, *The Federalist Papers* (New York: Bantam Books, 1988), p. 47.
2. William Peters, *A More Perfect Union* (New York: Crown Publishers, 1987), p. 213.
3. Election statistics from Common Cause, *Common Cause Campaign Finance Monitoring Project.*
4. Statistics about George Bush's President's Dinner are from the April/May/June 1992 issue of *Common Cause Magazine* (Volume 18, Number 2), entitled "George Bush's Ruling Class."

Chapter 2

Government Guaranteed:
The Savings and Loan Crisis

1. U.S. Bureau of the Census, *Statistical Abstract of the United States: 1989 edition* (Washington, D.C.: Government Printing Office, 1989), p. 496.

2. For a detailed chronicle of this new S&L age and the band of thieves it attracted, see Stephen Pizo, Mary Fricker, and Paul Muolo, *Inside Job* (New York: HarperCollins, 1991).

3. Ibid., p. 378.

4. Nathaniel C. Nash, "Staying Calm—Maybe Too Calm—in the Midst of a Crisis," *The New York Times*, June 26, 1988, III, p. 7.

5. Nathaniel C. Nash, "Bank Board's Wild Week of Round-the-Clock Deals," *The New York Times*, January 3, 1989, p. A1.

6. Please note that the numbers shown here are for federal outlays for deposit insurance, line item 373 of the federal budget. These numbers tend to understate the cost of the S&L crisis because they also include the fees from healthy depository institutions which, in more normal times, typically run between two and four billion dollars a year. Office of Management and Budget, *Budget of the United States Government, Fiscal Year 1995, Historical Tables* (Washington, D.C.: Government Printing Office, 1994), pp. 46-47.

7. Brooks Jackson, *Honest Graft*, rev. ed. (Washington, D.C.: Farragut Publishing, 1990), pp. 169-173.

8. Ibid., p. 270.

9. Ibid., p. 204.

10. For more details on these Savings and Loan owners, see Pizo, Fricker, and Muolo.

11. Jackson, pp. 297-299.

12. Judith Miller, "S.E.C. Charges American Financial," *The New York Times*, July 3, 1979, IV, p. 1.

13. Statistics on Charles Keating and Lincoln Savings from Pizo, Fricker, and Muolo, pp. 358-359, 390, 432-433.

14. Jill Abramson, "Keating Five Hearings Depict a Senate Marred By Money, Staff Power and a Lack of Courtesy," *The Wall Street Journal*, November 27, 1990, p. A18.

15. For a transcript of this meeting, see Pizo, Fricker, and Muolo, pp. 513-525.

16. Helen Dewar, "Five Senators' Links to Keating Were Forged in Different Ways," *The Washington Post*, February 28, 1991, p. A14.

Chapter 3
The Fiscal Abyss

1. Unless otherwise noted, national debt and budget deficit data is from *Economic Report of the President, 1994* (Washington, D.C.: U.S. Government Printing Office, 1994), p. 359. Throughout the book, inflation (year to year consumer price index changes, p. 339) and unemployment statistics (pp. 310, 314) are also from this source.

2. Statistics for interest and net interest (paid to the public) on the national debt are from *Budget of the United States Government, Fiscal Year 1995, Historical Tables*, pp. 53-57.

3. These statistics, calculated from figures in *Budget of the United States Government, Fiscal Year 1995, Historical Tables*, somewhat understate (by less than 1%) total federal investment expenditures because they do not include miscellaneous physical capital expenditures.

4. Calendar of budget events from "Countdown to Crisis: Reaching a 1991 Budget Agreement," *The New York Times*, October 9, 1990, p. A20.

5. Population projections require making assumptions in three areas: births, deaths, and net immigration. Fertility rates are assumed to increase over the next few years before leveling out at 17 births per 1,000 population (adjusted for percentage of female population of childbearing age). It is assumed that declining mortality rates increase life expectancy from 75.4 years (in 1990) to 79 years (in 2050). Net immigration is assumed to fall from 1.8 million (in 1991) to 800,000 (in 2000), before beginning to grow at 1/2% per year. Beginning

statistics are from the *Statistical Abstract of the United States: 1993.*

6. The primary trust fund for social security is the old age and survivors insurance fund. The other social security trust fund is the disability insurance trust fund (assets, at end FY 1993, of $10 billion). Statistics from *Budget of the United States Government, FY 1995, Historical Tables*, p. 227.

7. These estimates require a variety of assumptions including population projections (see footnote 5), real GDP growth (3%), inflation (3%), and adjustments for the higher level of benefits promised to future social security beneficiaries compared to current beneficiaries. In 1991, the federal government estimated the social security shortfall under the open system method at $1.24 trillion and under the closed system method at $7.1 trillion. Government estimates from *Budget of the United States Government, FY 1992*, pp. II–270-271.

8. Paul Kennedy's best seller *The Rise and Fall of the Great Powers* (New York: Random House, 1987) provides numerous examples of this phenomenon, with a special emphasis on military overreach.

9. Calculated from statistics in *Statistical Abstract of the United States: 1993*, p. 852.

10. James Brooke, "Inflation Saps Brazilians' Faith in Democracy," *The New York Times*, July 25, 1993, p. A10.

11. *Budget of the United States Government, FY 1995*, p. 4 and repeated again on p. 13.

Chapter 4

The Breakdown of Laissez Faire

1. Adam Smith, *The Wealth of Nations* (New York: Random House, 1937), p. 14.

2. Ibid., p. 397.

3. John Maynard Keynes, *The Economic Consequences of the Peace* (New York: Penguin Books, 1988), p. 271.

4. For a compilation of historical stock index prices see Phyllis Pierce, ed., *The Dow Jones Averages 1885-1985* (Homewood, Illinois: Dow Jones-Irwin, 1986).

5. John Kenneth Galbraith, *The Great Crash, 1929* (Boston: Houghton Mifflin Company, 1988), p. 174.

6. U.S. Department of Commerce, *The National Income and Product Accounts of the United States, 1929-82* (Washington D.C.: U.S. Government Printing Office, 1986), p. 218.

7. Ibid., p. 1.

8. *Budget of the United States Government, Fiscal Year 1995, Historical Tables,* p. 13.

9. John Maynard Keynes, "From Keynes to Roosevelt: Our Recovery Plan Assayed," *The New York Times*, December 31, 1933.

10. Say's law was formulated by French economist Jean-Baptiste Say and incorporated into classical economic thought by economist David Ricardo. For the place of Say's law in the historical development of economic thought, see Robert L. Heilbroner, *The Worldly Philosophers* (New York: Simon & Schuster, 1986), p. 100. For Keynes's dismissal of Say's law, see John Maynard Keynes, *The General Theory of Employment, Interest, and Money* (New York: Harcourt Brace Jovanovich, 1953), p. 26.

11. John Maynard Keynes, *The General Theory of Employment, Interest, and Money* (New York: Harcourt Brace Jovanovich, 1953), p. 32.

12. Ibid., p. 3.

13. Ibid., p. 348.

14. Ibid., p. 320.

15. U.S. Department of Commerce, *Historical Statistics of the United States: Colonial Times to 1970* (Washington D.C.: U.S. Government Printing Office, 1975), p. 126.

16. *Budget of the United States Government, Fiscal Year 1995, Historical Tables,* p. 13.
17. *Historical Statistics of the United States: Colonial Times to 1970,* p. 126. Note that a timing difference does exist— unemployment data is for calendar years, while deficit data is for fiscal years (July to June).

Chapter 5
The Cold Winds of War

1. From President Harry Truman's speech before a joint session of Congress on March 12, 1947.
2. Statistics from the Statistics & Reports Division, Agency for International Development, November 17, 1975.
3. Joseph Alsop, "Why We Lost China," *The Saturday Evening Post,* January, 7, 14, 21, 1950.
4. David Halberstam, *The Best and The Brightest* (New York: Penguin Books, 1972), pp. 146-147.
5. On January 26, 1950, the United States and South Korea signed a mutual defense assistance pact which authorized the presence of the U.S. Army's Korean Military Advisory Group in South Korea. The advisory group numbered approximately 500 in January 1950. See *The New York Times,* January 27, 1950, p. 7.
6. Dean Acheson, *Present at the Creation* (New York: W.W. Norton, 1969), p. 357.
7. Neil Sheehan, *A Bright Shining Lie* (New York: Vintage Books, 1988), p. 466.
8. Ibid., pp. 283-289.
9. Stanley Karnow, *Vietnam* (New York: Penguin Books, 1984), p. 248.
10. Ibid., p. 680.
11. Sheehan, p. 189.

12. Halberstam, pp. 414-415.
13. Ibid., p. 234.
14. Ibid., p. 339.
15. Karnow, p. 183.
16. Sheehan, p. 741.

Chapter 6
Postwar Pitfalls

1. Halberstam, pp. 732-741.
2. *Statistical Abstract of the United States: 1993,* p. 263.
3. Calculated from statistics in National Energy Information Center, Federal Energy Administration, *Monthly Energy Review* (Washington D.C.: Government Printing Office, October 1974), p. 36.
4. Calculated from statistics in Energy Information Administration, U.S. Department of Energy, *Monthly Energy Review* (Washington, D.C.: U.S. Government Printing Office, June 1980), p. 76. Statistics are for self-serve unleaded regular gasoline.
5. For an insightful look at the individuals and events leading to the hostage seizure in Iran, see Eric Rouleau, "Khomeini's Iran," *Foreign Affairs*, Fall 1980, pp. 1-20.

Chapter 7
Living for the Moment: America in the 1980s

1. For a statistical overview of short-term interest rate volatility from 1979-1981, see *Economic Report of the President, 1982,* p. 311.
2. John Brooks, "Annals of Finance—The Supply Side," *The New Yorker*, April 19, 1982, pp. 131-134.

3. Calculations using statistics from *Economic Report of the President, 1993*, pp. 348, 364, 374, 376.
4. Ronald Reagan, First Inaugural Address, January 20, 1981.
5. For some detailed examples of how the overleveraging of America impacted workers, see Donald J. Barlett and James B. Steele, *America: What Went Wrong?* (Kansas City: Andrews and McMeel, 1992).
6. Haynes Johnson, *Sleepwalking Through History* (New York: W.W. Norton, 1991), pp. 172-185.

Chapter 8

A Noticeable Lack of Substance

1. Johnson, p. 400.
2. Elizabeth Kolbert, "Test Marketing a President," *The New York Times Magazine*, August 30, 1992.
3. For detailed examples of the relativistic nature of Washington politics see William Greider, *Who Will Tell The People* (New York: Simon & Schuster, 1992).

Chapter 9

Running on Empty: America's Economic Problems

1. Adam Smith, *The Wealth of Nations* (New York, Random House, 1937), pp. 4-5.
2. For a detailed account of Japanese targeting of America's television industry, and the failure of the U.S. government to do anything about it, see Pat Choate, *Agents of Influence* (New York: Alfred A. Knopf, 1990).
3. The Treasury Department even published a paper that claimed that there was no direct link between budget deficits and interest rates. See *The Effects of Deficits on Prices of Financial Assets: Theory and Evidence* (Washington, D.C.: U.S. Treasury Department, 1984).

4. Calculated from statistics in *Economic Report of the President, 1994*, p. 388.

Chapter 10
The Foreign Challenge

1. Calculated from statistics in The World Bank, *World Tables 1993* (Baltimore: John Hopkins University Press, 1993), pp. 348-349, 628-629.
2. *Economic Report of the President, 1990*, p. 413.
3. Calculated from statistics in World Bank: *World Tables 1993* and *Economic Report of the President, 1990, 1993*.
4. Warren Buffet quoted in Jaclyn Fierman, "The Selling of America," *Fortune*, May 23, 1988, p. 64.
5. For a good overview of Deming's work see Mary Walton, *The Deming Management Method* (New York: Perigee Books, 1986).

Chapter 11
Back to Basics: What Role for Government?

1. Franklin D. Roosevelt, State of the Union Address to Congress, January 4, 1935.

Chapter 12
Avoiding the Abyss

1. See Chapter 3, Table 9.
2. Peter G. Peterson and Neil Howe, *On Borrowed Time* (New York: Simon & Schuster, 1988), p. 268. This book and Peter G. Peterson's new book *Facing Up* (New York: Simon & Schuster, 1993) both provide a detailed look at how the growth in entitlement programs threatens America's future.

3. This was raised from 50% by the Omnibus Budget Reconciliation Act of 1993. *Budget of the United States Government, FY 1995*, p. 56.
4. *Statistical Abstract of the United States: 1993*, p. 849.
5. *Statistical Abstract of the United States: 1993*, pp. 844-845.
6. Robert Pear, "$1 Trillion in Health Care Costs is Predicted," *The New York Times*, December 29, 1993, p. A12.
7. See Chapter 3, Table 9.
8. Robert A. Levine, "Rationing Care? Let the Patient Do It," *The New York Times*, April 25, 1993, p. F11.
9. Pear, p. A12.
10. "Substance Abuse is Blamed for 500,000 Deaths," *The New York Times*, October 24, 1993, p. 20. The study, "Substance Abuse: The Nation's No. 1 Health Problem," was sponsored by the Robert Wood Johnson Foundation.
11. Robert J. Samuelson, "Health Care: How We Got Into This Mess," *Newsweek*, October 4, 1993, p. 31.

Chapter 13
Revitalizing America's Economy

1. P. J. O'Rourke, *Parliament of Whores* (New York: The Atlantic Monthly Press, 1991), p. xviii.
2. Statistic is from 1991. *Statistical Abstract of the United States: 1993*, p. 378.
3. All public employees are covered by defined-benefit plans. In 1989, 52% of private plan participants were covered by defined-benefit plans. *Statistical Abstract of the United States: 1993*, p. 377.
4. "Government Finds Wider Gap on Financing of Pensions," *The New York Times*, November 23, 1993, p. D12.
5. Ibid.
6. Maggie Mahar, "The Great Pension Raid," *Barron's*, December 2, 1991, p. 8.

7. *Budget of the United States Government, FY 1992*, p. II–270. Using currently accrued method of accounting.
8. Matthew L. Wald, "In Quest for Electric Cars, He Adds the Power of Faith," *The New York Times*, March 6, 1994, p. 3:12.
9. Carl J. Weinberg and Robert H. Williams, "Energy from the Sun," *Scientific American*, September 1990. This special issue is dedicated entirely to articles on world energy.
10. *Economic Report of the President, 1994*, pp. 388-389.
11. *Budget of the United States Government, Fiscal Year 1995, Historical Tables*, pp. 126, 132.
12. For detailed examples of state and local governments that have privatized various functions and reinvigorated the way they operate, see David Osborne and Ted Gaebler, *Reinventing Government* (Reading, MA: Addison-Wesley Publishing, 1992).

Chapter 14

Taxes: the Necessary Evil

1. For more information on the flat tax proposals of the early 1980s, see Robert E. Hall and Alvin Rabushka, *Low Tax, Simple Tax, Flat Tax* (New York: McGraw-Hill, 1983).
2. Robert D. Hersey Jr., "Obeying the Tax Laws: Small Business' Burden," *The New York Times*, January 30, 1994, p. F4.

Chapter 15

Investing in Human Capital

1. *Statistical Abstract of the United States: 1993*, p. 177.
2. *Budget of the United States Government, Fiscal Year 1995, Historical Tables*, p. 52.

Chapter 16
A New Era of Political Economy

1. Theodore Roosevelt, State of the Union Address, December 3, 1907.
2. Harold W. Stanley and Richard G. Niemi, *Vital Statistics on American Politics*, Fourth Edition (Washington, D.C.: CQ Press, 1994), p. 264.
3. Presidential campaign costs include $158 million in public funds—$92 million in public funds for the general election and $66 million in federal matching funds for presidential primaries. *Statistical Abstract of the United States: 1993*, pp. 287-288.
4. Both the amendments proposed by Madison and those passed by the House were in the form of actual changes to the original wording of the Constitution. The Senate modified the wording so that the proposed amendments could be added as addenda, leaving the original wording of the Constitution intact. For wording of proposed amendments see Bernard Schwartz, *The Great Rights of Mankind* (New York: Oxford University Press, 1977), pp. 238-246.
5. Peter Applebome, "Guinier Ideas, Once Seen as Odd, Now Get Serious Study," *The New York Times*, April 3, 1994, p. E5.
6. Timothy Egan, "Federal Judge Strikes Down Law Limiting the Terms of Lawmakers," *The New York Times*, February 11, 1994, p. A20. On March 7, the Arkansas Supreme Court struck down that state's term limit law. The Arkansas ruling has been appealed directly to the U.S. Supreme Court.
7. Thomas Jefferson, in a letter to Samuel Kercheval, July 12, 1816. Quoted from William Peters, *A More Perfect Union* (New York: Crown Publishers, 1987), pp. 235-236. A substantial portion of this quote can be found on the walls of the Jefferson Memorial in Washington, D.C.

Chapter 17
The Challenge of History

1. Max Farrand, ed., *The Records of the Federal Convention of 1787* (New Haven: Yale University Press, 4 vols, 1937), vol. 3, p. 560.

Chart Sources

CHART 1   FEDERAL BUDGET DEFICITS, 1940-1993 ($ BILLIONS). *ERP 1994.*

CHART 2   FEDERAL BUDGET DEFICITS, 1940-1993 (% GDP). *ERP 1994.*

CHART 3   NATIONAL DEBT, 1940-1993 ($ BILLIONS). *ERP 1994.*

CHART 4   NATIONAL DEBT, 1940-1993 (% GDP). *ERP 1994.*

CHART 5   INTEREST ON THE NATIONAL DEBT, 1940-1993. *Bud. FY 1995.*

CHART 6   GRAMM-RUDMAN-HOLLINGS DEFICIT TARGETS. *ERP 1994.* Stanley E. Collender, *The Guide to the Federal Budget : Fiscal Year 1992* (Washington, D.C.: The Urban Institute Press, 1991).

CHART 7   LAFFER CURVE. John Brooks, "Annals of Finance—The Supply Side," *The New Yorker*, April 19, 1982, pp. 131-134.

ERP - *Economic Report of the President* (Washington, D.C.: U.S. Government Printing Office, annual).

Bud. - *Budget of the United States Government* (Washington, D.C.: U.S. Government Printing Office, annual).

WT - World Bank, *World Tables* (Baltimore: John Hopkins University Press, annual).

Bibliography

Barlett, Donald L., and James B. Steele. *America: What Went Wrong?* Kansas City: Andrews and McMeel, 1992.

Barone, Michael. *Our Country: The Shaping of America from Roosevelt to Reagan.* New York: The Free Press, 1990.

Batra, Dr. Ravi. *The Great Depression of 1990.* New York: Dell Publishing, 1988.

Bowen, Catherine Drinker. *Miracle at Philadelphia: The Story of the Constitutional Convention, May to September 1787.* Boston: Little, Brown and Company, 1986.

Bruck, Connie. *The Predator's Ball: The Junk Bond Raiders and the Man Who Staked Them.* New York: Simon & Schuster, 1988.

Burnham, David. *A Law Unto Itself: Power, Politics, and the IRS.* New York: Random House, 1989.

Chancellor, John. *Peril and Promise: A Commentary on America.* New York: Harper & Row, 1990.

Choate, Pat. *Agents of Influence: How Japan's Lobbyists in the United States Manipulate America's Political and Economic System.* New York: Alfred A. Knopf, 1990.

Collender, Stanley E. *The Guide to the Federal Budget: Fiscal Year 1992.* Washington, D.C.: The Urban Institute Press, 1991.

Dionne, E.J. Jr. *Why Americans Hate Politics*. New York: Simon & Schuster, 1991.

Freidman, Benjamin M. *Day of Reckoning: The Consequences of American Economic Policy*. New York: Vintage Books, 1989.

Galbraith, John Kenneth. *The Great Crash, 1929*. Boston: Houghton Mifflin Company, 1988.

————. *The Culture of Contentment*. Boston: Houghton Mifflin Company, 1992.

Gorbachev, Mikhail. *Perestroika: New Thinking for Our Country and the World*. New York: Harper & Row, 1987.

Greider, William. *Who Will Tell the People: The Betrayal of American Democracy*. New York: Simon & Schuster, 1992.

Gross, Beatrice, and Ronald Gross, eds. *The Great School Debate: Which Way for American Education?* New York: Simon & Schuster, 1987.

Gwertzman, Bernard, and Michael T. Kaufman, eds. *The Collapse of Communism*. New York: Times Books, 1990.

Halberstam, David. *The Making of a Quagmire*. New York: Random House, 1965.

————. *The Best and the Brightest*. New York: Penguin Books, 1972.

————. *The Next Century*. New York: William Morrow & Company, 1991.

Hall, Robert E., and Alvin Rabushka. *Low Tax, Simple Tax, Flat Tax*. New York: McGraw-Hill Book Company, 1983.

Hamilton, Alexander; James Madison; and John Jay. *The Federalist Papers*, ed. Garry Wills. New York: Bantam Books, 1982.

Heilbroner, Robert L. *The Worldly Philosophers: The Lives, Times, and Ideas of the Great Economic Thinkers*. New York: Simon & Schuster, 1986.

Jackson, Brooks. *Honest Graft: Big Money and the American Political Process*. Washington, D.C.: Farragut Publishing Company, 1990.

Johnson, Haynes. *Sleepwalking Through History: America in the Reagan Years*. New York: W. W. Norton and Company, 1991.

Johnson, Paul. *Modern Times: The World from the Twenties to the Eighties*. New York: Harper & Row, 1983.

Karnow, Stanley. *Vietnam: A History*. New York: Penguin Books, 1984.

Kennedy, Paul. *The Rise and Fall of the Great Powers: Economic Change and Military Conflict from 1500 to 2000*. New York: Random House, 1987.

Keynes, John Maynard. *The Economic Consequences of the Peace*. New York: Penguin Books, 1988.

————. *The General Theory of Employment, Interest, and Money*. New York: Harcourt Brace Jovanovich, 1953.

Kuttner, Robert. *The End of Laissez-Faire: National Purpose and the Global Economy After the Cold War*. New York: Alfred A. Knopf, 1991.

Miller, James A. *Running in Place: Inside the Senate*. New York: Simon & Schuster, 1987.

Osborne, David, and Ted Gaebler. *Reinventing Government: How the Entrepreneurial Spirit is Transforming the Public Sector*. Reading, Massachusetts: Addison-Wesley Publishing Company, 1992.

Peters, William. *A More Perfect Union: The Making of the United States Constitution*. New York: Crown Publishers, 1987.

Peterson, Peter G., and Neil Howe. *On Borrowed Time: How Growth in Entitlement Spending Threatens America's Future*. New York: Simon & Schuster, 1988.

Peterson, Peter G. *Facing Up: How to Rescue the Economy from Crushing Debt & Restore the American Dream*. New York: Simon & Schuster, 1993.

Phillips, Kevin. *The Politics of Rich and Poor: Wealth and the American Electorate in the Reagan Aftermath*. New York: Random House, 1990.

Pilzer, Paul Zane, with Robert Deitz. *Other People's Money: The Inside Story of the S&L Mess.* New York: Simon & Schuster, 1989.

Pizzo, Stephen; Mary Fricker; and Paul Muolo. *Inside Job: The Looting of America's Savings and Loans.* New York: Harper-Collins, 1991.

Reich, Robert B. *The Next American Frontier.* New York: Times Books, 1983.

————. *The Work of Nations: Preparing Ourselves for 21st-Century Capitalism.* New York: Alfred A. Knopf, 1991.

Schlossstein, Steven. *The End of the American Century.* New York: Congdon & Weed, 1989.

Sheehan, Neil. *A Bright Shining Lie: John Paul Vann and America in Vietnam.* New York: Vintage Books, 1988.

Smith, Adam. *An Inquiry into the Nature and Causes of the Wealth of Nations*, ed. Edwin Cannan. New York: Random House, 1937.

Smith, Adam. *The Roaring '80s: A Roller-Coaster Ride Through the Greed Decade.* New York: Penguin Books, 1988.

Stockman, David A. *The Triumph of Politics: The Inside Story of the Reagan Revolution.* New York: Avon Books, 1987.

Thurow, Lester C. *The Zero-Sum Society: Distribution and the Possibilities for Economic Change.* New York: Basic Books, 1980.

————. *The Zero-Sum Solution: An Economic and Political Agenda for the 80's.* New York: Simon & Schuster, 1985.

————. *Head to Head: The Coming Economic Battle Among Japan, Europe, and America.* New York: William Morrow and Company, 1992.

Waldman, Michael. *Who Robbed America? A Citizen's Guide to the Savings & Loan Scandal.* New York: Random House, 1990.

Walton, Mary. *The Deming Management Method.* New York: Perigee Books, 1986.

Acknowledgments

The author would like to take the opportunity to thank the individuals whose assistance was invaluable in the preparation of this book. I am grateful to Todd Stoltzfus for his research efforts and his ability to find important, yet frequently obscure, statistics. I am indebted to Amy DeLouise for her extensive editing efforts; to Bruce Bower for his advice and counsel; and to Charlie Puritano for his skills with the cartoonist's pen. I would like to thank my brother, Thomas J. Spath, for his extensive editing comments. In addition, I am grateful to Tom Ayers and A. Jonathan Speed for their comments and constructive criticism.

I would like to thank my parents, Thomas F. and Mary E. Spath, for their editorial comments and their constant encouragement and support. I would also like to thank Mary and Jim Keene at Glenbridge Publishing. After a long book writing effort, an author gets tremendous satisfaction in finding the right home for his manuscript. At Glenbridge, I have found such a place.

Index